Norman Lebrecht

THE LIFE AND DEATH
OF CLASSICAL MUSIC

Norman Lebrecht, assistant editor of the *Evening Standard* in London and presenter of BBC's *lebrecht.live,* is a prolific writer on music and cultural affairs, whose weekly column has been called required reading. Lebrecht has written eleven books about music, and is also author of the novel *The Song of Names,* which won the Whitbread First Novel Award in 2003.

www.normanlebrecht.com

ALSO BY NORMAN LEBRECHT

Mahler Remembered
The Maestro Myth
When the Music Stops
The Complete Companion to 20th Century Music
Covent Garden: The Untold Story
The Song of Names

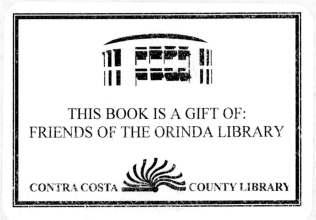

The Life and Death
of Classical Music

Featuring the 100 Best and 20 Worst
Recordings Ever Made

Norman Lebrecht

Anchor Books

New York

AN ANCHOR BOOKS ORIGINAL, APRIL 2007

Copyright © 2007 by Norman Lebrecht

All rights reserved. Published in the United States by Anchor Books, a division
of Random House, Inc., New York, and in Canada by Random House of
Canada Limited, Toronto. Published in Great Britain as *Maestros, Masterpieces,
and Madness* by Allen Lane, an imprint of Penguin Books, London.

Anchor Books and colophon are registered trademarks of Random House, Inc.

The Cataloging-in-Publication Data for *The Life and Death of Classical Music*
is on file at the Library of Congress.

Anchor ISBN: 978-1-4000-9658-9

Author photograph © Sam Long

www.anchorbooks.com

Printed in the United States of America
10 9 8 7 6 5 4 3 2 1

Contents

In memory of
Klaus Tennstedt (1926–1998)
a studio nightmare

List of Illustrations

Acknowledgements

As so often in a work of untold history, the ones who deserve greatest thanks are those who asked to have their names kept out of the book. Many of my other informants are acknowledged in the notes and have been thanked by the author in person. I am eft with the agreeable task of expressing my gratitude to those who, at one stage or other, provided encouragement or assistance in getting the story of classical recording finally on the record.

To my colleagues at the *Evening Standard* Veronica Wadley, Fiona Hughes, Sally Chatterton, and MaryAnn Mallet; at BBC Radio 3 Roger Wright, Tony Cheevers, Jessica Isaacs, Paul Frankl, Olwen Fisher and Cameron Smith; at Scherzo (Spain) Luis and Cristina Sunen; at www.scena.org (Canada) Wah Keung Chung and Mike Vincent; to my agents Jane Gelfman and Jonny Geller; to my publishers Marty Asher and Simon Winder; to my assiduous copy-editor Trevor Horwood and to my attentive reader Catherine Best.

And to all of those people in and out of the record business, some no longer alive, who shared with me their insights, ideas and access over the years:

Antonio de Almeida; Peter Alward; Peter Andry; Shirley Apthorp; Nicole Bachmann; Robert von Bahr; Mike Batt; Richard Bebb; Roxy Bellamy; Gunther Breest; Lucy Bright; Paul Burger; Marius Carboni; Schuyler and Ted Chapin; Matthew Cosgrove; Didier de Cottignies; Chris Craker; John G. Deacon; Peter Donohoe; Cor Dubois; Albrecht Dümling; Tony Faulkner; Ute Fesquet; Johanna Fiedler; Michael Fine; Ernest Fleischmann; Maureen Fortey; Simon Foster; Medi Gasteiner-Girth; Sir Clive Gillinson; Judy Grahame; Michael Haas; Ida Haendel; Gavin Henderson; Antje Henneking; Klaus Heymann; Bill Holland; Katharine Howard; Alexander Ivashkin; Peter Jamieson; Mariss

Jansons; Jane Krivine; Gilbert E. Kaplan; Madeleine Kasket; Lotte Klemperer; Michael Lang; Mona Levin; Naomi Lewin; Susi and Martin Lovett; Richard Lyttelton; James Mallinson; Nella Marcus; Richard Marek; Lucy Maxwell-Stewart; Monika Mertl; Henry Meyer; John Mordler; Melanne Mueller; Christopher Nupen; Dr Stephen Paul; Ted and Simon Perry; Costa Pilavachi; Karen Pitchford; Christopher Pollard; Martha Richler; Terri Robson; Stephen Rubin; Peter Russell; Isabella de Sabata (Lady Gardiner); Karen Schrader; José Serebrier; Yehuda Shapiro; Sylvana Sintow; Ed Smith; Sir Georg and Lady Solti; Denise Stravinsky; Sheila and Adrian Sunshine; Inge and Klaus Tennstedt; Maria Vandamme; Alison Wenham; John Willan; Dolly Williamson; Claire Willis; Dr Marie-Luise Wolff.

THE LIFE AND DEATH
OF CLASSICAL MUSIC

Introduction: Past Midnight

A week before Christmas 2004 the president of a major classical record label gave a farewell dinner for the vice-president of another, who was taking early retirement. It was an intimate affair in an exquisite restaurant in the Pimlico district of London. Present, besides the host, were another label chief, a jovial singers' agent and myself – just a few good friends and their tolerant partners who had heard all the best yarns many times over and knew exactly when to laugh.

As fine wines flowed and reputations were cheerily trashed, it struck me how unusual this party might seem to a greasy-pole climber in the more ruthless worlds of media, or car rentals. You could never imagine the head of Hertz, say, giving a feast for the number two at Avis. But classical recording had always been a convivial activity and, now that it was nearing nemesis, there was no reason to dispense with civilities. After all, as someone remarked, the band played on even as the *Titanic* sank.

A year earlier I had written a column announcing the end of classical recording. Nothing had since disturbed that thesis. Deutsche Grammophon, the arbiter of classical purity, was employing its star mezzo-soprano, Anne Sofie von Otter, in songs by the Seventies band Abba. *Gramophone*, the classical review magazine, had pop crooner Elvis Costello on its cover. Sony Classical, heir to the Columbia legacy, was forcibly merged with its historic rival Victor, now German owned. A century of recorded heritage was tossed from hand to corporate hand, as if worthless.

Productivity was at its lowest since the Great Depression, a trickle of two or three releases monthly from so-called major labels and another handful from sole traders. The days when DG and EMI each flourished ten new titles in the month before Christmas seemed mythical barely a decade on. As we sat past midnight retelling glories and follies, recalling indispensable records that were planned and never made and others that should never have seen light of laser, we shared a golden glow of something whose significance had yet to be defined. What, exactly, had the classical record contributed to modern civilization? Who had been the driving forces, and who the destroyers? Where did this hybrid object – part art, part engineering – fit into the kaleidoscope of contemporary culture? These questions had never been comprehensively addressed and the need to understand them acquired a tangible urgency as the last producers were turning out the lights.

Unlike photography, recording could not claim to be a pure art since the impetus was commercial. Nevertheless, by some symbiotic quirk, the organs of recording acquired an artistic personality and a spiritual dimension. The Decca Sound differed materially, or so it was said, from RCA Living Stereo and both could be told apart from Mercury Living Sound. The act of making and playing a record involved a quasi-religious ritual: the cleansing of the surface, the placing of the needle. No private sanctum was complete without several versions of major works in divergent interpretations – the Beethoven symphonies conducted variously by Arturo Toscanini, Herbert von Karajan, Claudio Abbado, Simon Rattle, Nikolaus Harnoncourt. Whether this cult amounted culturally to more than a row of has-beens was impossible to adjudicate until a line was drawn beneath the recording century and the entirety was assessed as a single artefact.

From the endpoint, where we sat, it became clear that classical recording had changed the world in more ways than previously told. It had brought Western civilization within everyman's reach. No hamlet was too remote to hear Shakespeare and Goethe, Shostakovich and Gregorian chant. A child in Szechuan, enchanted by a sound, grew up into a celebrated virtuoso. Conversely, pentatonic Szechuan tunes, captured on early records, found their way into Western symphonies. Classical recording shrank the world to fit anybody's fist, long ahead of mass tourism and multiculturalism.

Certain recordings united nations in grief and reflection. A Bruckner symphony signalled, for Germans, the end of the Third

Reich; Samuel Barber's Adagio for Strings mourned, for Americans, the death of presidents Roosevelt and Kennedy. Classical recording, over the course of a century, reordered musical priorities. In 1900 Beethoven was the most important composer that ever lived. By 2000 he had given way to Mahler, a symphonist whose metamorphosis from non-person to most-popular was wrought not by live performance or broadcasts but through classical recordings by Leonard Bernstein and Otto Klemperer which changed musical taste.

That such a useful activity could collapse at the end of the century, supplanted by the froth of ephemeral celebrity, is a cultural loss of some magnitude, equivalent to the drowning of Venice. It came about when labels were pushed by corporate owners to chase the popular buck. Decca signed a quartet of girls in bodysuits. EMI embraced a *Playboy* centrefold. America's foremost cellist went hillbilly. A Welsh warbler gobbled up the promotion budget of Sony Classical, then declared that she was done with classics. A civilization was ending. It could not be allowed to die without eulogy or explanation.

I began, in my weekly newspaper column and on my website, to enumerate the milestones – the hundred classical records that, in some way or other, altered the world and its music. These were not necessarily the most perfect records, nor the most ambitious, but they were ventures which – singly or taken together – signified the legacy. A voluminous response from readers the world over revealed an engagement that was both catholic and passionate. It appeared that classical records mattered profoundly, even to people who never bought records and did not listen much. They were, in some way, a cornerstone of cultural certainty.

Readers wanted to know why. Why symphonies had been displaced by crossover, why the regular flow of durable masterpieces had stopped, why new artists were not selling. I had no empirical answer since the historical background was opaque and largely untold. The more I strove to select a hundred recordings by an objective criterion of cultural significance, the more I had to discover about the circumstances of their creation. Great recordings do not come about by accident, or stand alone in time. I needed to furnish the critical discussion of the hundred greatest recordings in this book with an account of how they came about, from Caruso's first scratchings to the serenity of CD. I expected this industrial history to be brief and uneventful, only to find myself overwhelmed by fantastical storylines. Who would have imagined that one famous label came about as the child of a Nazi war criminal and a concentration camp victim? Why would a strictly orthodox Jew finance a gay men's collective? What made one record chief fly to Hong Kong with a million dollars in two suitcases? These romances cried out to be investigated. Once word got round that I was writing the inside story of classical recording, artists, producers and executives opened their hearts and archives to my inquiries. Much of what follows is hitherto undocumented, the oral lore of a civilization that is no more.

Our farewell dinner ended in tears. Among the gifts on the table was a DVD recording of the late Carlos Kleiber, a conducting titan who had cost our departing friend millions of dollars in cancelled projects. Moisture welled in our friend's eyes. He thanked our host, hand on heart. He would watch the DVD as soon as he got home. Working, and mostly not working, with Kleiber had been an incomparable privilege. His executive life had been made tolerable by helping a few mortals of genius achieve a fragment of their potential. If the history of recording was over, so be it. The music would endure.

PART I

Maestros

1. Matinee

One afternoon in 1920, a young pianist sat down in a shuttered room in the capital of defeated Germany and played a Bagatelle by Beethoven. At the return of the main theme, one of his fingers fractionally strayed, touching two keys instead of one. 'Donnerwetter!' (dammit!), cried Wilhelm Kempff. He looked around and saw crestfallen faces. 'That was very beautiful,' said the machine operator, 'but the recording is now ruined.'[1]

This lapse, recalled by Kempff years later, amounts to a defining moment in the annals of performance – the moment a musician realized that recording required a different discipline and temperament from public concerts. Kempff, had his finger slipped on stage, would have played on regardless, knowing that few would detect the flaw, or remember it afterwards. On record, though, the imperfection was engraved for all time, growing larger and uglier with each replay. There was no hiding place, no camouflage available on disc for inferior technique or inchoate interpretation. The artist stood exposed to eternal scrutiny, stripped of illusory diversion.

Sound recording had begun in 1877 with the inventor Thomas Alva Edison shouting 'Mary had a little lamb' into a phonograph and acquired a mass market in 1902 with the first brass-horn arias of the Neapolitan tenor Enrico Caruso. But the birth of recording as a musical act, separate and distinct from live performance, came in 1920 with the undeletable exclamation of a German artist in the aftermath of the First World War. Kempff, a protégé of Brahms' friend Joseph Joachim, was rooted in gaslight romanticism but sufficiently aware of swirling currents to realize that recording presented more than just an opportunity to earn a fee. What it offered, once an artist had overcome the fear of error, was the chance to achieve a perfect score. For the first time in cultural history, accuracy and speed transcended inspiration as the object of performance, and there was no shortage of young men like Kempff who wanted, quite literally, to set a record with their playing.

Wiser heads demurred. The professional pianist Artur Schnabel, a man of lofty mind and caustic wit, argued that recording went 'against the very nature of performance' by eliminating contact between player and listener, dehumanizing the art.[2] Music, he said, was a one-time thing, once played never to sound the same again. Schnabel turned his back monumentally on mechanical impertinences. Kempff, meanwhile, faced fresh dilemmas, moral and aesthetic. Recording, he discovered, was innately competitive. Where, before the war, no one could have asserted empirically that Ferrucio Busoni was a *better* pianist than Ignacy Jan Paderewski, now it was possible to measure Kempff against Wilhelm Backhaus and, music in lap and stopwatch in hand, checking every note in the Moonlight Sonata and timing each movement against Beethoven's metronome mark, *prove* that Kempff was materially superior. Strife ensued. Artists became bitter enemies and listeners were confused. Soon, it was not enough to have one Moonlight in the living-room cabinet; two or three sets displayed intellectual breadth and civilized tolerance. Where emperors in Vienna once staged live contests between Mozart and Clementi, the suburban homeowner in Peckham or Pittsburgh now played Rachmaninov against Vladimir Horowitz for a satisfyingly close shave. An element of sporting competition entered the musical game.

Kempff, who lived to the great age of ninety-five, was a studio master. His articulation was explicit, the notes separated as if bejewelled, his interpretations eschewing an excess of individuality. He recorded the popular classics twice, bought a castle near Bayreuth and was exclusive to Deutsche Grammophon from 1935 to his death in 1991. Yet, while his records entered thousands of homes, Kempff was never a household name. Lacking stage magnetism, he did not visit London or New York until 1951 and many who queued for hours to hear Kempff repeat his estimable studio interpretations came away feeling defrauded. Where was the raptness, the subtle variants of colour, when this nondescript little fellow sat upon an empty platform? Kempff, they complained, was a synthetic invention – a soloist who could never have flourished before the anonymity of recording. His fame came from work done in the dark, away from social and political realities. In his memoirs Kempff is untouched by the century's traumas, by Hitler or mass hysteria, unaware that, when he played in occupied Krakow, he was less than an hour's drive away from Auschwitz.[3]

Schnabel, by contrast, was acutely attuned to public mood and eventually dropped his resistance to recording on an assurance that his work would be sold only in Europe and the British Empire until American audiences had a chance to compare his living presence with the shellac substitute. The principle of eye contact remained uppermost in his mind. Gregarious and polyglot, a commanding presence at the keyboard, Schnabel created a new edition of the thirty-two Beethoven sonatas and played them serially, start to finish, in seven Berlin recitals for the 1927 centenary of the composer's death. He repeated the cycle twice in London while recording for His Master's Voice. The last box in the 100-disc series, sold by advance subscription, appeared in 1939. Schnabel, in this set, introduced a twin-edged concept of integrity: the complete works, performed by the supreme authority. But the idea of the complete cycle had another advantage in that it sold people things they never wanted or knew existed. Subscribers who signed up for the Moonlight, the Hammerklavier and the imposing opus 111 received, together with these summits, discs of less interesting sonatas. Schnabel's Beethoven showed that great composers could be marketed to the self-improving middle classes as a mantelpiece essential, like *Encyclopaedia Britannica*, the plays of Shakespeare and a potted aspidistra.

Schnabel did not take easily to recording and the producer had to bring in his pretty niece to turn pages to give him an illusion of audience. 'I suffered agonies and was in a state of despair,' he reported. 'Everything was artificial – the light, the air, the sound – and it took me quite a long time to get the company to adjust some of their equipment to music.'[4] The recordings, however, are the antithesis of synthetic. They ripple with spontaneity and are riddled with wrong notes, scintillating in their contempt for precision and their search for inner meaning. Schnabel, said the Chilean pianist Claudio Arrau on his death in 1951, was the first 'to illustrate the concept of the interpreter as the servant of music rather than the exploiter of it'.[5]

His record allies had no qualms about exploitation. They took Schnabel's notion of integrity and sold it as doorstoppers to a world that furnished its homes with big boxes. If Kempff's expletive defined music ex machina, Schnabel's blessing put the whole of Beethoven within mundane domestic reach.

Sounds that were collected before these events are chiefly of archaeological interest. To listen through aural debris to Francesco Tamagno (1850–1905), Verdi's original Otello, or to Alessandro Moreschi (1858–1922), the last castrato, is a fascinating experience but one that cannot be endured for much longer than holding one's head down a wishing well. The pitch is wobbly, the static obtrusive and any impression of the singer's musicality requires an imaginative leap on the listener's part. Mighty Melba comes forth enfeebled, Tetrazzini underpowered, Galli-Curci unbeautiful. Mint copies of these objects fetch thousands of dollars (a prolific collector was the oil billionaire, John Paul Getty), but artistic satisfaction is hard to come by on these hand-cranked receptacles.

The first recordings to overcome extraneous noise were ten arias taken by a young American, Fred Gaisberg, from a bumptious Neapolitan, Enrico Caruso, in a Milan hotel one floor above the suite where Verdi, the year before, had died. Gaisberg, as a kid in Washington DC, had hung around after school with men who tinkered in sheds. A useful pianist, winner of a city scholarship, he accompanied singers and whistlers on Edison cylinders, fretting at their inadequacy. In 1893 he met Emil Berliner, a German-Jewish immigrant who had invented a flat disc and was, besides, 'the only one of the many people I knew connected with the gramophone who was genuinely musical and possessed a cultured taste'.[6] Gaisberg, aged nineteen, offered himself to Berliner as an all-purpose factotum, playing the piano when required, raising cash, demonstrating the disc to Bell Laboratories, finding artists. He was the first professional producer of records and, a hundred years later, many still considered him the greatest.[7] In the trinity of recording fathers, Edison engraved sound on surface, Berliner invented the gramophone and Gaisberg created the music industry.

Berliner joined up with Eldridge Johnson, a motor mechanic of Camden, New Jersey, to manufacture gramophones as the Victor Talking Machine Company. Gaisberg set up his first recording studio in 12th Street, Philadelphia, across the river from Camden. In 1898 Berliner sent him permanently to the London branch of his Gramophone and Typewriter Company, soon to be renamed His Master's Voice after an emblematic painting of dog and horn was bought from a passing artist, Francis Barraud. A Berliner nephew who sailed with Gaisberg went on to Hanover, to found the Deutsche Grammophon Gesellschaft. Twenty-five years old and full of vim, Gaisberg roamed with his brother Will as far out as the Russian Caucasus and down into India, capturing remote sounds of throat singers and wedding bands for late-imperial customers. The arch-producer never married; the gramophone was the love of his life.

At La Scala, Milan, in March 1902, he liked the leading tenor in Alberto Franchetti's ephemeral opera, *Germania*. Gaisberg approached Enrico Caruso the morning after through a pianist, Salvatore Cottone, and asked if he would like to make records. The singer, alert to imminent debuts at Covent Garden and the Metropolitan Opera, demanded £100 for ten arias. Gaisberg requested authority from London and was curtly refused: 'Fee exorbitant, absolutely forbid you to record.' He went ahead regardless. Short, fat and ugly, Caruso was an unlikely star but the public was swayed in those days by what it heard, not by what it saw on stage and in dim press photographs. On record, Caruso sang with enviable ease, his baritonal quality stabilizing the recorded image and overcoming pop and crackle. The result was an instant bestseller, the first gramophone hit. By the end of the year he was world famous and fabulously rich. Within two decades – he died of pleurisy in August 1921, aged forty-eight, while mastering Eleazar in Halévy's *La*

Juive – he earned $2 million. Thirty years later Mario Lanza's movie of his life took in $19 million. It was a voice that never stopped selling (CD 1, p. 160).

Caruso's Red Labels convinced the rest of his profession that recording was more than just a gimmick. The first ten tracks offer an object lesson in good breathing and authentic verismo style. Caruso, said Luciano Pavarotti, who recorded a pop elegy to his memory, 'is the tenor against whom all the rest of us are measured . . . With his incredible phrasing and musical instincts he came closer than any of us to the truth of the music he sang.'[8] After Caruso, singers recorded routinely. The last Golden Ager to hold out was the thunderous Russian bass Feodor Chaliapin, whose resistance melted on witnessing the triple benefits: prosperity, publicity and a ticket to posterity. The retired Adelina Patti, living in a castle in Wales, summoned Gaisberg to perpetuate her formidable voice. '*Maintenant,*' she exclaimed on hearing his playback, '*maintenant je sais pourqois je suis Patti*' (now I know why I am Patti).

Other instruments were less convincing. Orchestras, shrunken and warped, sounded as if locked in a bathroom and heard through a rush of water. Fiddlers squeaked, pianists tinkled. To musical ears and an idealistic mind, the results were odious and the outcome obvious. Gaisberg, writing from Milan in April 1909, told his kid brother to cash in and get out:

Say, Will, I have been doing a good deal of thinking of late and have come to the conclusion that the Gramo business is finished. The novelty is gone and days of big profits are over. Gramophone (shares) will never see 40/- again and the Co will settle down to a basis of eight to 10% dividends . . . It will be better for them to liquidate right away than to drag on indefinitely . . . I feel very discouraged generally about the outlook of things and only warn you that this is your last chance to save money.[9]

Few in the business believed that recording would last any longer than such parallel gimmicks as the stereoscope and the hot-air balloon. Already there were other mechanical means of receiving music at home. Marcel Proust, repined in his Paris bed, would listen to Pelléas et Mélisande from the Opéra night after night down the tinny telephone. The First World War, with its portable gramophones and fevered demand for dance music, staved off the inevitable, but radio followed soon after with the first public broadcasts from Philadelphia in 1920 and live music from the British Broadcasting Company in London two years later. The Columbia label, founded in 1889 as Victor's chief competitor, went into liquidation. The remaining labels wrote off their patents and stock and signed up in 1925 with Bell, which had developed an electrical method of making recordings, based on telephone and microphone advances. The future, as Lenin was telling the Soviet Union, lay in electrification.

Electrical recording allowed artists to stand away from the microphone and orchestras to achieve verisimilitude. 'A whisper fifty feet away, reflected sound, and even the atmosphere of a concert hall could be recorded – things hitherto unbelievable,'[10] marvelled Gaisberg. The electrical players were flatbed instruments with frontal speakers – an ignoble replacement for the magnificent horn, but the public response was enormous. In one week in 1926, Victor sold $20 million worth of Victrola players; its entire profit the year before had been just $122,998. It was as if Caruso had been born all over again. In the sleepy Austrian town of Salzburg, a teenaged inventor, Wolfgang von Karajan, rigged up a player of his own making on the town bridge and turned up the volume. Within minutes the centre of the town was thick with crowds and he was ordered by the police to take the contraption down. 'Those people were dumbfounded,' noted his brother, the conductor Herbert von Karajan. 'The sound of music actually emerging from a box like that created a sensation.'[11]

It was the dawning of the age of mass entertainment and shared experience. Commentary to a world heavyweight fight between Gene Tunney and Jack Dempsey, relayed on radio, was released on five discs. The aviator Charles Lindbergh was recorded on landing after the maiden transatlantic flight. Fifteen glee clubs sang Adeste Fideles at the Met, a swelling of 4,850 voices. Church bells were recorded in English hamlets, birds singing in the Auvergne. The composers Igor Stravinsky and Sergei Rachmaninov, refugees from the Russian revolution, found a new home on records. Béla Bartók, who had roamed Balkan villages with a recording machine, worked the folklore he had collected into his string quartets – the first masterpieces to owe their existence to the act of recording. In Germany Paul Hindemith, Kurt Weill and Stefan Wolpe introduced disc playing in live recitals. Weill went so far as to compose a gramophone aria for his 1927 opera, The Tsar Has Himself Photographed.

Symphonies and string quartets continued to resist the medium. Discs could carry only four minutes of music and musicians had to plan side breaks. When Edward Elgar conducted his own works for Gaisberg, the set carried a health warning: 'The tempi on these records do not necessarily represent the intentions of the composer.' Richard Strauss, though, had no such qualms and professional conductors took to the studio, some reluctantly but almost without exception. A music industry photograph of 1929 traps five glowering maestros at a celebratory dinner in Berlin – Arturo Toscanini, Wilhelm Furtwängler, Bruno Walter, Otto Klemperer, Erich Kleiber; all were famed far beyond their cities as a result of making records.

Toscanini, artistic director at La Scala, premiered a work by Ottorino Respighi, The Pines of Rome, which interpolated a nightingale's song – the first recording to be incorporated within a concert work. In America, Leopold Stokowski arrayed his orchestra in a 'Philadelphia Sound', a benchmark for luxuriant precision. The repertoire grew more adventurous. Columbia, back in business for the 1928 centenary of Schubert's death, launched an international competition for composers to finish off the Unfinished Symphony, the result to be recorded. This was a medium ravenous for novelty, indiscriminate of taste. A label might put out jazz one day, a symphony the next. It was the era of anything goes.

And then it crashed. In the Wall Street aftershock, record sales in the US dropped from 104 million in 1929 to just 6 million the following year. In the UK, HMV and Columbia sales dropped from 30 million to 4.5 and the labels were forced into a merger as Electrical and Music Industries, Ltd. It was thirty years before EMI recovered its 1929 sales volume. Decca, a new record label, was taken over by a resourceful young Welshman called Edward R. Lewis, who bought part of US Brunswick and kept Decca afloat on Bing Crosby and Al Jolson imports.

In America, classical recording ceased and stars were fired by the dozen. 'I remember coming back to my office after lunch to find a cable reading "Dropping De Luca and Horowitz. Any interest?"' recalled Gaisberg's assistant, David Bicknell. 'And not only cables – the artists started to arrive in person. [Jascha] Heifetz was one of the first. Fred invited him to lunch.'[12] Gaisberg, in his circumspect way, rose above the panic. Nearing sixty, he held no executive title and earned less than the EMI directors, but he understood better than any man alive the dynamics of the industry. Gaisberg repeated his warning that recording could come to an end at any time. Its best hope was to preserve the best art of its time. 'He had wonderful instincts regarding the direction in which the whole gramophone industry was moving,' said Bicknell. 'And one of the decisions he took was to switch from recording small pieces – which had been the lifeblood of the record business since it started: that is, operatic arias, single piano pieces and so on – to building a library.'[13]

For Gaisberg, Schnabel's Beethoven cycle (CD 7, p. 167) was the cornerstone of a strategy that would remove classical recording from relative triviality to a plane of curatorial responsibility and economic tranquillity. Flimsy showpieces might sell well in times of plenty, but when the going got tough the world needed Beethoven as never before. By 1939, when the world again went to war, the Schnabel cycle had raked in profits of half a million dollars and Gaisberg was revered as a latter-day saint. To the Victorian mansion that EMI had bought on Abbey Road, in residential St John's Wood, Gaisberg brought the great and the good to inscribe an immortal legacy. Elgar conducted the teenaged Yehudi Menuhin in his violin concerto; Jascha Heifetz introduced the

Sibelius concerto (CD 9, p. 170); Pablo Casals recorded Bach (CD 11, p. 172); Gigli, Supervia and Chaliapin sang their hearts out; and Paderewski, lion of Poland, inscribed his final testament. Gaisberg treated all artists with deference, yet without him few would have passed into history. Although British by acculturation, he embodied, in the view of his assistant Bicknell, 'many of the greatest American virtues, namely: first: his fearless interest in dealing with difficult, celebrated and formidable people, never hesitating to tell the truth whenever it was necessary, however unwelcome it might be. Second, his approachability. Finally, his youthful outlook which he retained right into old age.'[14] Gaisberg, who died, aged seventy-eight, in September 1951, had accompanied the industry of recording from toolshed beginnings to corporate establishment, shifting its centre of operations from inventor's America to investor's Britain. It would take a second world war and a brutal dictator to reverse the trend, placing classical records in the heart of a mass consumer market and the home of the brave.

The rise of fascism brought Italy's new Duce, Benito Mussolini, and its most important musician, Arturo Toscanini, into instant conflict. A totemic figure since he conducted the Requiem at Verdi's funeral, Toscanini was a fanatical precisionist in a land of lazy sunshine, a fundamentalist interpreter who preached fidelity to the letter of the score while making textual adjustments as he saw fit. Irresistibly propulsive, his performances of Italian opera and German symphonies were imbued with revivalist fervour. Trim, short and coal-eyed, Toscanini joined the 1919 fascist parliamentary list out of patriotic zeal but grew disillusioned with blackshirt violence. On the eve of Mussolini's March on Rome in October 1922, Toscanini said there was no man he would rather murder. He refused to let the Fascist Hymn be sung, or the Duce's portrait hung, in La Scala. A tyrant to musicians, physically assaulting those who failed to meet his exacting expectations, Toscanini was resolute in defending his opera house from political indoctrination and from any authority greater than his own.

In April 1923 Mussolini visited La Scala and had his picture taken with its glowering music director. An uneasy truce ensued until, in 1929, Toscanini left La Scala to head the New York Philharmonic. Returning home in summer, he was roughed up by Party thugs and confined to house arrest. His anti-fascism crossed borders when Hitler came to power in Germany. Toscanini walked out on Bayreuth over a ban on Jewish artists and, at no small personal risk, sailed to Palestine to conduct an orchestra of refugees. Dismayed at the state of the world, he told his mistress in January 1935 that 'I would like to end my career next year, once I have finished my fiftieth year of conducting.'[15] He advised the New York Philharmonic to replace him with the Berlin conductor Wilhelm Furtwängler, who was having a rough ride with the Nazis. When Furtwängler decided to stay in Germany, Toscanini never spoke to him again.

Word of Toscanini's frustration reached David Sarnoff, founder of the Radio Corporation of America (RCA), which owned the National Broadcasting Company (NBC) and Victor Records. Sarnoff, a Russian-born cigar-chomper with a reverence for high culture, sniffed an opportunity. He despatched Samuel Chotzinoff, brother-in-law of the violinist Jascha Heifetz, to offer Toscanini an NBC orchestra comprising the best musicians in America. His fee would be $40,000, tax free, for twelve concerts – four times Philharmonic rates. Record royalties would provide a welcome nest-egg for the grandchildren. Toscanini signed on the line.

His return to America was heralded with a hyperbole worthy of the second coming (it was, in fact, his third). An opinion poll in *Fortune* magazine showed that two out of five Americans knew his name. Sarnoff introduced him on air as 'the world's greatest conductor'. Twenty million tuned in on Christmas night 1937 to his inaugural concert, comprising Vivaldi's Concerto Grosso in D Minor, Mozart's Symphony No. 40 in G minor and the first symphony of Brahms. Toscanini was called back seven times to take his bows. The reviewers were awestruck. The *New York Times* called him 'predominant in his art'. The *Tribune* acclaimed 'a peak of unexampled popular success'. Chotzinoff informed *Cosmopolitan* readers that, for each nation, Toscanini was the 'supreme' interpreter of its music: for Germans in Beethoven and Wagner, for Austrians in Haydn, Mozart and Schubert, for the Italians in everything, the French in Debussy, the English in Elgar. He was the only conductor anyone would want to hear, which is exactly what Sarnoff wanted everyone to read.

When Pearl Harbor brought America into the war, Toscanini's anti-fascism made him a national hero. 'Your baton,' said President Roosevelt, 'has spoken with unmatched eloquence on behalf of the afflicted and the oppressed.' Everybody called him 'The Maestro' as if there were no other. 'He quite candidly believes that he is not merely the greatest conductor in the world, but the only good one,'[16] observed RCA Victor's musical director, Charles O'Connell, himself a part-time conductor.

'Sitting as close to Toscanini as I did,' wrote principal viola player William Primrose, '. . . I believed without qualification that everything he did was incontestable. After I left the orchestra and listened to him as a member of the audience I was no longer as certain.'[17] 'Toscanini did not really like to make records,' wrote a fellow violist, Milton Katims. 'He took no apparent interest in the problems involved and rarely, if ever, went into the control room to check the results of a take. But he was aware of the difference in the quality of sound of his records and those of other conductors.'[18]

Paramount as he was, his records were marred by the cramped acoustic of NBC's Studio 8H, fracturing filigree timbres and exacerbating what Furtwängler would cruelly characterize as the 'uncomfortable brilliance' of American orchestral sound. 'Excitement,' wrote the composer Virgil Thomson, a lone sceptic in the critical claque, 'is of the essence in Toscanini's concept of musical performance.' Even Thomson, though, admitted that 'one gets hypnotised'.[19]

Sarnoff decreed that 'all Toscanini records, regardless of any commitment to any other artist or any consideration of the necessities imposed by announcement, advertising, distribution and the like, must be put on the market within thirty days.'[20] The entire company was geared to magnify Toscanini's indomitable image. O'Connell, a garrulous fellow who irked the Maestro with under-praise, was fired on his orders, never to work again. Sarnoff himself felt the lash when Toscanini, hearing that his orchestra was being used for classical pops concerts, refused to conduct again at NBC. Sarnoff talked him into making records with the splendid Philadelphia Orchestra at vast expense. Toscanini agreed, then vetoed the release. When Stokowski won hotly contested rights to the US premiere of Shostakovich's Leningrad symphony, Toscanini got Sarnoff to wrest the piece off him and hand it over to the network's number one maestro. Absolutism was never quite enough for him. At Carnegie Hall, in concert with his son-in-law Vladimir Horowitz, he raised $10 million in war bond sales and a million more in the interval by auctioning off his score of The Star-Spangled Banner. On VE-Day he conducted the nation's Victory Symphony. On 18 March 1948 Toscanini gave America's first televised symphony concert.

His predominance reordered the hierarchies of recording. An industry that had waxed rich on singers and soloists now hinged upon the myth of a Mosaic leader who waved a stick in the desert air and produced an outpouring of sound. The maestro was to become the figurehead of classical labels. RCA signed Serge Koussevitsky in Boston and Philadelphia's Eugene Ormandy, along with the prolific Stokowski. Columbia surged back into contention, bought in a 1938 poker game by William Paley, son of a Russian-Jewish cigar manufacturer and founder of the Columbia Broadcasting System (CBS). Paley snatched RCA's 'best record salesman', a deceptive aesthete called Edward Wallerstein, who renamed Columbia records 'Masterworks' and boosted classical sales from just over $1 million in 1939 to $12 million in 1945.

The source of this prosperity was an English-born composer, Goddard Lieberson, whom Wallerstein hired as a maestro magnet. Tall, expertly manicured and witty in several languages, Lieberson at twenty-eight was a founder of the American Composers Alliance and a friend of Igor Stravinsky's. He had written a romantic novel, *Three for Bedroom C*, that became a Gloria Swanson B-movie, and had a finger in many pies. Lieberson went on the road with an open chequebook. In Cleveland he signed the Christian militant

Artur Rodzinski, in Minneapolis the high-octane Greek, Dmitri Mitropoulos. Both would be promoted by the label to the New York Philharmonic. In a flagrant turf war, Lieberson then poached Ormandy from RCA, which grabbed Pierre Monteux in San Francisco and Eugene Goossens in Cincinnati. Both labels financed continental tours by their conductors, spreading symphonic gospels. Orchestral concerts became a central feature of urban life, sustained by returning servicemen, educated on the GI Bill. The brow of Middle America rose by several furrows.

Toscanini, who had sparked this cultural revolution, was too frail to savour its fulfilment. On 4 April 1954, after a memory lapse on air in Wagner's Tannhäuser overture, he laid down his baton. At his death in 1957, just short of his ninetieth birthday, he left 160 recordings, a legacy of relentless tempi, rigid structures and febrile sonorities. His rivals in the iconic Berlin photograph came into the rewards. Bruno Walter enjoyed an Indian summer on CBS Masterworks while Kleiber and Klemperer served Decca and Vox. Furtwängler bit his lip and signed for EMI. 'When I heard my first recording, I actually felt ill,' he said. His approach to conducting, the antithesis of Toscanini's 'ruthless clarity',[21] was conditioned by mood and moment. The Beethoven violin concerto, recorded in 1944 Berlin, was so darkly coloured it sounded like Götterdämmerung. The same work, recorded with Menuhin in 1947, was bathed in romantic regret. Furtwängler was a conductor for all seasons. In 1950s Vienna, two music students, Claudio Abbado and Zubin Mehta, joined the Philharmonic chorus in order to observe his mesmeric rehearsals. A ten-year-old Israeli kid, Daniel Barenboim, came by to seek his blessing. There was a priestly aura to this willowy, self-contradictory intellectual.

Furtwängler's death in 1954 closed a creative chapter in conducting history, but no sooner was he gone than his aesthetic influence redoubled. Conductors aimed to synthesize Furtwängler's cerebral instinctuality on record with the metronomic exactitude of Toscanini. The resultant mongrel, known as 'Toscwänglerism', delighted the record industry, which thought it had achieved the best of both worlds.

2. Middlemen

It had taken half a century for record labels to grow an identity. Back in 1914 there were seventy-eight labels, from Aerophone to Zonophone. Mergers, liquidations and transatlantic alliances reduced the number but not the confusion. EMI shared its 'dog and horn' with RCA in the US. Decca was known in America as 'London'. EMI issued US Columbia and Victor products in Europe. Both US labels were owned by major broadcasters. In Britain, EMI and Decca regarded radio as the enemy.[1] US labels were run by Jews; in Britain there was hardly a Jew in studio or boardroom.

Over time, house style evolved into brand. RCA stood for big stars, big sound; CBS had a liberal, epicurean image: one was Middle America, the other Manhattan; one Republican, the other Democrat; one was market leader, the other tried harder. RCA inhabited the Rockefeller Center; CBS recorded downtown on 30th Street in a deconsecrated Greek Orthodox church. In Britain, EMI was conservative, Decca radical; one British bulldog, the other slinky Siamese. EMI occupied a mansion in St John's Wood. Decca's studios were eight bus stops north in Broadhurst Gardens, West Hampstead, an area thick with continental immigrants.

High-profile producers provided a finishing touch to label style. Goddard Lieberson, the face of CBS Masterworks, was a man about town, usually seen with Vera Zorina, movie-star wife of George Balanchine. 'He worked very hard at it, putting himself about – it was not easy being on first-name terms with Noël [Coward] and Marlene [Dietrich],'[2] said a colleague. Zorina married Lieberson in January 1946. The party was given by opera's glamour pair Lily Pons and Andre Kostelanetz. As a wedding gift, Paley made Lieberson president of Masterworks.

His decisive act was to use the label as a newspaper, alighting on the new Broadway shows and bringing them out on record just as the reviews hit the streets. Kismet went into studio three days after curtain-up and was on sale in a week. South Pacific, with Ezio Pinza and Mary Martin, ran 1,900 nights on Broadway, 2,700 in London, and sold a million records. Lieberson, ecstatic, plunged the profits into high art and core heritage. Voices from the American Civil War appeared on Masterworks, along with the forbidding atonalists Schoenberg and Webern. For the first time, a label took on the complete works of a living composer, its director's best friend. 'I am a Masterwork,'[3] said Igor Stravinsky, cherishing the accolade.

CBS was young, hungry and punching above its weight. Its scientists came up with a record that played forty minutes a side, ten times as long as standard 78 rpms. Peter Goldmark, a nephew of the Hungarian composer, had been listening to the Toscanini–Horowitz recording of the second Brahms piano concerto (CD 12, p. 173) when, irritated by disc changes ('like having the phone ring at intervals while you're making love'[4]) he whipped out a ruler and, counting eighty grooves to the inch, calculated how many would contain a symphony and at what speed they would have to play. One-third of one hundred – thirty-three and one-third rotations per minute – was the answer.

Wallerstein warned that the long-playing record would damage pop singles, but Paley was keen to score points off Sarnoff and in April 1948 summoned his RCA rival to hear the new format. 'Within a few bars of audition,' said Goldmark, 'Sarnoff leaped out of his chair. I played [the LP] for ten seconds and then switched back to seventy-eight. The effect was electrifying, as we knew it would be . . . Turning to Paley, Sarnoff said loudly and with some emotion "I want to congratulate you and your people, Bill. It is very good."'[5]

No sooner was he back at Rockefeller Center than Sarnoff ordered his boffins to come up with a competing format, the 45 rpm extended-play EP. On 21 June 1948, at the Waldorf Astoria, CBS Masterworks launched the LP with 100 new albums, topped by Nathan Milstein in the Beethoven violin concerto and a Frank Sinatra selection. Uptake was slow at $4.85 a disc and $30 a player, but Lieberson's South Pacific hit the stacks ten months later and converted America to the LP. RCA's format, useless for classical, proved perfect for pop. The schism sharpened: CBS went highbrow, RCA low.

Jazz masters, excited by the chance to play lengthy improvisations, flocked to the church on 30th Street. 'After Columbia started LP, we became the hottest label in jazz,' said producer George Avakian. 'Miles [Davis] saw what was going on, so he kept after me because he knew that if he were successful on Columbia that would be far better for him than any other label.'[6] Dave Brubeck, Louis Armstrong, Duke Ellington and Thelonious Monk followed the sensitive producer John Hammond. The first Davis album was named Miles Ahead, for that was where the label now was.

Other technologies were unreeling. In a San Francisco garage, a demobbed GI called Jack Mullin was tinkering with a pair of Magnetophon tape machines that he had taken with an officer's permission from a radio studio south of Frankfurt-am-Main. Mullin informed the crooner Bing Crosby, a nervous broadcaster, that he could pre-record parts of his radio show. Crosby appointed Mullin his producer and both CBS and NBC embraced magnetic tape. There would be no more cutting grooves into molten wax. Tape let musicians retake sections of a work and create a recording from multiple versions. The pace of change was picking up, and the next development was just round the corner.

In Britain, Decca was first to seize the future and EMI last. As Decca went over to LP, EMI announced it would 'continue to produce standard (78-rpm) records in undiminished quantities'.[7] It took four years for EMI to sack its managing director, Sir Ernest Fisk, in which time (the next chairman told Wallerstein) his procrastination had practically put them out of business.[8] EMI, like many post-war British firms, was run by 'captains of industry', a term which denoted recent army service at modest rank. Executives wore pin-striped trousers and musicians were sent home if they turned up without suit and tie. War raged between constituent labels. David Bicknell took over Gaisberg's HMV; Walter Legge ran (British) Columbia; Oscar Preuss was head of Parlophone. If Preuss let slip that he was doing a concerto, Legge would sneer 'awfully sorry, old chap – I did that last month,'[9] and make off with the idea.

A natural musician, half-trained but with an ear for the extraordinary and a certainty of style, Legge was an egotistical intriguer with a sadistic streak. Rumpled and smoke-wreathed, he was a menace to lone women in dark corridors. 'I was the first of what are called "producers" of records,'[10] he bragged. 'I was the Pope of recording.'[11] During the war he had organized concerts for the forces and put together a band of London's finest musicians for EMI. Unknown to EMI, the Philharmonia was wholly owned by Legge, who took a royalty on its records as a supplement to his salary.

He refashioned EMI around two conductors, both signed in Vienna in January 1946 at a time when they were under an Allied ban. Wilhelm Furtwängler had been Hitler's favourite conductor and Herbert von Karajan a puppet of propaganda minister Joseph Goebbels (until he married a half-Jewish woman in 1942 and took a career dive). Both were soon cleared by tribunal but Furtwängler could not forgive Karajan for having tried to usurp his position in Berlin. Legge, knowing their antipathy, played the conductors cruelly off against each other. While in Vienna he signed a dozen singers, among them the bombshell Elisabeth Schwarzkopf, whom he later married.[12] They made an incongruous couple, the roly-poly Englishman and his curly-haired blonde, and together they posed as the creative face of EMI while Furtwängler and Karajan racked up the raves.

David Bicknell, Legge's corporate antipode, was 'a decent sort of chap, happiest at Hayes amid a pile of contracts'.[13] He married a manly Italian violinist, Gioconda de Vito, with a faint moustache and variable intonation. Legge circulated ribaldries about their sexuality. Bicknell once laid a friendly hand on his shoulder. 'Touch me again,' snarled Legge, 'and I'll kill you.'[14] Legge was always on the go, Bicknell stayed home. Legge lived high on expenses; Bicknell was frugal. A producer, called to his house in the middle of the night to unravel a Legge crisis, was received by Bicknell in a simple iron bedstead, an army lamp on the table. Bicknell, a public school man, received regular promotions at EMI. He wound up as head of the International Artists Department, controlling Legge's contracts. When Legge threatened that Karajan would quit unless he, Legge, was named sole producer, Bicknell delivered a masterly put-down. 'The Company,' he said, 'has never accepted the stipulation that an artist's contract should be dependent on the availability of one of its servants.'[15]

Legge, in his own mind, was nobody's servant. He reduced artists to tears and drove the young Kathleen Ferrier to leave EMI and join Decca (CD 14, p. 176). His conduct after the Beethoven concert that reconsecrated the Bayreuth Festival in 1951 was recalled by Furtwängler's appalled widow, Elisabeth:

Walter Legge came in and, like a child, my husband looked at him and just said 'Nah?' He wanted Legge's reaction, as he thought a lot of him. 'I have heard much better Ninths from you,' was his reply . . . You can't know how this affected him! Immediately he thought: 'Something must have happened, there must have been something that was no good.' He did not sleep at all right through the night and then the next morning we had to go to Bayreuth again, and he asked Wieland Wagner: 'Please tell me, how was the Ninth Symphony yesterday?' and he said: 'It was just marvellous.' But Furtwängler was still distressed and uncertain. As I was driving him home to Salzburg, suddenly he said: 'Stop.' He got out of the car and walked away – for almost 30 minutes he was gone and I started to be afraid. Then he was back and he said: 'Right, we can go on now, that is all finished.' He was a big walker, he walked to make himself free.[16]

Furtwängler accused Legge of 'an outrageous personal breach of trust'[17]; Sir Thomas Beecham referred to him as 'a mass of egregious fatuity'.[18] But rival producers conceded that 'over and over again he made records that were the envy of all of us'.[19] His artists included the pianists Dinu Lipatti, Solomon and Claudio Arrau, the young conductors Guido Cantelli, Carlo-Maria Giulini and

Wolfgang Sawallisch. In July 1952 Legge threatened to resign unless he got the go-ahead to sign a fat Greek soprano at La Scala. His first recording with Maria Callas was Tosca (CD 23, p. 186). It became the biggest selling opera of all time and Callas never worked with any other producer.

Legge launched in America under the sign of the Recording Angel – 'a small, well-fed cherub who seems to be doodling with a long quill'.[20] Angel, run by opera enthusiasts Dario and Dorle Soria, had the opera racks to itself since Lieberson insisted that Americans 'don't like opera – they like singers and are content to hear them over and over in the same arias'.[21] Angel was in no position to wrestle with American giants but it carved a distinct market share, albeit of a conservative tint. Legge was averse to modern music and living composers, looking resolutely backwards. It was the other British label that waved the banner of progress.

Decca was democracy incarnate. Having survived the choppy 1930s by the narrowest of margins, its engineers joined the war with gusto, inventing all manner of radar and navigation devices and exploring the outer rim of sonic science and the bottoms of the world's oceans. Back from the depths, Decca in June 1945 launched full frequency range recordings – ffrr, for short, 'the first time anyone could hear the full range of frequencies the ear could detect'.[22] Decca's navigator department, which continued to develop marine systems for Nato, was the most profitable in the company for years ahead, a hedge against classical losses.

Limitlessly inventive, engineers were the driving force at Decca and a legend across the industry. 'Producers with other labels tended to dictate to the engineers exactly what they wanted and what [equipment] should be used, all without any explanation of context. At Decca, engineers and producers listened to operas and recordings ages before the first session of a project. It was a real team, and in terms of pay they were treated equally,'[23] noted a leading producer. Where Legge expected his engineers to lug all the equipment, at Decca everyone pitched in.

Exceptionally in class-ridden Britain, Decca demolished social barriers. Arthur Haddy, the chief sound engineer, spoke in a thick Essex Estuary accent and called everybody 'boy'. His number two, Kenneth Wilkinson, would sit at the console, eyes shut, a Player's cigarette drooping from his lips, his fingers touching the buttons of the mixers like a clinical diagnostician's. In rehearsal breaks Wilkie would walk around the studio adjusting musicians' chairs. If he disliked the tempo he would mutter 'my daughter couldn't dance to that',[24] and a prudent producer would take heed. Dress at Decca was casual. In studio, everyone wore squeak-proof tennis shoes.

The chairman, Edward Lewis, was an aloof, abrupt Welshman. His passion was the summer game of cricket – he would hire county players to perform odd jobs in the company during the English winter – but his reactions had been sharpened in the Depression and he rose swiftly to a challenge. When Legge formed his Philharmonia Orchestra, Lewis understood that he had to compete. Lacking foreign currency, he got his Swiss distributor to line up the best orchestra in Europe in exchange for artistic control and a seat on the board. Maurice Rosengarten did not need asking twice.

Moshe-Aron Rosengarten was a strictly orthodox Jew who did no business after lunchtime on Friday, refusing to answer telephone or doorbell until Saturday night. A self-made wheeler-dealer, born in a Polish village, he owned a Swiss concession to a range of household goods, including gramophones, radios and televisions, and set up a string of yodel labels to service the local market. 'He knew nothing about music, but he had a tremendous nose for what might sell,' said Decca producers. He was, they agreed, 'something of a genius'.[25] Rosengarten signed two ensembles for Decca – the matchless Vienna Philharmonic, and the Suisse Romande. Some found it odd that so devout a Jew should work with unreformed Viennese Nazis and the Swiss conductor Ernest Ansermet, an avowed anti-Semite. To Rosengarten, it was just business. The Viennese were the best, the Suisse Romande dirt cheap. Their politics were irrelevant.

From a modest office on Zurich's Badenerstrasse, Rosengarten took command of Decca's post-war output. All record plans were subject to his approval. 'It was never a good idea to sound enthusiastic about a project,' said one producer, 'he would always shoot it down. You were best off seeming reluctant and letting him talk you into it.'[26] His brother-in-law, Leon Felder, played yes-man at repertoire conferences, watching the boss closely to see which way he had to vote. Rosengarten followed some invisible instinct. 'He was a frustrating man,' said Decca administrator Nella Marcus. 'You would go to Zurich and he'd keep you waiting for hours, often into the next day. Mr Felder would come out and say, "He's so busy". I must have shown my irritation because when Mr Rosengarten finally emerged, he announced, "Mr Felder, Miss Marcus is going shopping. When she comes back we will talk business."

'So they sent me off in a chauffeur-driven car to a fashion store. I came back with a lovely coat. Mr Rosengarten was so excited: "What did you buy? Is it leather? Mr Felder, do you think it's leather?" So Mr Felder went around sniffing it, sniff-sniff . . . It was a funny way to run a record business.'[27]

Known as 'Uncle Mo', Rosengarten's relations with Lewis verged on the symbiotic. 'There wasn't one day in all those years that they didn't talk to each other,' said Rosengarten's daughter, Sarah.[28] As demand picked up, Rosengarten signed a third orchestra, the Concertgebouw in Amsterdam. Needing extra hands at the console, Decca hired a Swedish violinist who had put together Beecham's Royal Philharmonic Orchestra, in opposition to Legge's Philharmonia. Victor Olof Arlquist (he dropped the surname) was a highly competent musician, so competent that he once took over a concert in his street clothes when Beecham had to attend a sick wife.[29] Known as 'the Baron', Olof would shout down mild conductors like the Dutchman Eduard Van Beinum and the Czech refugee Rafael Kubelik. He was much admired by George Szell, another Decca conductor, soon to become Cleveland's rigorist chief.

Other maestros were less tolerant of Decca's know-alls. Furtwängler refused to accept their microphone settings, rendering Brahms' second symphony flabby and opaque. Sergiu Celibidache, who deputized in Berlin during Furtwängler's denazification, found Decca so uncongenial that, after a Tchaikovsky Fifth with the London Philharmonic, he refused to make another sound recording so long as he lived. Decca's domestic crop was headed by a Blackburn telephonist, Kathleen Ferrier, whose organic contralto captivated Bruno Walter at the 1947 Edinburgh Festival. Their recording of Mahler's Das Lied von der Erde, with the Vienna Philharmonic, was one of the wonders of the age; her death of breast cancer, aged forty-two, in 1953 was universally mourned. Decca's golden boy was Benjamin Britten, whose masterpiece Peter Grimes was staged seven weeks after the war. Britten recorded for no other label, giving Decca the gloss of genius that Stravinsky brought to Columbia. Confidence soared and there seemed no limits to Decca's ambitions.

In 1951 a Decca team went to Bayreuth to record the Ring, only to find that there was no contract. The producer, John Culshaw, transfixed by what he heard, grew convinced that he could achieve a better Ring, less error-strewn, in studio. Culshaw, a wartime radar operator, had got his first job at Decca by means of a deep-voiced charm, subtle intelligence and serene good manners. 'He was a generous person, not jealous of other people,' said his sound engineer, Gordon Parry. 'Even if you interrupted him, he was the one who stopped talking – he very politely waited for you to finish,' said a producer, Erik Smith.[30] When Culshaw started talking about casting a Ring, colleagues told him he was crazy: Rosengarten would never pay and no worthwhile Wagner conductor would take orders from Decca techies. Culshaw smiled. He was an unusual blend of patient visionary and restless activist who twice resigned from Decca, writing two novels and a Rachmaninov biography, while never losing sight of his goal: to bring the Ring into people's homes. Even when out of Decca he flew often to Zurich to meet Rosengarten at a kosher restaurant. The Swiss introduced him to a young conductor, eager as himself. Georg Solti had lived out the war in Zurich as a visaless Hungarian refugee, living rent-free with a tenor in exchange for Tristan lessons. Rosengarten said 'we must do something for the boy' and booked him to accompany the German violinist Georg Kulenkampff. Solti said, 'I don't want to play the piano. I want to be a conductor.' Rosengarten replied, 'We shall see.'

Thirty-two years old when the war ended, Solti made his way to Munich, where a Hungarian contact got him the job of music director at the crucible of National Socialism. 'It was only after several years that Munich began to discover I was conducting everything for the first time,' he laughed.[31] Rosengarten gave him a conducting contract, dated 21 November 1950, for fourteen sessions over two years, £50 a session (against royalties of 4 per cent), with a £50 travel allowance 'for any recordings outside Munich'.[32] Solti had the contract framed and hung it gratefully above his desk to the end of his life.

Culshaw heard him conduct Walküre in May 1950 and decided he had found his Ring master. Solti was raw, energetic and open to suggestion. He saw in Culshaw an ego-free partner who wished him no harm. Culshaw recognized in Solti a furiously hardworking talent. Theirs was the opposite of a Faustian pact: both were in it for the ends, not the means, and both went in with eyes wide open. There was no male rivalry between them, since Culshaw was gay and Solti aggressively heterosexual. Over dinner, they shyly agreed that they rather liked one another.

Olof dismissed Solti as 'uncontrollably brash' but Rosengarten favoured Culshaw's verdict. In 1954 Culshaw left to work for Capitol in America. He had been gone a few months when Olof, after a falling out with Frank Lee, head of the Artists Department, defected to EMI, taking with him all of Decca's secrets and his personal assistant Peter Andry, an Australian flautist. 'I was working happily in Vienna,' said Andry, 'when one day Victor said to me: I've had enough, and we're going. I was being paid about five hundred pounds a year. He got me fifteen hundred. So we went. He'd been having trouble with Rosengarten, who never wanted to pay artists properly, and there were people at Decca of the greatest incompetence – Frank Lee, a man in a green suit. It all got too much for Victor.'[33]

Panic ensued. Lewis called Culshaw in New York and urged

him to return, warning that Capitol was about to be bought by EMI. Rosengarten, next on the line, ordered him to Vienna to take over Olof's session. 'There was a tremendous row,' said Gordon Parry, who was recording Wagner's Wesendonck Lieder. 'Victor was summoned to Zurich and told to quit Vienna because of his EMI contract. Culshaw came out and I got threatening words from Mr Haddy, who was my direct boss, to say that I must cooperate with Culshaw, I must be very strict about this.'[34]

Culshaw had never been to Vienna, nor dealt with its duplicitous player-managers. It was a leap into the deep but it took him one large step closer to the grail. There was no better orchestra for his Ring than the Vienna Philharmonic, no better venue than the Sofiensaal, a disused imperial steambath. He was in Rosengarten's good books and his friendship with Solti was almost familial. Culshaw's mother would look after Solti's dog while he went on holiday. A letter from Solti to Culshaw, opening with threats of resignation, culminated in fond salutation: 'love to you and the boys'.[35]

'The boys' is how musicians talked about Decca – whether for its practical mechanics, its puerile idealism, or its preponderance of homosexual men at a time when gay love dared not speak its name. Discretion was the norm for gay men in the arts, but Decca was a safe house, as out as it was possible to be. Gordon Parry, pink-blond and perpetually on the prowl, was flagrantly bisexual. In the Decca apartment above the Sofiensaal, he went pounding on bedroom doors at night crying, 'Come on beau! It's only a bit of mutual masturbation!' 'Gordon did everything to excess,' said Andry. 'He was flamboyant, extrovert and manipulative,' said another colleague. 'He could turn nasty if thwarted.' 'There were some very aggressive gay people at Decca,' said a vulnerable young producer. 'Nowadays they'd be charged with sexual harassment.'[36]

Culshaw himself showed little interest in sex. 'As far as sex was concerned with John,' said one of his team, 'it was either nothing or a great enigma. I never sensed anything going on.'[37] Although some Decca boys were straight, the ethos was distinctly gay. 'Decca was pink, where EMI was blue, or grey,' said a gay

Decca producer. 'It's what made interesting people want to work for us.'[38] Decca's composers of choice were Britten, Michael Tippett and Peter Maxwell Davies, a different sexual aesthetic from EMI's straight flush of Elgar, Delius, Vaughan Williams and Walton. Nevertheless, when green-suited Frank Lee was caught with a catamite in Zurich on a company trip, he was sacked on the spot. The Decca brand was a delicate balance of Culshaw's gay culture and the biblical values of Lewis and Rosengarten, together forging a proselytic sense of mission. 'Decca was more than a job, it was a family,' said Andry. 'You wouldn't find that camaraderie anywhere else. At EMI, they clocked off at six and went home.'[39]

Germans, in the rubble of defeat, went groping for a grasp on civilization. Deutsche Grammophon, bombed out of Berlin, moved back to Emil Berliner's Hanover. The war was not to be mentioned. 'This chapter of its history does not reflect well on Deutsche Grammophon,' states the official record. 'The company's business policies [were] heavily influenced by the Third Reich, as is apparent from the recordings the company was required to make by the ruling regime, which do not correspond to Deutsche Grammophon's usually high standards.'[40] Tapes of Goebbels speeches and Hitlerite hymns littered the vaults. And there was worse in the boardroom.

The label had a new owner. A 1941 share-swap between electrical giants AEG and Siemens & Halske resulted in AEG owning Telefunken and Siemens taking DGG. The label was assigned to Ernst von Siemens' electro-acoustical division. A grandson of the founder, club-footed from birth, Ernst led a privileged existence in a lakeside villa, surrounded by great art. A regular concertgoer, he met Herbert von Karajan and funded him to record Brahms' first symphony in occupied Amsterdam. Karajan asked if Siemens had any Mendelssohn in his library. 'Of course,' said Siemens. Karajan requested a particular score.[41] In Nazi Germany this transaction amounted to a bond of trust, for a word from either man would have landed the other in a Gestapo cell. For Siemens, music was a pleasant diversion from the grim realities of running a business in a genocidal state that his family, an early financial supporter of the Nazis,[42] had helped to create.

In the year it took over Deutsche Grammophon, Siemens & Halske began to buy slave labour from the SS. Starting with 2,000 Jewish women from Ravensbrück concentration camp, the atrocities intensified as the war went on, using inmates from occupied countries in some of the most murderous camps, including Auschwitz-Birkenau, which Siemens & Halske helped to build. A Siemens board memorandum of 23 February 1943 notes that 60,000 bunk beds were being used by its forced labourers and more were urgently required.[43] Ernst von Siemens was an attending member of that board, complicit in the crime. After Hitler's defeat, his chairman (and cousin) Hermann von Siemens was arrested by the Americans and briefly interned, but he was never charged and, on release, was allowed to resume his place at the head of West German industry. The company expressed no regret for its crimes against humanity and offered no reparations until, in 1998, the belated threat of a US boycott prompted Siemens to set up a Holocaust compensation fund. In all, 100,000 men, women and children were dragged from their homes across the continent of Europe and pressed into servitude, under threat of death, brutality and bombardment, in the factories and laboratories of Siemens, where they made anything from V-2 rockets to classical records.

This morally soiled organization took the lead in restoring German music to former glories. Ernst von Siemens founded an Archiv label in 1945 to record organ music in baroque churches that had escaped bombing. Helmut Walcha, a blind organist from Leipzig, played Bach at the Jakobkirche in Lübeck. Few copies were pressed but the act was symbolic. Germany was repossessing its rightful legacy and the recordings were made on magnetic tape, a German invention. The soundman, Erich Thienhaus, would go on to train, in a Tonmeister course at Detmold, the producers and engineers of Germany's recording future.

The task of cultural reconstruction was daunting. Since no foreign artist would record for a label called 'Deutsche', Siemens needed an impeccable go-between. He did not have to wait long before she appeared in his salon. Elsa Schiller had survived two years in Theresienstadt, the 'model' Czech concentration camp where cultural events were staged to fool the Red Cross. Schiller kept a low profile and, in October 1944, evaded a mass transport to Auschwitz. Born in Vienna, raised in Budapest, she had been a professor at the Liszt Academy before a lust for life took her to 1920s Berlin, where she conducted a chamber orchestra. Harried by the Nazis, she moved from one female lover's flat to the next until a threat of betrayal landed her in Gestapo hands.

After liberation, she crawled cadaverously home to Berlin. The music critic Hans Heinz Stuckenschmidt, Schoenberg's biographer, spotted her in the street and got her work as a pianist on the American radio station, RIAS. Like many whose careers had been frozen by Hitler, Schiller resumed work with pent-up fervour. She told the Americans they needed an orchestra and hired a Hungarian to conduct it. Ferenc Fricsay, thirty-three years old, had given the 1947 Salzburg premiere of Gottfried von Einem's Death of Danton and was about to become chief at Berlin's City Opera. His radio orchestra, he promised, would outshine Toscanini's.

Berlin lacked high-quality concerts. The Philharmonic was in poor repair and the Russian sector had no orchestra at all. With most concert halls in rubble, Schiller booked a disused cinema, the Titania Palast. Solo recitals she recorded in the music room of the Siemens Villa on Gärtnerstrasse, seized by the Allies but still occupied by Ernst von Siemens who treated RIAS artists as his guests and welcomed Schiller to his home.

In February 1948 Stalin blockaded Berlin. German conductors stayed away and it was left to Fricsay to maintain morale during the Allied airlift. 'It was cold, there was no heating, no water,' he recalled. 'Women and men were up half the night to use electricity when it came on. At ten the next morning, unslept, they came to rehearsal. Despite all that, it was a glorious time.'[44]

Critics marvelled at his Toscanini-like clarity. A pupil of Bartók's (whose Bluebeard he conducted at the City Opera), Fricsay was soft-spoken, precise, ethereal. 'I was too young to hold two such responsible jobs,' he reflected. 'I made mistakes . . . but I think I did a great deal towards rebuilding musical life in Berlin. And I had partners at the RIAS orchestra with whom I worked happily and who became my friends.'[45]

Schiller, by then head of music at RIAS, was doing deals with Deutsche Grammophon. When they asked to record her dance band, she demanded new suits for her threadbare players. Siemens consulted her privately on artistic policy. She sold him Fricsay as repertoire builder. On 12 September 1949 Fricsay cut his debut disc in a suburban church in Dahlem, the Jesus-Christus-Kirche, with a trailblazing Tchaikovsky fifth symphony. It was the beginning of the new DGG. He went on to perform French music, unheard in Berlin for fifteen years. The elegant pianist Monique Haas and the conductor Igor Markevich, Diaghilev's last protégé, left town with DGG contracts. A repatriated prisoner-of-war, twenty-two years old, turned up for an RIAS audition. 'Can you sing Winterreise?' Schiller demanded. She sat with him until one in the morning, producing his broadcast. Schiller, recalled Dietrich Fischer-Dieskau, was

the embodiment of . . . [an] artistic director who was in sole charge of such a company. She always spoke to the point. In fact, her candour could be cutting. She could not, would not, put up with sanctimoniousness and fawning. She put down a young conductor who had apologised once too often for his presence in front of an orchestra: 'Please, not so much modesty. You're not good enough for that.'[46]

At the 1950 Berlin press ball, Siemens asked Schiller formally to join Deutsche Grammophon as programme director. The label had undergone a radical redesign,[47] separating genres by colour: Polydor pop was red, Archiv was silver and DGG was the Yellow Label – uncomfortably, the colour that once set Schiller apart from German society. Siemens was about to enter LP production. Schiller told him he needed nothing less than an industrial revolution. Label attitudes were patriarchal and production mostly manual; record sleeves were sewn by ladies at treadle machines. A new LP was a bespoke item costing 32 Deutschmarks, a fortnight's wages for a bank clerk, but the products were not intended for the working classes. Siemens aimed to accrue prestige and provide pleasure for his own kind. Elsa Schiller demurred and kept him waiting for months.

What finally swayed her was the opportunity to produce a cycle of Mozart operas, having argued that it would be a national disgrace if Mozart was sung only on English labels during his 1956 birth bicentennial. Die Entführung aus dem Serail, the first release, drew fire from Stuckenschmidt for its untimely frivolity. Fricsay replied: 'Through Mozart, we become better people.'[48] Schiller's Wieder-gutmachung – making good again – involved signing Jewish artists to the Yellow Label. When Fricsay left Berlin after the US Senate discovered it was spending tax money on a foreign orchestra (something it would never do at home), she lined up Lorin Maazel for RIAS and DGG. Hearing reports of a quartet of three Austro-German refugees and a British Jew, she invited the Amadeus to Berlin. 'She was a very lively personality,' said Siegmund Nissel, the second violinist. 'We had just been offered a contract by EMI. Soon afterwards, Frau Schiller got in touch. I said, "I am terribly sorry, I have already agreed with EMI . . ." She said, "Would you allow me to come to London and talk to them?"

'Some time later she called: "I didn't get you, but at least I got you the same conditions from EMI that you would have got from us".'[49] Nissel, embarrassed, asked EMI to split the contract with DGG. Six years later, Schiller won exclusive rights. 'She was a very shrewd Jewish lady,' said Martin Lovett, the cellist. 'She would look through you and weigh you up in a way I only ever experienced from Margaret Thatcher. I was a bit uncomfortable recording for the Germans, but Sigi's father had been in Dachau. Who was I to object?'[50]

'In Germany I always wondered who I was shaking hands with,' said Siegmund Nissel. 'You had to put it out of your mind. Deutsche Grammophon was the best firm for us. They made records of marvellous quality and gave us enormous time to make them.' It took less than a decade for Schiller to rehabilitate the German label.

★

To the west, another giant stirred. Philips of Holland was famous for close-shaving men's razors and women's depilators; it also made light bulbs, radios and record players. Frits Philips, the family's rising star, was anxious to secure a flow of good LPs for his turntables. He bought the local Decca dealership, HDD, and proposed a global merger to Edward Lewis. When that offer was rebuffed, he snatched CBS sales away from EMI and founded his own label.

Early releases were feeble. Philips poured forth light music of unfathomable triviality, fronted by the bandleader Geraldo. Classics, based in sleepy Baarn, wore a muddy-brown sleeve colour – milk-chocolate, in polite parlance – and unfamiliar faces, but the somnolence was deceptive. Amsterdam, lacking an opera house, had an intense concert life. Eduard van Beinum, the Concertgebouw music director, gesturally inelegant and unhealthily overweight, was a refined Francophile who attracted rare and unusual artists. Clara Haskil, a Romanian refugee in Switzerland, melted Dutch hearts in Mozart, recorded for Philips and earned, at the age of 57, enough money for the first time in her life to buy a piano. Claudio Arrau, the silken Chilean, recorded Beethoven sonatas. Arthur Grumiaux and Henryk Szeryng were the key violinists, Maurice Gendron the label cellist. These quiet musicians were no match for RCA's 'million dollar trio' of Rubinstein, Heifetz and Gregor Piatigorsky, but the Dutch, deploring tall tulips, were building a label without stars, a label where music came first. Philips was the sixth and last of the great classical labels, completing a set of so-called 'majors' that controlled the distribution game – the networks, the discounts, the deals – and colluded at times over prices (for which they were fined) and programming. No start-up ever succeeded in breaking up their cosy colloquy.

Which is not to say that others did not try. George Mendelssohn, a Hungarian in Los Angeles, lit upon a diaspora of talent – the pianists Shura Cherkassky, the violinist Ruggiero Ricci and the brothers Jakob and Bronislaw Gimpel. No relation to the great Felix, the would-be music mogul styled himself George de Mendelssohn-Bartholdy and named his label Vox. He grabbed hold of Otto Klemperer, who had wrecked his American career with manic-depressive escapades and was heading off to conduct the state opera in Hungary, a rash move in the gathering Cold War. Mendelssohn got Klemperer to record a few symphonies in Paris and Vienna. Back in LA, the pair entered a record store and asked for Beethoven's Fifth, conducted by Klemperer.

'Sorry,' said the assistant, 'we've only got Toscanini and Walter . . .'

'But we want Klemperer.'

'These are the best recordings,' said the sales guy. 'Why do you want anyone else?'

'Because I am Klemperer,' growled the conductor.

'And I guess your pal's Beethoven,' grinned the assistant.

'No, he's Mendelssohn,' roared Klemperer.

'Wow,' exclaimed the clerk. 'You know, I've always loved your Wedding March.'

Another ex-Hungarian named his New York label Remington after a phonograph company that went bust in 1921. Don Gabor, cousin of glamour-puss Zsa Zsa, recorded Bartók at the piano and, working as a packer at RCA, picked up a few distribution tricks. He launched Remington in 1946 on a red label, mistakable for Victor's Red Seal. Laszlo Halasz, chief conductor at New York City Opera, was his musical adviser and Marcel Prawy, lawyer to the movie actors Jan Kiepura and Marta Eggerth, his Vienna fixer. Prawy got Vienna Philharmonic players (under exclusive contract to Decca) to record for Remington under such pseudonyms as Pro Musica and Vienna State Opera Orchestra.

Subterfuge was the lifeblood of little labels. Vox issued Beethoven's first symphony under 'Conductor X' after Artur Rodzinski refused to put his name to it. It recorded the conductor George Ludwig Jochum, brother of DGG's Eugen, and violinist Walter Schneiderhan, not to be mistaken for the Vienna concertmaster, Wolfgang. Gabor was run out of stores by ruinous reviews, but not before he had tapped such promising talents as the pianists Jorge Bolet and Jörg Demus. Vox discovered Ingrid Haebler and Alfred Brendel who, after voluminous activity in Vienna, transferred to Philips.

Some of the upstarts had taste, others good ears. Mercury, founded in New York in 1945, was driven by C. Robert Fine, a sound engineer, and his fiancée Wilma Cozart, sometime secretary to Antal Dorati, music director in Dallas and Minneapolis. They got Rafael Kubelik to conduct Ravel's score of Mussorgsky's Pictures at an Exhibition in Chicago in a sound so distinctive that the *New York Times* reviewer said it felt like the orchestra's 'living presence', a term the Fines swiftly trademarked. 'We wanted the performance to seem so lifelike that the listener could "see" it before his eyes,' explained Cozart in a press release.

Knowing how US orchestras worked, Cozart could usually get round union barriers and overtime premia. When these proved insurmountable, Mercury came to England. 'One August,' said Neville Marriner, leader of the London Symphony Orchestra's second violins, 'we worked thirty days on the trot, three sessions a day, alternating from Dorati to Pierre Monteux. You couldn't have bought a better education.'[51] So large did Mercury loom for a while that its director of music, Harold Lawrence, became the LSO's next general manager.

Westminster, another New York indy,[52] hooked up with a UK independent, Pye-Nixa, one of whose labels was set up by the father of child star Petula Clark, who was still recording half a century later.[53] Westminster issued the world premiere recording of Mahler's seventh symphony with Hermann Scherchen. Frustratingly it appeared in 1953, just weeks before Hans Rosbaud's performance appeared on Urania, a shadowy outlet for German radio tapes, often conducted by ex-Nazis.

In France, Bernard Coutaz got into his Citroën 2CV and drove an engineer and organist from one cathedral to the next, recording baroque sonatas. Based in Arles, where Vincent Van Gogh lost his ear, Coutaz and his Harmonia Mundi opened untapped realms of early music. In London an Australian heiress, Louise Hanson-Dyer, launched L'Oiseau Lyre (the lyre bird) as a baroque niche but could not resist supporting her struggling compatriots. She gave a gawky soprano at Covent Garden a recital LP. Later, on Decca, Joan Sutherland became the top-selling soprano on record, after Callas.

Klemperer's life on Vox ended rancorously when another baton finished off Mendelssohn's Scottish Symphony in his absence – 'a gross public deception,' he called it.[54] The formidable giant joined EMI, where Legge tended his temperamental swings with unexpected sensitivity. Klemperer loudly scorned records, which, he said, were a poor substitute for live music. 'Listening to a recording,' he sonorously proclaimed, 'is like going to bed with a photograph of Marilyn Monroe.'[55]

3. Midpoint

Halfway through its century, classical recording reached a set of turning points. EMI set the ball rolling with a $3 million bid for US Capitol. Decca formed a counter-alliance with RCA. CBS tied up with Philips. Old enemies became Orwellian allies. EMI's new chairman, Joseph Lockwood, was a miller's son from Nottingham who had organized national animal-feed supplies during the war. He took one look at the music business and decided the classical tail could not continue to wag the popular dog. 'It was a conscious decision of mine to support pop music and play down the importance of the classical people a bit,' he explained, 'not to discourage them, but not to let them think they owned the bloody place.'[1]

In future, Lockwood decreed, no record could be made without approval from an International Classical Recording Committee (ICRC) comprising the heads of the largest regions. Unless a majority agreed that a project would show profit in their territories in three years, the record would not be made. The fiat was received with horror by the classical sector. 'What will I tell Karajan?' wailed Legge, but the clamp stayed until executives got round it in backroom deals. At international conferences, Paris would submit an inflated sales projection for a Beecham LP in exchange for London's reciprocal overestimation of Georges Prêtre.[2] The figures were pure fiction.

Lockwood fumed and tightened his scrutiny. 'He once visited our department at Hayes' (EMI Records, Export Dept, Branch Supplies), said a junior clerk. 'I was about twenty-two. He was introduced to me at my desk and asked me two very pertinent and detailed questions about my work. I never worked out how a chairman could possibly know so much.'[3] A crusty bachelor, the chairman had an eye for sharp young men. He appointed George

Martin, twenty-eight, as EMI's youngest-ever director, head of Parlophone. An oboist by training, it took Martin little more than a couple of years to overturn the musical economy.

That same midpoint moment brought Goddard Lieberson in 1955 to the presidency of CBS Records, in place of Edward Wallerstein. Signing his letters 'God', Lieberson was the last classical man to head a major label. He gave the pop side to Mitch Miller, an ex-classmate of his at Eastman Musical School and oboist in the school band. Miller meant business. He fired Frank Sinatra (years later, meeting him on the street, Miller said 'Hi, Frank'; Sinatra said, 'Just keep on walking') and became overnight the mightiest man in pop. Piratically opportunistic – he put Frankie Laine's cover version of High Noon in the shops three weeks ahead of the official soundtrack – Miller won his own singalong show on CBS television, selling 20 million records. 'He had too much power and not enough taste,' wrote the pop historian Donald Clarke.[4] Miller liked Johnny Mathis-style smooch and the sepia sound of a fading America, untouched by social discord. To kids on street corners, CBS looked old and out of touch.

Lieberson went searching for another South Pacific. 'Goddard backed My Fair Lady when everyone else turned it down at backers' auditions,' said a producer, 'and he was respected enough to go on the road and make suggestions for cuts and improvements. At recording sessions, he was the real star.'[5] In studio, observed CBS photographer Don Hunstein, 'he would sit in Savile Row suits, keeping the atmosphere friendly with little jokes. The president of the company was the working producer of these show records.'[6] With the president at the console and the A&R boss singing along, CBS Records was a hands-on cottage industry operating out of five floors at 799 Seventh Avenue. In the southern US, its LPs were sold by Philips (or Philco) reps, along with personal grooming products. Total sales amounted to $277 million, and one in five records sold was classical.

Down on the mean streets, a storm was gathering. On 12 April 1954 a southern bandleader, Bill Haley, and his group, the Comets, rattled the world's vertebrae with Rock Around the Clock, which inaugurated rock 'n' roll. A gritty movie, *The Blackboard Jungle*, used the song as its soundtrack. The idea came not from the star, Glenn Ford, but from his nine-year-old son, Peter. Kids were calling the shots in music, and Mitch Miller did not like that one little bit. In a caustic address to a convention of radio disc jockeys, he laid into rock merchants for pandering to the under-age. 'You abdicated your programming to the corner record shop, to the eight- to fourteen-year-olds, to the pre-shave crowds that make up 12 per cent of the country's population and zero per cent of its buying power,' he raged. But Mitch was wrong. Teens were rolling in prosperity pocket money. They bought music that was loud, rhythmic, melancholic, sexually assertive. Kids, from here on, were the driving force, responding to a beat that was set on the streets, not in media towers.

Rhythm and blues brayed forth from independent labels in Chicago, Cincinnati and Detroit, getting heavy radio play through deejay bribes, known as payola. Listeners couldn't care less so long as the music rocked. The major labels, terrified, could not tell a hit from the whooping cough. A hip-swiggling crooner who drove girls wild left Mitch Miller stone cold. In November 1955 his RCA rivals paid Sun Records thirty-five grand for Elvis Presley, plus five thousand to his personal manager. Six weeks later, two days after his twenty-first birthday, Elvis sauntered into a Nashville studio and delivered himself of Heartbreak Hotel. It would sell 300,000 in three weeks, a million by springtime. By the end of 1956 Elvis had sold $22 million worth of discs and merchandise in the US, half as much as the whole of the classical market.

Rock took longer to conquer Germany, where the Cold War was hotting up and billions were being pumped into rebuilding West Berlin as a showcase for capitalist plenty against communism's empty windows. Office blocks soared on bombsites and cultural life was fuelled by Bonn government subsidy and secret CIA payments. Elvis was unheard of in Berlin until he joined the US Army and served, from October 1958 to March 1960, in a tank battalion at Friedberg, dating the granddaughter of Olga Chekhova, a notorious Soviet spy.

Musical life in Berlin centred on the Philharmonic Orchestra and its new music director, Herbert von Karajan. On its first US tour in February 1955 the orchestra faced an anti-Nazi demonstration at Carnegie Hall. Back home, Karajan was awarded a Liberty Bell by the Mayor of West Berlin. The symbolism was explicit. Karajan was not just music director but a moral leader in the fight for freedom.

A photograph taken on 27 April shows him at lunch in a rooftop restaurant with the influential critic Stuckenschmidt and the orchestra's grey-faced manager, Gerhart von Westermann. Karajan, suntanned chin resting on upturned left hand, looks neither man in the eye yet commands rapt attention. A satisfied smile flickers on his lips. This is a cat that has collared the cream, a conductor who can do as he pleases, the most powerful maestro on earth. In addition to Berlin, he had taken command of the Vienna State Opera and the Salzburg Festival, and held positions at La Scala Milan and the Philharmonia in London. The one area where his writ fell short was the record industry, but there too the wind was blowing his way.

Vienna Philharmonic players, employed at the State Opera, urged Decca to make records with him. Karajan was keen, believing Decca had a sonic advantage and its new RCA partnership could get him access to the valuable US market. Also beckoning was Deutsche Grammophon. Ernst von Siemens invited him, as a personal favour, to an audio demonstration. 'They made an experiment for him in the studio – "Look, maestro, this is what we can do with a crescendo."'[7] Karajan, impressed, held discussions with Elsa Schiller. 'She understood this business better than anyone, apart from Legge,' he discovered.[8]

When his EMI contract expired in August 1957, he invited competing bids. Decca came top, DGG second, EMI bottom, with a pittance (Bicknell put his money on Barbirolli against Karajan). Legge was mortified, fatally disempowered. Months later, Karajan marched into the Sofiensaal to open his Decca account.

He handed his coat to Gordon Parry, who let it drop to the floor. At Decca there were no flunkeys. 'Don't stand up,' said Karajan. It had not crossed anyone's mind, but they saw his point: the Decca boys towered above the maestro, who was sensitive about his five-foot four. Karajan proceeded to whip up a spectacular Holst Planets for Decca, along with Strauss waltzes and a memorable Madam Butterfly and Aida. But he never warmed to Culshaw and the contract ended in six years, leaving Karajan with a grasp of Decca's advanced techniques which he duly took to Deutsche Grammophon.

Among the Germans he was met with much bowing and scraping. Karajan led off with Richard Strauss's A Hero's Life. 'The sessions took place on three consecutive March mornings in 1959 in the Jesus-Christus Church,' wrote producer Hans Ritter. 'I had been warned that Karajan's signing of a contract depended on whether he was satisfied with our trial recording. When I took the tapes to him in Vienna, he admitted that he had been anxious to make a good impression on us, as he badly wanted the contract. Unfortunately, I made only two more recordings with him.'[9] The record, with melting solos by concertmaster Michel Schwalbé, was beautifully engineered but it failed to sell and Karajan demanded the producer's head.

His next LP was a set of Brahms and Dvořák dances, Hungarian and Slavonic; it sold 55,000 in a year and went on selling. He went on to make 330 recordings on DGG, powering the label to world leadership and turning the public-funded Berlin Philharmonic into his private recording machine, its rehearsals and concerts routinely taped and edited for release. Each summer near Salzburg, DGG would throw a party at Schloss Füschl where Karajan mingled with his 'family', but behind the happy smiles no one felt secure in his approbation. After Ritter, Karajan was produced by Otto Gerdes, a part-time conductor with several DGG recordings to his credit. One morning, having given a concert the night before, Gerdes greeted Karajan jovially as 'Herr Kollege'. He was sacked on the spot.

★

The Next Big Thing was nearly ready. 'General' Sarnoff, smarting from LP defeat, ordered full speed ahead on stereo. Two-channel recording had been around since 1932 when Stokowski got Bell Labs to record a Skryabin symphony and, in London, EMI's Alan Blumlein recorded Mozart's Jupiter Symphony with Beecham. Stokowski gave a stereo demonstration at Carnegie Hall in April 1940, described by the *New York Times* as 'the loudest sound ever created', but the public was unready to invest and interest faded until, in 1954, the advent of FM radio demanded a record response. If automobiles had two speakers, record systems would have to match up, or die.

Jack Pfeiffer, a new RCA recruit, went to Boston in March 1954 to try out stereo in Berlioz's Damnation of Faust with the Frenchman Charles Munch. He went on to Chicago, where Fritz Reiner was conducting A Hero's Life, and decided to risk the session on just two microphones. 'The clarity and definition that we got – of course, a lot of it had to do with the acoustics of the hall, the quality of the musicians, Reiner's balances, and so forth – were so dramatic. It was completely different from anything we had ever heard before.'[10] In the Brahms D-minor concerto with Arthur Rubinstein (CD24, p. 187), Pfeiffer added a third pick-up microphone for zoning in on solo passages. By trial and error, he had established standard stereo recording technique.

Pfeiffer's results were trademarked as RCA Living Stereo and sold to audiophiles at a prohibitive $18.95 a disc. It took four years for RCA and CBS, eager to avoid another 'war of speeds', to agree a joint format. In the meantime, every session was recorded in duplicate, mono and stereo, just in case.

Post-production was undergoing a parallel revolution. Jascha Heifetz, said Pfeiffer, 'loved to work with his hands. He liked automobiles, firearms, all sorts of things. He had every tool in the world there in his workshop in California. Never used any of them, of course. Because of his feel for tinkering, when he discovered tape editing he became fascinated. Not that he wanted to edit for the sake of editing, but it gave him an ability to put things together in a way he never could before. He was never totally satisfied with his recordings.'

Tape editing provided an illusion of perfection that detached recording from concert humanity. Some musicians objected. The Olympian Otto Klemperer entered an Abbey Road suite where an editor, spools of tape around his neck, was replacing a broken horn note in a Mozart concerto. Mount Klemperer erupted. 'Lotte,' he barked at his faithful daughter, 'ein Schwindel!'[11] (it's a fraud!).

On the second day of 1955 a Canadian pianist made his US debut on the tiny stage of a modern art museum, the Phillips Collection in Washington, DC, with a recital that bordered on the bizarre. Instead of Mozart, Schubert and Chopin, Glenn Gould opened with a pavane by the remote Elizabethan composer Orlando Gibbons and a fantasia by his Dutch contemporary Jan Peterszoon Sweelinck. There followed five works of J. S. Bach, the Beethoven Hammerklavier sonata, and, after intermission, the modernist sonata of Alban Berg, succeeded by the abstruse opus 27 Variations by Anton von Webern. By way of encore, he repeated the forbidding Webern.

So soon after Christmas, attendance was sparse, but the *Washington Post*'s critic Paul Hume was on the edge of his seat. Hume hailed 'a pianist with rare gifts for the world . . . we know of no pianist anything like him, of any age.' Among the listeners was Alexander Schneider, second violinist of the Budapest String Quartet, who rushed back to New York to tell David Oppenheim, head of Columbia Masterworks. 'We listened to a recording by Dinu Lipatti,' recalled Oppenheim, 'and I said, "Why can't we find another one like that?" And Sasha said there was one, a person in Toronto named Glenn Gould, who was, alas, a little crazy, but had a remarkable, hypnotic effect at the piano.'[12]

Gould's New York debut at Manhattan Town Hall on 11 January drew another meagre crowd – 250, by Gould's count – but among them were the rising pianists William Kapell, Gary Graffman and Eugene Istomin, along with Oppenheim, who kept looking round nervously for rival scouts. Next morning, he signed

Gould to a two-year contract, to start with Bach's Goldberg Variations, a cerebral suite never commercially recorded.[13] The artist was twenty-two years old.

His sessions, over four days in June, turned into a media gawk fest. 'There's something happening in the studio on 30th Street,' gushed publicist Deborah Ishlon. 'We've got this nut and everybody's talking how absolutely marvellous he is.'[14] Sitting exactly fourteen inches above ground, Gould soaked his arms to the elbows in scalding water 'to relax them' and popped pills of untold provenance to cope with minute changes in air quality. He wore a headwrap and several sets of gloves – but no shoes, the better to pedal with his toes. He sang, hummed and howled while playing. Critics spotted that he played with his wrists below keyboard level, almost a physical impossibility. 'I think he was totally aware of the fact that he probably created a strange personality, but that's what he wanted to do,' said his producer, Howard H. Scott. 'He was a marvellous marketing executive . . . he marketed himself perfectly.'[15]

The Goldberg Variations appeared on Masterworks on 3 January 1956, priced $3.98, with a cover comprising thirty action photographs of Gould, one for each variation. The LP was an instant icon, its spine number – ML 5060 – acquiring mystic resonance. It was the top-selling classical record of 1956, clearing 40,000 copies, and it pumped Gould's reputation so high and wide that Khrushchev asked to hear him in Moscow and Karajan booked him for Salzburg and Berlin.

Gould took a minute interest in the recording process. 'Recording him was unlike working with anyone else,' said producer Paul Myers.

We made the first book of the Well-Tempered Clavier, and he would record each Prelude and each Fugue anything up to ten or twelve times (nearly always note-perfect). Then, he liked to 'edit' the material ('This section should sound more *pomposo*; I think that part is too subdued'). Most pianists edit to correct mistakes. Glenn rarely made mistakes (he also rarely practised, seemingly transferring his thoughts to his fingers as a natural process) and he edited to change emphases and create his interpretations . . . He always insisted that he was not a pianist. He liked to describe himself as 'a composer who expresses ideas through the keyboard' . . . He was also quite modest, saying: 'If you want Beethoven Sonatas as they should be played, buy Schnabel. I just like to experiment.'[16]

In concert, he scowled and winced at the conductor and sat cross-legged on his stool until a second before entry. When Leonard Bernstein took him home for dinner, his wife Felicia unwrapped the filthy turban and subjected his lank brown hair to a wash and trim. Lieberson took him to lunch. They discussed twelve-note rows in Berg's opera Lulu (still unseen in America) and a contract that would bind Gould to CBS exclusively and for life. Lieberson told him to record whatever he liked. At a gala dinner years later, Gould sang out a Lieberson Madrigal, mocking CBS ('We're all uncommercial here, our sales get worse from year to year') and lampooning the president's irritation with his pet conductor ('No, no Lennie, no you can't, why must you be so damn avant, damn avant, damn avant garde?').

Bernstein was Lieberson's other carte-blanche artist, and biggest headache. As a fresh-faced kid he had erupted onto the *New York Times* front page in November 1943 when he took over a Bruno Walter broadcast at a few minutes' notice. The next year he wrote a Broadway show, On the Town, followed by two symphonies, one based on the prophet Jeremiah, the other on a W. H. Auden theme, the Age of Anxiety. He gave lectures at Harvard. There was nothing, it seemed, that he could not do.

But Lennie spelled trouble. He was sexually rapacious with men and politically active in leftist and Zionist causes. As McCarthy paranoia gripped the US, Bernstein was spurned by his home-town Boston Symphony Orchestra and wound up unemployed in Manhattan, his passport seized by the State Department. He composed two more musicals – the satirical Candide, which flopped, and West Side Story, which dragged Broadway into urban ethnic conflict. Lieberson, who recorded both shows, regarded

Lennie more as a Broadway composer than a symphony conductor but he kept him on a small contract for contemporary music.

Then, in 1957, the New York Philharmonic ousted its socially awkward music director, Dmitri Mitropoulos, in favour of the 38-year-old Bernstein, who had ostentatiously married. Lennie took the orchestra on an inaugural trip to Russia and warned CBS he was getting offers from RCA. 'I want to be free to record whatever I wish. I don't want anyone to tell me such-and-such cannot be done,'[17] he announced. Bernstein's lawyer spelled it out: 'a twenty-year contract with minimum guarantees against maximum royalties and the right to record anything he pleased, any time he desired'.[18] Masterworks boss Schuyler Chapin went to Lieberson, who okayed the deal. Bernstein then tore up the twenty-page contract and sent back a single-sheet letter of agreement. 'You tell me what you need, I'll tell you what I'd like to do, and together we'll develop a good catalogue,' he told Chapin.

Where do we start? said Chapin. Mahler, said the maestro. 'I plan to play all of the symphonies over the next few seasons and I want to record them all. The public is ready to respond to Mahler. His time has come.'[19]

That line, 'my time will come!', was Mahler's own. With a centenary approaching in 1960, it was reasonable for the New York Philharmonic to put on a symphonic cycle, selling 2,000 seats a concert over several years. But a record label needed to shift many times more LPs to break even and Mahler was a man on the margins, adored by European émigrés and few others. There were ten symphonies to sell and Bruno Walter, Mahler's acolyte, was already recording the First and Ninth with the Columbia Symphony Orchestra. CBS was on the point of putting out competing versions of unsaleable symphonies.

Bernstein set out the case for Mahler with blazing conviction. 'Mahler's music is about Mahler,' he postulated, 'which means simply that it is about conflict. Think of it: Mahler the Creator vs Mahler the Performer; the Jew vs the Christian; the Believer vs the Doubter; the Naif vs the Sophisticate; the provincial Bohemian vs the Viennese homme du monde; the Faustian philosopher vs the oriental mystic; the operatic symphonist who never wrote an opera . . . Out of this opposition proceeds the endless list of anti-theses – the whole roster of Ying and Yang – that inhabit Mahler's music.'[20] In the dawning of the Age of Aquarius, he presented Mahler as all things to all men – and it seemed to work.

If Bernstein's verbal advocacy was glib, the sweep of his argument and the passion of his performances won the day. Using every media opportunity – most popularly his Young People's Concerts on CBS TV – Bernstein made Mahler the composer for modern times. While Rafael Kubelik issued a parallel set on DGG, lyrical and serene, it was Bernstein who set Mahler at the centre of world attention.

He applied the same proselytic gifts promiscuously and some-times ill-advisedly to a raft of American contemporaries: Copland, Barber, Diamond, Fine, Rorem and Schuman. His enthusiasms embraced the underpowered Nielsen and Milhaud and his com-missions included Luciano Berio's gigantic Sinfonia, a musical commentary on Mahler's Resurrection Symphony. Remarkably, the public trusted his flights of fantasy, despite withering criticism from Harold Schonberg in the *New York Times* and the routine Tchaikovsky and Rachmaninov that Eugene Ormandy offered on regular Philadelphia visits. Bernstein, over eleven years, set New York afire and the hall was filled nightly with eager young faces, some contorted in perplexity.

Yet, for all his appeal, Bernstein was a disaster on record, outsold by Ormandy and Philadelphia[21] and seldom among the CBS top sellers except with Rhapsody in Blue (coupled with An American in Paris) and Aaron Copland's Billy the Kid and Rodeo suites.[22] The costs were often self-annihilating. Under union rules, unless the Philharmonic recorded within two days of a concert, players were entitled to a full session fee every fifteen minutes.[23] Recording Bernstein's score for Elia Kazan's film On the Waterfront, coupled with the West Side Story suite, cost fifty grand. The shocked maestro offered to forgo royalties until it broke even (to general surprise, it did), but few other ventures covered their costs. Mahler apart, his classical and romantic records were poorly received on both technical and analytical grounds. CBS sound erred on the side of murk and Bernstein's interpretations lacked the warmth of Walter or the icy perfectionism of sharp-eared Georg Szell. Nevertheless, despite financial losses and critical assaults, Bernstein gave CBS what it needed – a youthful, brash and trendy image. In the classical racks it leaped a whole generation ahead of RCA, whose boss, George Marek, still considered Toscanini 'the greatest musician that ever existed'.[24] RCA went in for big signings, grabbing the pianist Van Cliburn after he won the 1958 Moscow Tchaikovsky Competition, but its stars were ageing and unable to match Bernstein and Gould on Lieberson's glamour label.

In the hiatus between mono and stereo, John Culshaw seized his moment. Stereo, he told Maurice Rosengarten, would vindicate his vision of opera for the home. The Ring would bring wide-open spaces to suburban sitting rooms. Gordon Parry had brilliant ideas for simulating anvils, horses and clashing swords. Culshaw had enticed Kirsten Flagstad out of retirement to sing Fricka in Das Rheingold. Others pencilled in were George London and Hans Hotter as Wotan, Birgit Nilsson as Brünnhilde, Wolfgang Windgassen as Siegfried and Fischer-Dieskau as Gunther. Late in 1957 Rosengarten and Lewis gave Culshaw the green light for Rheingold. 'You had to fight for what you believed in at Decca,' said Nella Marcus, Culshaw's assistant, 'but then they would stand by you.'[25]

Culshaw assembled two full teams, stereo and mono, taking on a pair of Mozart scholars, Christopher Raeburn and Erik Smith, as junior producers. Parry rigged up Decca's stereo 'tree' – 'a central trio of microphones, plus left and right outriggers, with extra spot-mikes as necessary'.[26] Positions were chalked on the floor. Every last Norn knew exactly where she had to stand and sing.

There was one last-ditch hitch. Rosengarten, hearing an LP of Flagstad in the third act of Die Walküre, decided to drop Solti and complete the opera under the Augustan Hans Knappertsbusch. Culshaw was conflicted, but did his best: 'We tried to drag [Kna] kicking and screaming into the twentieth century of the gramophone record, the era of the listener-at-home who hears without any visual aid and without the community of the theatre. It was an alien world for him. He was a nineteenth-century professional, and to the end of his life the gramophone was a new-fangled toy.'[27] With a huge heave of relief, Culshaw told Solti he had been reinstated.

The night before recording began the pair were going over the score in the bar of the Imperial Hotel in Vienna, where Wagner had once stayed, when Walter Legge sauntered in.

'What are you doing here?' he demanded mock-innocently.

'Recording Rheingold,' said Solti.

'Very nice,' snorted Legge, 'but you won't sell fifty copies.'

On the afternoon of 24 September 1958 the Decca Ring began with a Flagstad piano rehearsal. Culshaw, in his vivid account of the adventure, *Ring Resounding*, failed to convey its extreme precariousness. The Vienna Philharmonic simmered with spite at Solti, the brash Hungarian Jew, no match for their wonder-Karajan. RCA kept poaching Culshaw's best studio men and Rosengarten constantly prevaricated. All hinged on the launch of Rheingold. In May 1959, the set shot into the *Billboard* charts one slot below Elvis Presley. The next opera was safe, but no sooner had Rosengarten given the go-ahead for Siegfried than Solti agreed to conduct an RCA Otello in Rome on the designated dates. 'I really am angry about the Otello business,' said Culshaw, urging his friend to reconsider 'in your best interests' (but adding courteously that 'if you decide against Otello, you should notify RCA quickly, in fairness to them').[28] Culshaw followed up with an ultimatum: 'Very unlikely able delay confirmation Ring dates . . . cannot guarantee to prevent another conductor taking over.'[29] Faced with loss of Ring, Solti gave Otello a miss.

Siegfried, the second in the cycle, came out on five LPs against Rheingold's three. It was a much tougher sell but Culshaw took on a Canadian publicist, Terry McEwen, whose encyclopaedic knowledge of vocal lore roused US critics to untold heights of hyperbole. Götterdämmerung was comparably acclaimed in 1964, Die Walküre the following year. Solti and Culshaw played extracts of the complete cycle to packed public meetings in London, Manchester and Cambridge. A radio station in upstate New York played the whole set in a day.[30] More than any other record, Decca's Ring made stereo a domestic necessity.

Solti, now an international celebrity, was treated by Rosengarten as if he were still a refugee boy on the streets of Zurich. 'How did it go?' asked Nella Marcus as he came out of a meeting. 'It was like this,' said Solti. 'Mr Rosengarten put an ashtray on the coffee table. He said: "When the ashtray is on your side, you talk; when it's on my side, I talk." Not once, did he push the ashtray to my side of the table.'[31]

Solti held the flagship role at Decca, as Bernstein did at CBS and Bernard Haitink, the Concertgebouw conductor, at Philips. They were hardworking studio all-rounders. Bernstein was at his best in contemporary music, Solti had the edge in opera and Haitink was a solid symphonist. The leader of the fleet, however, was racing ahead on Deutsche Grammophon.

Herbert von Karajan in 1962 quit his jobs at the Vienna Opera and Salzburg, having already relinquished La Scala and London. He had a better plan: rule by records. With the Berlin Philharmonic working full time in its custom-built ochre concert hall, he could control the world's turntables from his own production centre.

Karajan found a kindred spirit in Glenn Gould, who abruptly gave up travelling and renounced public concerts, declaring that records were a superior musical form. 'I was working with Glenn in 1964, when he decided to quit the concert stage,' said Paul Myers. 'He felt that people were waiting to pounce when he made a technical mistake (he rarely did). Probably the most important reason (which he rarely admitted) was that he was very self-conscious (from his conducting with a free hand to his curious groaning form of singing) and he felt that people came to watch him rather than listen to him.'[32] Karajan, smitten by Gould's leap of faith, offered to fly his Berliners to Toronto to make records together. The pianist was tempted but refused to yield editorial control. A prolonged stalemate set in.

Karajan plunged instead into DGG's biggest undertaking, a project so costly that fans were asked to pay for it by advance subscription. He had recorded the Beethoven symphonies with the Philharmonia over several years. Now he approached them as an integral cycle, issued indivisibly as a boxed set, priced at a forbidding $40. The production cost was 1.5 million Deutschmarks (close to $400,000) and EMI's David Bicknell gloated that DGG was heading for 'a colossal financial catastrophe'.[33] But Karajan had prepared his ground. Weeks ahead of release, he took his orchestra to play Beethoven in Paris, London and New York to high acclaim. The set, when it appeared, was elegantly presented and lavishly endorsed by weighty authorities. Stuckenschmidt, forsaking critical detachment, gushed:

Karajan's aim is tonal perfection and rhythmic precision. Thanks to his wonderfully acute ear and his highly rationalised rehearsal work he is *the greatest living exponent* of the art of training an orchestra. His attitude to Beethoven . . . is totally different from that of Furtwängler. To him, transparency and luxuriant colour are of the utmost importance. However, with his rare sense of tone, he reveals as if by magic details in Beethoven's symphonic textures, which come to us as new discoveries.[34]

A younger hagiolater, Karl Heinz Ruppel, wrote of Karajan as an epic hero in much the same terms as Bernstein had spoken of Mahler. Karajan, said Ruppel, aspired to

the creation of order between the diametrically opposed elements of his artistic nature; between glowing warmth and coldness, fervour and dispassionate distance, temperament and discipline, vitality and reflection, intuition and intellect, imagination and technique. It is an enormous achievement to keep up the high degree of tension between these forces . . . more, to direct them toward one goal – the representation of the musical work in its objective form, i.e. that intended by its creator.[35]

Such adulation had not been heard in post-war Germany and it was excesses like these that prompted Culshaw to warn that Karajan 'filled the void left by the death of Hitler in that part of the German psyche which craves for a leader'.[36] The conquest of Beethoven was Karajan's moment of Hitlerian hubris. Apart from the Pastoral Symphony, which sounded leaden and inflexible, the interpretations were sleek, convincing and beautifully mastered, the sound balanced by a new engineer, Günter Hermanns, who became a Karajan fixture. The set sold massively in Germany and emphatically around the world. Apart from Toscanini on RCA and EMI's reboxed Karajan monos there was no competition to DGG's Beethoven set, which became the cornerstone of stereo collections. It was a masterstroke of market anticipation, cementing Karajan's grip on the record industry and inspiring me-too cycles from André Cluytens, Josef Krips, Klemperer, Hans Schmidt-Isserstedt, Haitink and others.

At Deutsche Grammophon it marked a transition of power. On the last page of his Beethoven programme book, Karajan published an open letter to Elsa Schiller, praising her 'unwearying energy' in supporting his cycle. 'Personally, I can tell you that these were among the most beautiful hours of my artistic activity. You know well how much love and effort the Philharmonic players and I have wrung into the seven years of our collaboration and, most importantly, into the Beethoven project.' He signed off, 'In deepest artistic attachment, Herbert von Karajan.'[37]

This was Schiller's final act. She turned sixty-five in November 1962 and carried on for another year, signing the pianists Martha Argerich and Tamás Vásáry and hammering down deals with other artists. 'Our last meeting was not very happy,' said Martin Lovett of the Amadeus. 'We had just done the Beethoven quartets and she tried to persuade us to take a lump sum payment. She was retiring from DG and wanted to leave a good impression. We refused. It was a dirty trick. Those records earn us royalties to this day.'[38]

Fricsay's death from cancer in February 1963 distressed Schiller greatly. Two years later she lost her brilliant protégé, the harpsichordist and composer Peter Ronnefeld, who was chief conductor in Bonn when he was also struck by cancer, at the age of thirty.

Although Karajan lured her out to judge conducting competitions, Schiller faded from the scene long before her death in November 1974. Karajan assumed effective artistic control of the record label, dominating its central production. Ernst von Siemens, aware of the organizational vacuum, used Schiller's withdrawal to reorganize the business. He called Frits Philips in Holland and agreed to merge sales forces. DGG became 'the centre of a worldwide network of companies whose principal function is the creation of new products in the field of classical music.'[39] Siemens had fulfilled his aim, restoring German music to world dominance, with Karajan at its helm.

4. Millionaires

In 1962 EMI posted a £4.4 million profit on sales of £82.5 million. Its chairman, known internally as Sir Joseph Tightwad for the low salaries he paid, was knighted 'for services to industry'. Head office moved to Manchester Square in the West End, where Lockwood's morning arrival froze employees to the spot. 'Out!' he barked at a young man who had entered the elevator ahead of him. Old hierarchies prevailed. No one imagined that sales were about to treble and profits quintuple by a force beyond all reckoning.

One April morning, Parlophone boss George Martin took a call from a colleague who was being hassled by a desperate provincial agent. 'Send him along,' said Martin. The man's name was Brian Epstein. He was twenty-seven years old, loved classical music and worked in his parents' Liverpool furniture store. He looked after a Cavern Club band which had auditioned twice at Decca without result. Other EMI labels were uninterested. Parlophone was his last hope.

George Martin listened to the tapes and liked what he heard. He brought the Beatles to Abbey Road, watched them play and suggested a change of drummer.[1] He then signed the group to a slave contract that paid one pre-decimal penny in royalties per two-sided record and bound them to EMI for five years. The first Beatles single, Love Me Do, reached number seventeen in the charts. The second, Please Please Me, went to the top, unleashing a wave of Beatlemania. By the end of 1963 Beatles UK sales were £6.25 million and the boys shared a Royal Variety Show billing with Marlene Dietrich.

Then they went global. Capitol, EMI's US subsidiary, passed on the first two Beatles singles, which came out on Vee Jay, a Chicago indy. Neither charted higher than 116. Vee Jay turned down She Loves You, which appeared on Swan, a New York minnow. Epstein flew to New York in November 1963 with I Want To Hold Your Hand and played it to Brown Meggs, Capitol's East Coast Director. Meggs, a classical producer, saw its potential. Six weeks after the Kennedy assassination, I Want to Hold Your Hand became the first-ever British number one in the US charts.

Seventy-three million Americans watched the Beatles on the CBS *Ed Sullivan Show* on 9 February 1964, a third of the population. John Lennon, in an interview with the London *Evening Standard*, said 'We're more popular than Jesus Christ now.'[2] Each successive LP – Beatles for Sale . . . Rubber Soul . . . Sergeant Pepper's Lonely Hearts Club Band – was more sophisticated than the last. George Martin drew upon classical resources, hiring a string quartet as backing for Yesterday and the RPO horn player Alan Civil for McCartney's song, For No One. That synthesis set the Beatles apart from the pop universe. Martin introduced four-track recording at Abbey Road and spent three days working on a single Beatles track, as long as it would take other groups to cut a whole album. The second album of 1969 was provisionally titled Everest, the summit of their achievement. In the end, they named it Abbey Road, for the studios.

George Martin, on a £3,000 salary, put in for a raise. Tightwad turned him down, so he quit. The Beatles refused to work with anyone else. Martin, now a freelance, demanded a producer's royalty – the first in music history. The Beatles were rewriting the rulebook, and the financial parameters. Their revenues were phenomenal, then and for all time. Thirty years after their break-up, the group were making $20 million a year in royalties; two anthologies compiled in 1996 netted close to $1 billion from new listeners.[3] Nothing in the music industry would ever be the same again.

EMI soared and Decca drooped. In the US, Capitol vied with Elvis on RCA while CBS had Mitch Miller and his singalongs. Lieberson, too late, fired Miller in 1965 and replaced him with Clive Davis, a contract lawyer. Davis was a new type of record man, neither creative nor intuitive – 'I had no A&R training, no claim to having "ears"'.[4] What he knew was how to handle money. A middle-class boy from Crown Heights, Brooklyn, prematurely bald, Davis had no time for classical music which, in the Beatles boom, fell from one-fifth of label turnover to just 5 per cent. Heads were bound to roll.

Walter Legge was first to go. Lockwood ordered him to give up his Philharmonia royalties, worth £75,000 a year. Legge regarded the back catalogue as his pension, and in June 1963 resigned. He flew off to see Karajan in Salzburg, looking for a job. Peter Andry found him sitting in the waiting room. 'Ich bin drei Tage antechambriert' (I've been waiting here three days), said Legge.[5] 'I thought every company in the world would be at my doorstep,' he told an assistant, 'but there has been nothing – nothing at all.'[6] The rest of his life was spent as his wife's shadow. John Culshaw's was the next departure. His Ring complete, he joined BBC television as head of opera and classical music in 1967 and instantly regretted it. 'We used to meet for lunch once a month,' said Paul Myers of CBS, 'and he proposed [making] recordings, including some live concerts at Aldeburgh. Despite the BBC job, he still wanted to do freelance recording work.'[7] Loneliness set in. His friends – his family – were at Decca and he felt cruelly cut off. After leaving the BBC in 1975 he contracted a wasting virus on a trip to Australia and died in March 1980, at the age of fifty-five. Culshaw left behind an explosive canister, a memoir that exposed classical recording to objective scrutiny and exposed human chinks in Fortress Karajan. For many, John Culshaw was the supreme classical producer, a man inspired by the absence of audience and the thrill of technology. 'For Culshaw, the red light was a liberator, not a stifler,' said one of his trainees, 'the medium an art form in itself.'[8]

Critically, at CBS, Lieberson yielded to pressure and handed over to Davis in 1967. Earnings were stagnant at $5 million (pre-tax) and Broadway was dead. 'Goddard hated doing the cut-outs: deleting records that sold fewer than 400 a year,' recalled Peter Munves, head of Masterworks marketing. 'He'd do it, but he made horrible faces.'[9] Although CBS, RCA and Capitol were on level pegging with a 12 per cent market share, CBS was losing the rock war. Lieberson's consolation was that his classical label was still the best in America. RCA poached Ormandy and the Philadelphia Orchestra. They also made some fine operas in Europe – 'the best Tosca in twenty years – Placido Domingo and Leontyne Price,' reported Munves, who switched labels, 'but the deal with Rosengarten was that RCA had ten years, then the rights went to Decca. RCA was losing its opera catalogue. It was only a matter of time before they stopped classical recording altogether.'[10]

Clive Davis experienced an awakening at the Monterey Pop Festival in the Summer of Love, returning to the office in a flowered shirt. In the last quarter of 1969 he cancelled all classical releases, killing the Christmas market and sending a negative signal across the industry. At sales conventions he would schmooze through classical presentations. Janis Joplin, Blood Sweat and Tears, Bruce Springsteen and Billy Joel were his personal signings, joining Bob Dylan, Simon and Garfunkel and the Byrds at the summit of the charts. In the six years that Davis ruled, CBS market share leaped from 12 to 22 per cent and classics went down the drain. The writing was becoming visible on the wall.

It was not just pop that squeezed classical pips. The formula itself was failing for want of strong successors to the Schillers, the Culshaws, the Liebersons and the Legges. In 1956 Arthur Rubinstein sold 350,000 copies of Rachmaninov's second concerto, with Fritz Reiner. Fifteen years later, his retake with Ormandy sold just 20,000. Heifetz was falling well short of his $65,000 RCA guarantee and Horowitz could not earn out his $50,000 advance on CBS. Big names no longer spelled paydirt. Music lovers balked at buying the same old stuff all over again.

Labels, lacking imagination, relied on a hard core of habitual buyers, overwhelmingly male, who hung around record stores on the first of the month waiting to sample the new releases. They also congregated in record clubs and around the village pump of a monthly publication, the *Gramophone*. Founded in 1923 by the Scottish novelist Compton Mackenzie, *Gramophone* attracted 80,000 subscribers at peak and could make the difference between profit and loss for major labels. The *American Record Guide* (est. 1935) aimed to avoid 'stuffy British sentences or academic circumlocutions'; there were also *FonoForum* (Germany), *Diapason* (France), *Scherzo* (Spain) and others. *Gramophone*, though, was the industry's international journal of record and its regressive tastes confined labels to a corridor of safety.

Reviews were relentlessly polite, if not downright deferential. 'I don't like saying bad things,' admitted Edward Greenfield, the chief *Gramophone* critic who was reputed to sell more records than any man alive, bar Karajan.[11] Reviews were routinely shown to record bosses before publication and, in some instances, modified. It was a very cosy relationship, veering on the promotional.

There were fifty-three gramophone societies in London and 250 more around the UK.[12] Their members, seen at annual conventions, were white, middle-class, middle-aged. Some bought as many as a hundred LPs a year, a harmless hobby. Catering to this constituency, producers stuck to the familiar. When Lorin Maazel covered the Tchaikovsky symphonies for Decca – 'technically and musically the most brilliant on record', said *Gramophone* – CBS followed with a Bernstein set and DGG with a Karajan. Maazel's Sibelius was matched by Ormandy on CBS and Colin Davis on Philips. Karl Böhm's DGG Schubert symphonies went head to head with Istvan Kertesz on Decca, Eugen Jochum's Bruckner cycle on DGG did battle with Karajan. A *Penguin Guide*, compiled by Greenfield and two Gramophonistas, became an essential guide to the perplexed in many record stores.

Over time, the boxes grew bigger. For Beethoven's bicentenary in 1970, DGG issued the complete works, in twelve sets, on seventy-six LPs. Antal Dorati recorded the 104 symphonies of Haydn on fifty LPs in nine boxes for Decca (CD 55, p. 224). Böhm conducted the forty-one Mozart symphonies on fifteen discs for DGG. While these magnificent enterprises did justice to the lesser works of great composers, they were hardly a nursery for new audiences.

Attempts were made to chase the campus dollar. Young Daniel Barenboim played the twenty-seven Mozart piano concertos on EMI (against Géza Anda on DGG, Alfred Brendel on Vox and Vladimir Ashkenazy on Decca). His cellist wife, Jacqueline du Pré, breathed life into Edward Elgar's world-weary concerto. Their friends Zubin Mehta, Pinchas Zukerman, Itzhak Perlman, Ashkenazy and the guitarist John Williams wore trendy clothes and giggled a lot in Christopher Nupen's TV films. The new kids talked cool but played in strict discipline, respecting tradition even as much of their generation rejected it. Luchino Visconti's film of Thomas Mann's *Death in Venice* drove up sales of the Adagietto from Mahler's fifth symphony, but campus nights throbbed to the violent rock of Vietnam. Pop flowered in psychedelic LP sleeves. While naked girls smiled innocently on Blind Faith and Jimi Hendrix covers, classics stuck to studio portraits of artists, dressed up in tie and tails.

Composers who grooved with the times received short shrift on classical labels. John Tavener, an English etherealist, got his break on Apple, the Beatles' label. Arvo Pärt, the Estonian dissident, found a home at ECM, a 1969 Munich indy where jazz and classics interconnected. There were isolated exceptions. Deutsche Grammophon flew over Steve Reich for a three-LP set of Drumming, Six Pianos and Music for Mallet Instruments, Voices and Organ (CD 60, p. 229). In December 1967 CBS released Music of Our Time. 'Can you imagine?' said Reich. 'Twenty simultaneous releases of people like myself, Gordon Mumma, John Cage, Milton Babbitt, Stockhausen – I mean, forget it!'[13] Two thousand copies were pressed of each LP and most were reprinted. Terry Riley's A Rainbow in Curved Air top-scored with 12,000. John McClure, the chief producer, was ecstatic but Clive Davis sneered at such small beer and, after the conservative upswing of Richard Nixon's election, plans for radical albums by LaMonte Young and Philip Glass were quashed. Major labels, flummoxed by the unfamiliar, treated living composers like benefit seekers. The pop revolution never crossed classical thresholds. At Abbey Road, where George Martin gave the Beatles a string quartet, a corporate firewall stopped any counterflow. Classics were living in a fast-receding past.

The times, as Bob Dylan droned, were a-changing. Peace and love gave way to riots, war protests and strikes. 'It was a horrible period,' said Andreas Holschneider, professor of musicology at the University of Hamburg. 'I was spending all my time after '68 being hauled to student political meetings.' A faculty colleague, Hans Hickmann, offered him a production job at DGG's Archiv. Hickmann, 'always in a cloud of tobacco smoke',[14] died soon after of a heart attack, leaving the reticent Mozartian in charge of Archiv, reporting to one of Germany's biggest industrialists. 'Ernst von Siemens said to me, "If ever you have an item for which you cannot enthuse your colleagues or get company approval, come to me,"' Holschneider recalled. 'We would meet five or six times a year to discuss music, and every year I would get half a million Deutschmarks for a project.'[15]

Prudently at first, Holschneider turned Archiv from a retro label, recording baroque pops for the Christmas market, to a leader in the exciting new field of period practice, making music sound as it did when it was written. The transformation was not easily achieved. Archiv's top seller was the Munich conductor Karl Richter, who, as former organist at St Thomas's, Leipzig, claimed irrefutable authority in the music of Bach. Richter was the kind of musician who made Germans comfortable with their past, employing moderate speeds, minimum fuss and limited intellect. He pooh-poohed the authenticist movement. 'Who says that Bach wouldn't have used modern instruments if he'd had them?' he blustered. 'It might be informative and revealing to play Bach on historical instruments, but for me, it's only a modish phenomenon that will fade away.'[16] Richter died in February 1981, having comprehensively lost the argument.

The early music revival had been around for a while. It arose during the arts-and-crafts movement in England but found no convincing interpreters until after the Second World War, when a countertenor, Alfred Deller, caught the ear on a BBC broadcast and a chorus leader of the International Ladies Garment Workers Union in New York, Noah Greenberg, took up singing Purcell in period style. In the summer of 1948 a Dutch harpsichordist, Gustav Leonhardt, ended his studies in Basle and took a train to Vienna to study conducting. 'We met in a corridor of the Academy and started talking about his thesis on The Art of the Fugue [by Bach],' related his fellow-student, Nikolaus Harnoncourt. 'We decided to perform it, after about 200 rehearsals, with a quartet of [viola da] gambas – myself, my wife [Alice Hoffelner], Eduard Melkus and Alfred Altenburger who was later Vorstand [player-chairman] of the Vienna Philharmonic. We met, and we struggled.'[17] That was the start of the revolution in Europe.

Leonhardt, with his wife, Marie, formed an eponymous Baroque Ensemble; the Harnoncourts, with Melkus, created Concentus Musicus Wien. Both groups joined up in 1954 to record Bach cantatas with Deller. There was something of the Singing Family Trapp about these groups, the more so when sons and daughters joined in, but the ethos was high-minded: a search, note by note, for musical truth. Harnoncourt, a descendant of Habsburg emperors, earned his daily living as a cellist in the Vienna Symphony Orchestra under Herbert von Karajan. 'In those days, musicians were slaves,' he reported. 'Conductors used to order a musician to play his part alone, and I have never seen anything less than terror when this happened. Two players, friends of mine, suffered a complete nervous breakdown and were dragged away to mental hospitals for electric-shock therapy.'[18]

Resentful and bored, Harnoncourt hung around antique shops, fingering ornate viols. He bought a 1558 Cremona bass fiddle for a pittance. 'For me, an instrument was a tool, not a cult,' he said. In 1960 he persuaded Telefunken, a German branch of Decca, to record Bach on early instruments and Hickmann, 'a terrible musician', to take on music from the court of Maximilian. Both labels offered long-term contracts. 'So I went to Hamburg. In the morning I had a discussion with Hickmann and his group and in the afternoon I had a session with Telefunken. The Deutsche Grammophon people said, "You're the absolute best for any kind of dance music, from medieval to Johann Strauss." The Telefunken people said, "We like your way of working." So we said goodbye to Deutsche Grammophon.[19]

Karajan, hearing that one of his cellists had conducted a Bach record, banned Harnoncourt from his empire. 'I don't understand why our relations went bad,' said Harnoncourt. 'Karajan loved to perform Bach, but every time he produced a choral recording it would be compared to mine, not always favourably. I wrote to him once, and got a very nice reply, but it remained impossible for me to work in Salzburg.' After a trailblazing US tour in 1969, Harnoncourt quit the day job and became a missionary for early music. Holschneider tried again to lure him to Archiv. 'You're the best man for church music,'[20] he said. Harnoncourt declined, sticking to small-time Telefunken. Leonhardt, similarly, shunned Philips. Baroque musicians lived on boutique labels – Deller on Harmonia Mundi, the Catalan Jordi Savall on Astree, Dutchman Ton Koopman on Erato, often crossing over to collaborate. Leonhardt's Brandenburg concertos on Telefunken, taped in Haarlem churches in 1976, brought together his best pupils: Sigiswald Kuijken on violin, Anner Bylsma (cello), Wieland Kuijken (viola da gamba), Frans Brüggen (recorder) and Bob van Asperen (harpsichord). 'If one strives to be authentic,' warned Leonhardt, 'one will never be convincing . . . The crucial point . . . is the question of artistic quality.'[21] Brüggen pursued cleanliness of tone, obliging students to play scales for half an hour while he read a newspaper.

The more organic performers hung around Reinhard Goebel, a Melkus pupil who got himself sacked by Cologne University in 1973 for sneaking an unregistered gamba player onto campus. Goebel formed Musica Antiqua Köln, a group which made such a fetish of raw text and literal fidelity that critics called him the Ayatollah. Holschneider signed him for Archiv ('I learned many things from him,' said Goebel, 'above all, good taste'), but balanced his harsh provocations with user-friendly Englishmen Trevor Pinnock and John Eliot Gardiner, the latter married to violinist Elizabeth Wilcock, a Harnoncourt pupil.

The English had stood, on the whole, aloof from the European movement, keeping their own period currency. 'When we first played in England,' said Harnoncourt, 'we did not find one musician who understood what we were doing.'[22] The English revolution was sparked by David Munrow, a bassoonist at the Royal Shakespeare Theatre in Stratford-upon-Avon, who lit up sombre halls with his quaint enthusiasms. Munrow's Early Music Consort recorded for a gamut of labels, large and small. In 1971, on a soundtrack he composed for the BBC's *Six Wives of Henry VIII*, Munrow played shawm, chalumeau, racket and recorder. He, more than anyone, turned early music in Britain from a knot of sandalled zealots to a popular interest, and the players from second rate to first. Reckless of his energies and troubled in his love life, Munrow committed suicide in May 1976 at the age of thirty-three, leaving a legacy of expert period singers, among them James Bowman, Nigel Rogers, David Thomas and Emma Kirkby.

In the hard-bitten world of London orchestras a keyboard player called Thurston Dart used coffee breaks at EMI sessions to demonstrate how much better Bach sounded at lower pitch and faster speeds. 'We called him the Liberace of the harpsichord,' said EMI's Peter Andry. 'He was a large jolly fellow, very camp,' said the flautist Richard Adeney. Dart took over Boyd Neel's chamber orchestra and made it a period band, the Philomusica. 'He'd ring up and say, "We're doing the Brandenburgs, are you free?"' said Adeney. 'He was very opinionated. There was no discussion, or anything like that. His speeds were quick but the pitch was modern.'[23] He made a pioneering period record of the Brandenburgs in 1959 and re-edited the scores once more for Neville Marriner, whose recording he accompanied in 1970, shortly before his early death (others in that epic session were Munrow, Barry Tuckwell (horn), Philip Ledger (organ) and Raymond Leppard (alternate continuo)).

Marriner served as blotting paper for Dart's ideas when they first met, in a military hospital in 1944, recovering from pre-D-Day wounds. Marriner had been playing the violin in orchestras since he was sixteen. He formed a baroque trio with Dart and Peter Gibbs, a Philharmonia violinist, expanding it to a chamber ensemble, the Academy of St Martin in the Fields. The Academy played baroque style on modern instruments. Louise Dyer, owner of L'Oiseau Lyre, came to their first concert in the Trafalgar Square church and offered a contract. 'We immediately recorded all those Italian ice-cream merchants – Manfredini, Corelli, and so on,' said Marriner. 'So in one leap we had gone from being a friendly society to something almost professional.'[24]

Every player in the Academy was an expert in period practice and every voice had to be heard in rehearsals that became, said Decca producer Erik Smith, 'like a session of Parliament'.[25] 'We were immensely democratic,' sighed Marriner. 'Everybody talked at the same time during rehearsals. In a way I would wish it had never been so successful. I think the spirit of the music and the personalities involved were much more vivid when we were heading for the top.'[26] A set of Rossini string sonatas, orchestrated by Marriner, was the Academy's first hit. Then they recorded Vivaldi's Four Seasons, still a baroque curiosity. 'I have never before enjoyed Vivaldi so much,'[27] exclaimed *Gramophone*'s Edward Greenfield, and bookings rolled in from all five continents. 'I got very tired of jumping through the same hoop over and over again,' said Marriner, well on his way to becoming Decca's busiest baton.

Marriner was the least imperious of maestros. 'He tolerates a great deal,' wrote Smith. 'Once, impatient with a record producer, he stomped off and slammed the door. Promptly fell downstairs. Decided this kind of behaviour was not for him.'[28] The Academy became something of a training school for conductors as Leppard, Andrew Davis and Christopher Hogwood graduated from its keyboard to careers of their own. Hogwood was a thorn in Marriner's flesh. 'He suffered a great deal when he worked with us,' said Marriner. 'Chris and I don't agree much about style. I cannot accept imperfections of intonation and articulation.' Hogwood formed a rival Academy of Ancient Music, working on period instruments and hoping to emulate Karajan with complete cycles of Beethoven, Mozart and Haydn. There was not much call yet for that sort of thing, but Hogwood got lucky when Decca fell into a serious rift.

Culshaw had left a vacuum. 'Nobody knew who would succeed [as musical director],' said Christopher Raeburn. 'There were three producers, roughly at the same level – myself, Erik Smith and Ray Minshull. I never wanted the job, and I don't think Ray did, either. He wanted to remain a studio producer. But Culshaw had landed him with an enormous amount of head office responsibility and he was the obvious choice.' Culshaw first supported Minshull then, in a letter to Edward Lewis, retracted. On being told that Minshull had got the job, Culshaw asked him round for a drink and, in the presence of another producer, David Harvey, set fire to his Lewis letter as a conciliatory gesture. Minshull never forgave him. A featureless man, devoid of personal warmth, Minshull set about undoing Culshaw's edifice. Where Culshaw fostered team spirit, Minshull shared his plans only with Raeburn. 'I was delighted when Ray took over,' said Raeburn. 'He was the most marvellous senior colleague. But then I was never after his job. Erik, on the other hand, felt his position was a bit untenable.'[29]

Smith, who lived in Somerset, 'was supremely indifferent to company politics, far more interested in visiting museums'.[30] He did not like taking orders from Minshull and hearing that Philips 'were looking for new ideas in developing the considerable potential of artists',[31] he arranged to defect and took Marriner with him. Minshull signed up Hogwood, in direct competition. Marriner went on to aggregate a catalogue of 600 recordings of 2,000 works, more than anyone bar Karajan. The next busiest maestro on record was Harnoncourt, with 440. Early music was the Yukon of the late-middle period of classical recording.

Leonard Bernstein, recording *Der Rosenkavalier* in Vienna, sat in the Sofiensaal, head in hands, weeping, 'I can't . . . I can't.' An hour later he was throwing a party for the Decca boys. It was the middle of 1970, the Beethoven bicentennial. 'I'm two years younger than Beethoven was when he died and I still haven't written a masterpiece,' wailed Bernstein. His bipolar swings and delusions were symptomatic of a stalled career. Bernstein had quit the New York Philharmonic to concentrate on composing but the result was a dismally trite Mass for the Kennedys, and little else.

CBS were discussing his future recording plans when Paul Myers, vice-president for A&R, raised a critical challenge. 'Name one work,' said Myers, 'apart from his own music, that you would rather have Lenny's performance of than anyone else's.'[32] There was a chilled silence. When it ended, so did Bernstein's CBS career. Times had truly changed.

At the new CBS Black Rock on Sixth Avenue and Fifty-second, Clive Davis cracked down on classics until he was escorted off the premises by security guards in May 1973, accused of misappropriating $53,700 of company money doing up his Central Park West apartment and another twenty grand paying for his son's bar-mitzvah. Davis said he had done nothing wrong. He decorated the apartment to impress artists. Charges of fraud and false invoicing (which he denied) were dropped. He pleaded guilty to an unrelated tax evasion count and bounced back inside a year with Arista Records, hitting number one with Barry Manilow. In 2001 he was admitted to Rock and Roll's Hall of Fame as one of the heroes of the music business. Davis went so far as to boast that the compact disc had been named for his initials, CD.

After the scandal Lieberson was brought back, but it was not the same. 'A funny thing happened to me on the way to my retirement,' he told a sales convention, and the laughter was pained. Broadway was putting on *Hair* in full frontal and Pierre Boulez, who followed Bernstein in New York, was a French ascetic who hated Mozart. It was hard to summon much enthusiasm for making records. 'Goddard liked to emcee the sales conventions,' said Don Hunstein, 'taking the microphone after dinner and introducing the acts with a dry wit. The dress code had changed – everybody now dressed casual – but he always turned out in black tie and dinner suit. "I guess you all want to know why I'm wearing this," he began. "It's because my jeans didn't get back in time from the presser's." '[33]

He hung on for two years, handing over to a Davis sidekick, Walter Yetnikoff, and retiring to Santa Fe, where he fell victim to an aggressive cancer in May 1977. 'I was very angry about him dying on me,' said Yetnikoff. 'He left with a sterling reputation and he was doing what he wanted to do. He beat the system. And then the motherfucker died on me! It sounds facetious but I was really pissed.'[34] Even a deaf mute could tell that the tone had changed at the Tiffany Label.

Yetnikoff, a Brooklyn lawyer with an ego the size of the Empire State, sacked Paul Simon, lost Bob Dylan to the predatory David Geffen and signed Michael Jackson, a family-band child singer who was to became the highest grossing rock star of all time despite his growing weirdness in the society of small boys. Yetnikoff noticed nothing untoward about Jackson's conduct. 'I'd come out of a coma around 7 or 8 a.m.,' he confessed. 'By 9 I might have drunk a half a bottle of vodka. Then I would call someone at CBS, maybe the head of the network or accounting, and yell at them. I'd finally drag myself out of bed and get into the office around noon. The steward would immediately bring me a screwdriver.'[35]

Foul-mouthed, sexually hyperactive and a serial substance abuser, Yetnikoff's gross behaviour concealed a subtle, fertile mind. As a junior lawyer he had written the 1967 partnership deal by which CBS licensed its records to Sony in Japan. Sony's founders were classical music buffs. Karajan would stay at Akio Morita's home when visiting Japan, swimming naked in his pool. Other guests included Leonard Bernstein and Lorin Maazel. Morita's next in line, Norio Ohga, had trained in Berlin as a classical baritone and gave up a burgeoning opera career on a promise that he would one day run Sony. Both men were imbued with Western civilization, but what they really coveted was youth culture. CBS rock stars would raise the Sony profile across Asia. Yetnikoff, appreciating the importance of the deal, delivered the contract in pouring rain to Morita's home. The chairman was in bed with flu. Yetnikoff waited dripping in the lobby while fifty pages were read, digested and initialled.

Each company sank $1 million in the joint venture. By 1970 CBS-Sony was making $100 million a year. Ohga, tall and emotionally reserved, capable of intense concentration and extreme rage, bonded with eager-beaver Yetnikoff. They shared long evenings talking about the meaning of life and slept over at each other's homes. Yetnikoff, alert to the Asian bonanza, wanted CBS-Sony to pay back profits to the parent companies. Ohga prevaricated. Yetnikoff indulged him by having Masterworks record John Williams (CD 45, p. 211), Murray Perahia and Andrew Davis cheaply from its London office. 'The company no longer cared about classics and almost resented any new project,' said Paul Myers, head of international A&R. RCA, in me-too mode, shifted classical to London, where Andre Previn covered the Vaughan Williams symphonies and an Irish flute from Karajan's orchestra, James Galway, became a solo star. The office was run by Ken Glancy, a former Lieberson aide; when he was purged, 'the top management that followed was mostly either disinterested in or totally ignorant of classical music'.[36]

US labels had effectively given up recording American orchestras when, out of the blue, the Europeans swanned in. Boston, dropped by RCA in 1969, offered Arthur Fiedler and its million-selling Pops to Deutsche Grammophon, provided they took some symphonic repertoire with William Steinberg and Bernstein protégé Michael Tilson Thomas. The Boston Symphony Orchestra was non-union and the costs manageable.

Decca landed months later in Chicago in the entourage of Georg Solti. Unsettled since Culshaw left, Solti apparently called Minshull 'second-rate'[37] and threatened to leave the label unless it recorded his new orchestras. To his surprise, Rosengarten agreed. Solti's inaugural season in Chicago ended with an overseas tour; he stopped in Vienna to record Mahler's eighth symphony with the Chicago Symphony Orchestra and the chorus of the Vienna Opera, a snub to the local Philharmonic. Solti went on to make a hundred recordings in Chicago, selling 5 million discs. 'The English are not good at selling,'[38] he grumbled, but the facts spoke otherwise – thanks largely to Decca's New York bureau chief, Terry McEwen.

'Terry was a man of gargantuan tastes with the biggest expense account I've ever seen,' said the *New York Times* writer Stephen

Rubin, later a successful publisher. 'He was one of those people who couldn't stay at home nights. We'd have these incredible dinners with Régine Crespin, Tebaldi, Marilyn Horne, Bidu Sayao, and then back to his place to listen to a cassette he'd made of singers in weird roles and the wrong languages: we had to identify the artists. Terry had a ferocious passion for singers. A lot of his personal tastes fed into Decca Records, or London as it was known here. London was the singers' label in Terry's time, bar none.'[39]

Two world stars plopped into his lap. Joan Sutherland was queen of bel canto and Luciano Pavarotti, her fledgling partner, was potentially the tenor of the century. Culshaw had not liked him and Rosengarten had too many tenors on his books – Di Stefano, Corelli, McCracken – but Minshull signed the Italian and McEwen took to him on sight, one man-mountain to another, when Pavarotti came to New York in 1967 as cover for Carlo Bergonzi in a Karajan Verdi Requiem. McEwen took the tenor to be styled and snapped by fashion photographer Francesco Scavullo. 'Luciano, you're a nice guy,' he said. 'You need a real bastard to do your publicity.'[40] Herbert Breslin, a hustler of hype, was hired to put Pavarotti everywhere, and all other singers in the shade. For Sutherland McEwen created an image as grande dame of the grand tradition.

His achievements were not wholeheartedly appreciated. 'Ray Minshull was always rather uptight about him,' said Paul Myers, 'but most of us suspected that Terry had a strong influence.' 'The artists loved him,' said Breslin, 'in part, because he was extremely generous: who's not going to love a generous record promoter? He always hosted after-performance dinners, and parties, and pro- motions – all, of course, with Decca's money.'[41] McEwen put Solti on the cover of *Time* magazine in May 1973 as The Fastest Baton in the West, the maestro for Middle America. Other labels, landing with lesser podium stars, found the fame game sewn up.

Philips started in San Francisco with the young Seiji Ozawa, in a bid to penetrate the over-protected Japanese record market. Ozawa – mop-topped, polo-necked and matey with the Sony bosses Morita and Ohga – was the first Japanese to head a Western orchestra. Photogenic, energetic and slightly off-centre in his musical tastes (CD 65, p. 235), Ozawa moved up from San Francisco to Boston. Philips took over the Boston contract from DGG without difficulty, since the labels were moving to the next stage of union. Frits Philips, nearing retirement, agreed with Ernst von Siemens to pool their labels in PolyGram International. DG (the 'Gesellschaft' was dropped) and Philips were allowed to maintain separate identities for the time being but the Dutch, in any clash, were expected to submit to the Germans.

DG turned its American operation into a Karajan support system. The maestro was appearing seasonally at the Met and his influence on its young music director, James Levine, was considerable – a 'phenomenal inspiration',[42] said Levine. 'Karajan will never rest until he is deified in the United States,' said a record official,[43] and DG's New York chief Guenter Hensler thrust K rations aggressively into stores. Karajan's progress, however, was constrained by his Nazi past and DG decided that it needed an American counterweight. When Bernstein was dropped by CBS, DG picked up a Met recording of Carmen, with Marilyn Horne in the title role. It won a 1973 Grammy but unsold sets cluttered record-store dump bins. DG re-signed Bernstein to record Liszt's unmarketable Faust symphony, followed by his own three symphonies. The clincher was getting Karajan to waive his veto and, in the interests of DG America, invite Lennie to conduct the London Symphony Orchestra and the Vienna Philharmonic at the 1975 Salzburg Festival.

Low farce ensued. Hearing that Lenny was heading for Salzburg, the CBS London office plastered Bernstein posters on every vacant shop window. A mischievous forest of posters sprang up on the route that Karajan took each morning into work. The maestro was not amused, even less so when Lennie staged a triumphal last-minute entry along the front row of Festspielhaus seats, leaning over a balustrade to greet his many pals in the Vienna Philharmonic while Karajan was waiting in the pit to start Verdi's Don Carlos. The Austrian Chancellor, Bruno Kreisky, gave a state party for

Bernstein's fifty-seventh birthday. Bernstein's Mahler Eighth was hailed in the Austrian press as 'an incomparable event'. Karajan turned puce, but DG got its man. Bernstein signed exclusively to the Yellow Label in 1981.

These realignments left three labels holding sway over America's Big Five orchestras. Cleveland lined up with Decca, Philadelphia with Philips, New York with DG. Chicago's musicians refused to enter wage talks without a Decca man present. By 1980, the British label with Solti, Pavarotti and Sutherland had almost one-third of US classical sales. The Decca Sound settled on America like an army blanket, minimizing the differences between orchestras, but demand was waning as war vets grew old. Solti, for all his vigour, never matched Toscanini's fame and, when Ozawa lost his Beatles looks, Boston began a long slide into ennui. Levine, Tilson Thomas and Leonard Slatkin maintained their profile but orchestras looked to the European labels for their next music director.

EMI, out of the US running, was mired in a British decade of oil crisis and labour stoppages. Lockwood retired, handing over to John Read, an accountant from Ford Motors, who looked at the Beatles profits, rising year on year, and said 'the music business can run itself'. Read went looking for external money spinners. CAT body scanners were the hot item in medical diagnostics and Read spent a mint on buying marketing rights. Record producers, hauled out of studios, were despatched to hospitals. 'I was appointed head of the East European business,' related Peter Andry. 'I remember flying off with John Read to Russia to sell CAT machines, but we couldn't get the Russian women into the things. Their thighs were too big.'[44]

Read splurged further on buying defunct film studios with a view to revitalizing British cinema. He lost touch with music, so much so that when the Sex Pistols punk band expleted four-letter words on family-time television, he sacked them. 'Our view within EMI,' intoned Read, 'is that we should seek to discourage records that are likely to give offence to the majority of people . . . EMI should not set itself up as a public censor, but it does seek to encourage restraint.'[45] Restraint never sold a record and EMI's youth-cred went down the drain.

Classics were becalmed under Peter Andry who, aseptically patrician, hitched his hopes to Andre Previn, principal conductor of the London Symphony Orchestra, a man once married to a pop singer (Dory Previn) and now to a film star (Mia Farrow). In strikebound, power-cut Britain, such secondhand celebrity passed for sex appeal and Previn, nicknamed Andrew Preview, was a fixture on three-channel television, whether as a musician or as a salesman for EMI household goods. He was regarded as 'a first-rate conductor of second-rate music', outstanding in show-pieces like Carmina Burana and Rachmaninov's The Bells. Some LSO players, craving profundity, tried to oust him for Eugen Jochum, but Previn clung on for eleven years, inflicting a breezy superficiality on London's musical ecology.

Peter Andry, alert to his shortcomings, had a secret weapon up his sleeve. 'I had always kept in touch with Karajan,' said Andry. 'His secretary, André von Mattoni, would let me know when he was passing through, and I'd be there at the airport to have a few words, talk music, say how wonderful he was.' Karajan was having a falling-out with DG, which paid him a flat fee per LP at his request, in order to keep royalties out of the grasp of his second wife, Anita, whom he had replaced with a French model, Eliette. But the records sold immensely and Karajan worked out that the alimony dodge had cost him 6 million Deutschmarks. He asked DG to make good. The Germans, unwilling to accede to an unjustified demand, dithered. The Berlin Philharmonic, sensing discord, chipped in with demands for an increased session fee of 65 Deutschmarks per player hour, as much as Decca were paying in Chicago. Not viable, said DG. The atmosphere was turning acrid when Andry, with exquisite timing, offered to take over one-third of the next DG contract, fifteen sessions a year, meaning more money for maestro and musicians. Karajan, pleased to have made his point, signed for both labels. He then punished the Berlin players by diverting several EMI sessions to the Orchestre de Paris.

'My policy,' reflected Andry, 'was to keep the English-speaking world happy with Previn, and Europe and Japan with Karajan. My achievement was to keep classical business going within the milieu of a greatly expanding pop business. It obliged me to sit in dreary meetings and click my fingers to their noisy stuff. But Karajan and Previn made a wonderful team.' So wonderful, in fact, that Ernst von Siemens secretly approached Andry to become president of DG and Philips. Unwilling to move his family to Germany, Andry declined. Siemens returned with a bigger offer. 'Each time, I managed to improve my position at EMI,' laughed Andry, a dealmaker to his bones.

Where Legge loathed all rivals, Andry was eager to trade. He let DG record Carlo-Maria Giulini 'since he wasn't selling much on EMI', as well as Placido Domingo who misjudged his record career by appearing on too many outlets, none of which promoted him as Decca did Pavarotti. Exclusivity was the coinage by which labels did their deals. Typically, two executives would meet for lunch at a blushingly expensive restaurant in London or Salzburg where, after a liberal imbibing of rare vintages, the talent was laid out over coffee. 'I'll give you an Arrau and two Brendels for Previn to play Rhapsody in Blue with Haitink,' Philips might say to EMI, like two kids with cigarette cards in a playground.

'We want the Vienna Phil for Previn's Tchaikovsky,' EMI would reply.

'Tricky, DG have got Vienna tied up for the next Tchaikovsky. Still, DG want Elly Ameling from us, so I might get a deal. You wouldn't take a Dutch fiddler off my hands in the Brahms concerto?'

'Not unless you borrow our English cellist for the Delius.'

Callous as this may sound, these exchanges often worked in an artist's best interest. A soloist failing twice on Philips might have better luck with a third shot on EMI. If Ashkenazy (Decca) insisted that only Previn (EMI) understood him in the Rachmaninov concertos, Minshull and Andry would cut a deal that kept both artists happy. These swaps reassured the majors that their artists were an elite and that they were protecting the consumer from a flood of charlatans.

Talent was trawled nightly at recital halls, opera rehearsals and conservatoire graduations. Producers pooled new names at monthly meetings, making their decisions on the basis of passionate conviction. 'Andry said we were going to do Italian operas and it was a choice between Riccardo Muti and James Levine,' said producer John Mordler. 'I was sent to Vienna and heard Muti conduct Aida at the Staatsoper – it was electrifying. After that, there was no more talk of Levine.'[46]

On 2 December 1970 EMI brought Muti over to conduct the New Philharmonia in Croydon, on the unreviewed outskirts of London. The players, alert to a record deal, asked him to become principal conductor. For Muti – coal-black hair, razor-sharp tailoring and just past thirty – Christmas came early that year. After recording Cherubini's Requiem, he stamped his authority on Aida at Walthamstow Town Hall. The first take was desultory, too many musicians dispersed around a vast building. Muti listened to the playback with a brow darker than thunder. He stormed back into the heart of the hall and fired up a performance that left the cast sweat-soaked and uplifted. 'The magnetism was irresistible,' said Mordler, and the set (Montserrat Caballé, Domingo, Fiorenza Cossotto, Nicolai Ghiaurov and Piero Cappuccilli) was hailed as a classic. Sales, though, were stubbornly slow. In the thick of the oil crisis few would risk £12 (the price of a good restaurant meal for two) on a young maestro. An 'anonymous admirer', apparently the General Electric Company chairman Arnold Weinstock, chipped in £25,000 to get EMI to record Muti again in Bellini's I Capuleti e I Montecchi at Covent Garden.

He was not an easy colleague. Seducing an EMI blonde, he used her to demand the sacking of an executive he disliked. After the early buzz, Philharmonia audiences fell and the players were relieved when the aged Ormandy offered Muti his Philadelphia post. Muti livened up the old town with a dazzle of stars – Pavarotti, Renata Scotto, Maurizio Pollini and the Russian pianist Sviatoslav Richter, with whom he enjoyed an innate understanding – and dragged EMI warily into recording in America. Although his sales were low and his Beethoven symphonies bombed,

Muti, newly head of La Scala and talked of as the next Karajan, kept EMI and Philips flinging ever more despairing wads of cash at his combustible career.

EMI kept its door ever open to options. Simon Rattle, a wire-haired kid from Liverpool, twenty-one years old, won a cigarette-sponsored conducting competition with an EMI recording as part of the prize. He asked to perform Mahler's tenth symphony, a deathbed work completed in 1964 by a BBC producer, Deryck Cooke, with the émigré composer Berthold Goldschmidt. Senior conductors had scorned the score, Bernstein and Kubelik rejecting it for their cycles. Ormandy made a premiere recording on CBS and Kurt Sanderling another in East Germany, but the case for the Tenth was yet to be made. Rattle studied with Goldschmidt and expanded the more speculative passages with the brother-composers Colin and David Matthews. The music, he wrote, 'requires an unusual degree of creativity from the conductor . . . one comes face to face with the bare material in a way that a conductor of Mahler's generation would have been'[47] (CD 71, p. 242). The record, blazing with conviction, would fix the symphony in the canon. Before it was out, Rattle was named principal conductor of the City of Birmingham Symphony Orchestra in Britain's second city. He was on a vertical curve.

It took EMI fifteen years to break even on Rattle and he was not the toast of the tearoom when one of his enthusiasms, Nicholas Maw's Odyssey, sold just ninety copies on release. But EMI held firm and Rattle repaid the label with dogged exclusivity and, ultimately, the supreme trophy of Berlin.

And still the door stayed open. An East German refugee, Klaus Tennstedt, made an explosive US debut with a Bruckner Eighth in Boston. 'Once in a lifetime,' gasped the *Globe*. Lanky, weak-willed, and prone to alcoholic consolation, Tennstedt collapsed in tears in a Philadelphia rehearsal and suffered a complete breakdown soon after, unable to cope with success. He found an empathy with Gustav Mahler; an EMI producer, John Willan, nursed him through an unforgettably intense cycle (CD 89, p. 262). Tennstedt, said a wide-eyed Rattle, 'has the effect of energising an orchestra in his own way quicker than almost anyone'.[48] He was a one-off, not long for this world, but Willan captured the best of Tennstedt and when the bedraggled anti-hero returned from illness to the Royal Festival Hall, banners waved from the balcony: 'Welcome back, Klaus.' Even Karajan was impressed.

Amid EMI's thicket of batons, Karajan was never the main event that he was on DG. His ill-judged EMI comeback featured the Soviet dream team of Richter, David Oistrakh and Mstislav Rostropovich (see p. 283). There followed a Dresden Meistersinger and the late symphonies of Mozart and Tchaikovsky. EMI made a £652,719 profit on Karajan in the 1970s, plus a fixed overheads contribution of almost £1 million.[49] Andry, to stroke Karajan's vanity, assigned a red-haired lad from marketing to work on his image. Peter Alward flew to Berlin to arrange a fresh set of cover photographs. Given the runaround by Karajan's minder, Emil Jucker, he turned to Michel Glotz, the maestro's independent recording consultant, who stole half an hour of DG time for the EMI shots. Afterwards Karajan said to the young man, 'What are you doing tonight?' 'Going back to Munich, Maestro.' 'No, you will come to dinner with me.'

Back in London, Alward was called in to see Andry: 'I've just had Karajan on the phone. He wants you to be involved in all his recordings.' Half-English, half-German-Jewish, a fount of minutiae and industry gossip, Alward formed a bond with Karajan that proved crucial for the classical division when EMI finally fell apart in 1979 after a run of Read depredations. In crisis, Andry sent Alward to tell Karajan that EMI could not fulfil a long-cherished Tosca. 'We'll have to see about that,' retorted the litigious Karajan. After a moment or two he said to Alward, 'What if my next record for EMI was Vivaldi's Four Seasons with Anne-Sophie Mutter?' The combination of old master and German teenager in a surefire hit left EMI with a million seller and Alward with the impression that the wily maestro understood the record business better than any of its bosses.[50]

Woe betide anyone, though, who took him for granted. 'He never forgot a slight,' said the soprano Birgit Nilsson.[51] Emil Jucker, who did his dirty work for decades, was destroyed by a multi-million Karajan lawsuit. Told that Jucker had suffered a stroke during one of his performances, Karajan said, 'People who go against me always come to harm' (he also bragged that he had caught Rosengarten stealing royalties and won a huge settlement, an assertion hotly denied by the Decca man's heirs[52]).

The more records Karajan made, the more he sold, and the more critics took against him. Even *Gramophone* struggled to find praise for his fourth and fifth Beethoven cycles and musicians muttered that his seamless perfectionism was simply boring, though few spoke out. An exception was the free-spirited Richter, who avoided Karajan after a contretemps during the Beethoven triple concerto when the conductor refused his request for a retake in order to pose for photographs. 'It's a dreadful recording,' wrote Richter, 'and I disown it utterly . . . And what a nauseating photograph it is, with him posing artfully and the rest of us grinning like idiots.'[53] That image defines its era, a picture of the captive state of classical recording at the heyday of Herbert von Karajan.

The last formative figures slipped away in sorrow or disgrace. In March 1975 Decca sacked Gordon Parry, after an investigation for abuse of expenses. 'Once Culshaw left Decca there was no controlling hand and Gordon's talent for excess took over,' said James Mallinson. 'He walked out on me in the middle of a session – you can't have that,' said Christopher Raeburn. The creator of the Decca Sound went on to work as a sound consultant at the Royal Opera House, Covent Garden. Released within months he was jobless until a friend in the garment trade put him to work on the cutting floor. 'I'm a member of a team again,' he beamed, 'which is how I always saw myself at Decca.'[54] A visitor to his bungalow, in the featureless east of London, noticed that he had no record player. His death, in February 2003, passed unrecorded in the British press.

Rosengarten kept his hands on the reins to the last, his eye on the bottom line. He told producers to lash out on expenses, which were covered by London; their salaries, paid from Zurich, were tiny. A Decca producer in the mid-1970s earned £100 a month in take-home pay, but sat in £36 seats at the opera,[55] travelled first-class and stayed in five-star hotels.

One night in November 1975 the Soltis were having dinner with Sir Edward Lewis. 'That'll be Maurice,' said the chairman, when the phone rang.

'How is he?' asked Solti when Lewis returned.

'He's dead.'[56]

Rosengarten's seat on the Decca board went to his son-in-law, Jack Dimenstein, who talked of selling his stake to EMI. The chairman had other ideas. Three decades after their initial flirtation, Lewis reopened contacts with Philips. Polygram was on a roll. It had bought MGM Records and Verve and, with an Australian, Robert Stigwood, co-produced *Saturday Night Fever* and *Grease*, unleashing a tidal wave of disco music and a 1978 profit of $120 million. Awash in cash, Philips bought Decca for just £5.5 million. There was a last-gasp bid from GEC's Arnold Weinstock, Riccardo Muti's friend, but the shareholders decided that Philips made a better fit. In 1979 Decca became part of the Dutch–German combine. Its UK factories were shut down, its West Hampstead studios sold. Lewis, sick with leukaemia, barely outlasted the sale, dying in January 1980 'as if unable to witness any longer the piecemeal selling-off, like so much scrap, of his beloved company'.[57]

The hub of classical recording was now located in a brown field in Holland, the landscape flat as far as the eye could see. 'International Finance & Administration was in a lovely old villa set in very nice grounds and was fired with rather less than driving purpose,' said a British employee. 'It felt rather like a rest home. We were . . . among the first to employ Word Processors (Philips of course), which were exactly the size and shape of a small upright piano.'[58]

The soporific backdrop was deceptive, for the Dutch were quietly engineering an audio revolution. Philips had stumbled into acoustic invention with the Compact Cassette, an office tool one-eighth of an inch across which played tape at 1.875 inches per second. No cultural use was foreseen until businessmen began taping favourite songs for long sales trips and the record industry started issuing pre-recorded cassettes. Sony offered to recognize the Philips format in exchange for a free right to manufacture the machines. Japanese players soon outsold the Dutch and Philips regretted their generosity. Then the motor industry decided to add a tape player to the dashboard radio. Ford opted for a pocketbook-sized cartridge with an eight-track loop. Labels began issuing music on a third format and cassettes and cartridges slugged it out at high speed on multi-lane highways.

It was a close-run thing. In 1975 Americans bought $583 million worth of pre-recorded cartridges, a quarter of the total recorded-music market. But the rest of the world chose the cassette for its simplicity, versatility and a sound quality improved by Dolby noise reduction. Cartridges died out, but the cassette acquired notoriety as a vehicle for illegal duplication. Piracy, never formerly a threat, became a nervous preoccupation of the music industry. Walter Yetnikoff told Norio Ohga that Sony cassettes were killing his sales. Ohga replied that his machines were opening new markets for music. The industry split between hardware innovators and software conservationists.

Into this schism splashed the calamity of quad. Aiming to super-sede stereo, RCA in 1970 fostered a four-speaker system developed by JVC in Japan. Leopold Stokowski, near his ninetieth birthday, conducted the demos. CBS, in rapid response, unleashed Surround Quadraphonic (SQ). The systems were mutually incompatible. Records in one quad format were unplayable on the other, and both quickly died. Sony, meanwhile, presented a video cassette at a 1970 Tokyo press conference fronted by Herbert von Karajan. Video cassettes, said the maestro, would soon replace 'all phono-graphic records'.[59] Sony's Betamax system was state of the art. Matsushita challenged it with cheaper, grainier VHS. The result was settled when VHS bought rights to Hollywood movies, leaving Sony with nothing to show. Morita was mortified.

Philips, beavering quietly away, came up with Laservision, a flat disc that bypassed the Edison method of capturing sound as electronic waves and converted it instead into computer digits, stored beneath the impermeable surface of a plastic disc, readable by laser beam. Digital recording eliminated tape noise, flutter, wow, distortion and all the clicks and pops of LPs. Digital was the future, but Laservision was not quite there. Of 400 machines sold in Holland, half were returned to stores. Ohga, in hospital after a helicopter crash, received a Laservision demonstration in April 1979. Smitten, he talked Philips into forming a joint task force to crack the digital atom. The Japanese set a ferocious pace. When the Dutch havered over several modulation systems, Ohga phoned team leader Kees A. Schouhamer Immink and told him he had a week to make a choice, 'or management would make it for us'.[60] Size was set in Japan. 'Compact Cassette was a great success,' said Philips. 'We don't think compact disc should be bigger.' Morita discovered that this would limit playing time to less than an hour, equivalent to an LP. He demanded that CDs be large enough to accommodate Beethoven's ninth symphony, his wife's favourite work. The Dutch went up half a centimetre to beer-coaster size, giving eighty minutes' play. The hole in the middle of the CD was cut around the diameter of the smallest Dutch coin. Garage methods, akin to Johnson's and Berliner's, gripped the digital inventors. Sony set a deadline of May 1981, a meeting of the International Music Industry in Athens.

Sound was already being digitized on tape. Thomas Stockham, an MIT professor who had investigated Richard Nixon's Watergate tapes, built a Soundstream machine that he tried out at Santa Fe opera festival in 1976. He met a pair of Clevelanders, Jack Renner and Robert Woods, who asked if they could use it for wind music sessions on their label, Telarc (CD 67, p. 237). Conducted by Frederick Fennell on 4–5 April 1978, the first digital LP blew out demonstration speakers in stores. Telarc followed with Stravinsky's Firebird from the Atlanta Symphony Orchestra under Robert Shaw, and Mussorgsky's Pictures at an Exhibition, by the Cleveland Orchestra and Maazel. Decca digitally recorded the 1979 New Year's Day Concert in Vienna in digital sound, far brighter than analogue.

A month before Athens, at the 1981 Salzburg Easter Festival,

Morita and Karajan demonstrated the Digital Audio Disc. 'All else,' growled the conductor, 'is gaslight.' Karajan was a man in a hurry. He had suffered a stroke, followed by spinal surgery, and was in constant pain. At home in Anif, he compulsively viewed and edited his concerts on a giant screen, preparing a video legacy. He put pressure on Polygram to invest 100 million Deutschmarks in a digital pressing plant in Hanover. Ohga spent $30 million of CBS-Sony dividends on a parallel plant in Shizuoka Prefecture. In the race to launch, Nobuyuki Idei, the Sony head of production, suffered a breakdown and watched the presentation from a hospital bed.

At Athens, the industry split between horsepower and nuclear. When Ohga played his prototype CD, label owners rioted, accusing equipment makers of killing the golden LP. 'The truth is in the groove! The truth is in the groove!' they chanted. 'We barely escaped physical violence,' recalled Jan Timmer, a burly Philips boss.[61] EMI and RCA boycotted CD and purists declared it 'sterile'. 'It would not be the first time the Japanese have burnt their fingers,'[62] gloated Raymond Cooke, president-elect of the International Audio Engineering Society.

But the LP, whatever its loyalists protested, was doomed. 'Almost every record purchased nowadays has one defect or another and in a number of cases I have found so many bangs, pops, cracks and so on that it is impossible to listen with any semblance of enjoyment,' ran a typical reader's complaint in *Gramophone*.[63] The ritual of dusting a disc, laying it on the turntable, inspecting the needle and lowering the arm onto the surface felt antiquated in an automated age. Sales were collapsing. At EMI's Classics for Pleasure label, an English-sung Ring cycle conducted by the venerable Reginald Goodall sold precisely eighty-six copies. The bleakness of such figures was seldom admitted but every now and then a grim truth shone through. In the summer of 1982 a Polygram executive was trying to wheedle a *Sunday Times* journalist into writing about two pretty French sisters, Katia and Marielle Labèque, who had a freak hit in France – 100,000 sales of Gershwin's four-hand version of Rhapsody in Blue.

'How many outside France?' said the writer.

'Not released in the States, 3,000 UK.'

'That's not much . . .'

'Are you kidding?' exclaimed the salesman. 'Three thousand classical in the UK is enormous. Most releases don't sell a tenth of that . . .'

'Are *you* kidding?' echoed the writer, unable to believe the disparity of sales to hype.

Arranging to meet the sisters at the Westbury Hotel, near Oxford Street, where many musicians stayed, he saw two men scurry into a doorway at the end of the corridor as he approached the room. One he recognized as an EMI producer. The situation was surreal. Despite minuscule sales, the girls were being wooed by several labels.[64] 'If compact disc had not come along when it did,' said Archiv's Andreas Holschneider, 'we would all have been lost.'[65]

5. Miracles on Miracles

While waiting for digital, daisy labels flowered on English lawns. Brian Couzens, a freelance engineer, founded Chandos with his son Ralph in the Essex backwater of Colchester. They spotted two formidable conductors from the Soviet Baltic states and launched the prodigious careers of Neeme Järvi and Mariss Jansons. Hyperion was the dreamchild of Ted Perry, who paid for his sessions by driving an ice-cream van by day and a minicab at night; his breakthrough was the monodic chant of the medieval Hildegard of Bingen. Two ex-Decca boys, Jack Boyce and Harley Usill, founded Academy Sound and Vision (ASV). Weirdest of daisies was Nimbus, run by a French-Russian called Numa Labinsky from a castle in Wales. Count Numa claimed to represent 'the only surviving legacy of older schools of singing',[1] a noise that veered from growl to squeak; he also built the UK's first CD plant, at Wyastone Leys, Monmouth.

The business was turning bizarre but the majors saw nothing, heard nothing, beyond their own glass walls. CBS needed a new head of Masterworks. Joseph P. Dash, vice-president for strategic planning, was promised the job – only to get pipped by a rank outsider from Israel. Simon Schmidt, founder of the CBS Israel subsidiary which had 80 per cent of national sales, wanted a break from Middle East tension. 'He was a genius at business,' said an underling,[2] but out of his depth at headquarters. 'Schmidt caused chaos,' said Paul Myers. 'He fired half the staff, [saying] that he intended to buy cheap records from Hungary and sell them for full price on the US market.' 'You want to know how he hired a head of A&R?' demanded Dash. 'This is the truth, I heard it from Zubin's own lips.'[3]

Zubin Mehta, music director of the New York and Israel

Philharmonic orchestras, was asked by Schmidt to recommend an assistant. 'Zubin thought Simon wanted a personal secretary and named a woman called Catherine Reed who had once worked at the Kennedy Center in Washington. Next thing we know, she is vice-president of artists and repertoire. Catherine came into my office as I was looking at a cover for Prokofiev's ballet Romeo and Juliet,' recalled Myers, 'and demanded to know who was singing the lead.'

An erotic presence, Catherine Reed formed a close friendship with the buttoned-up president of CBS Inc., Thomas Wyman. She told Wyman that Schmidt was useless and the Israeli was fired. Dash, the next head of Masterworks, delicately refrained from asking Reed about her relationship with Wyman. 'She came into my office saying he wouldn't leave her alone, but after that no one dared touch her.' When the board sacked Wyman for mishandling a takeover, Dash reported, 'In a matter of days, I kicked out Catherine Reed.'

Dash, inheriting a $20-million turnover and no profit, plunged into 'crossover' – a not yet pejorative term, which involved some gentle genre bending. If Frank Sinatra could sing Kurt Weill and Joan Baez the Bachianas Brasileiras of Villa-Lobos, why not twin the world's best tenor with America's number-one pop writer? The catalyst was Milt Okun, a millionaire folk mogul, producer of Harry Belafonte, Miriam Makeba, Peter, Paul and Mary and a guy called Henry John Deutschendorf, Jr, who topped the charts as John Denver. Milt was smitten with Placido Domingo, who introduced him to Dash in his Covent Garden green room. 'We go out to dinner, with wives, without wives,' said Dash. 'I sign Placido Domingo on an exclusive crossover contract. My staff think I have lost my marbles. Then Milt delivers Placido and John Denver in Perhaps Love. It goes platinum, sells a hundred thousand. In a year, Masterworks is in profit.'

Glenn Gould called. He had decided to make his record with Karajan. While CBS wrangled with DG over which label went on the cover, Gould phoned Neville Marriner, now music director in Minnesota. 'I want to make a record with orchestra,' he said.

Marriner headed north to Toronto, heart in mouth. During a long night's chat, Gould told him that, on a good day, he might get two minutes of music into the can. 'That would be uneconomic,' said Marriner. They agreed that Gould would play the solo part of a Beethoven concerto in his studio and send it to Marriner, who would wrap an orchestra around it.[4] The conductor went away beaming, but heard nothing more. Days after his fiftieth birthday in September 1982, Gould suffered a fatal stroke and the piano lost an unfathomable legend. Dead, Gould began selling faster than alive. Each memorial release outstripped the last. The same was happening with Maria Callas on EMI, five years after her death. This was an alarming trend, the mark of a doomed civilization that worships its dead.

Gould's producer, Paul Myers, had moved to Decca, hoping for a happier atmosphere but finding an office thick with intrigue. 'Ray Minshull had trouble communicating sympathetically with staff,' he discovered. 'Ray was always secretive,' said producer James Mallinson, 'and the Polygram pressures just made it worse.' Mallinson left the company shortly after the night he won thirteen Grammies, prompting rumours – unfounded, he insists – that Minshull fired him out of jealousy. Michael Haas, a young gay producer, was beset by office gossip that he was sleeping with the boss. He reported the story to Minshull, who gave him 'years and years of artists on contracts not being renewed: Karl Münchinger, Horst Stein, Geneva recordings. The official administration was very unfriendly towards me, but Christopher Raeburn remained a loyal supporter and so did Solti. He was generous and extremely kind, the most impressive "Mensch" I have worked with.'[5]

Decca, bottom of the pecking order in Polygram, fought with its sisters like cats in a sack. A clash-prevention system designed to stop the three labels covering the same repertoire was constantly breached. During one month all three issued Bruckner's fifth symphony; another year each produced a *Tristan und Isolde*. Harried producers, trapped between corporate discipline and the insistent demands of Karajan, Haitink and Solti, hit the bottle. As drugs were to rock, booze became the classical companion. Several senior men were sent to dry out at sanatoria; one DG producer committed suicide in a Black Forest clinic.

Tensions eased when Andreas Holschneider became chairman of the clash committee. 'Coming from Archiv, the smallest label, and from an academic background, I was seen as relatively neutral,' he said. 'I did the job for some years. In the view of my bosses I did it quite well. In the end, I was asked to become head of Deutsche Grammophon.'[6] His timing was immaculate: there had never been a better moment to take charge of a classical enterprise.

The rainbow dawn broke on 31 August 1982 with an announcement from Tokyo that a four-walled consortium of Sony, CBS-Sony, Philips and Polygram had perfected Compact Disc. On 1 October Sony's CDP-101 player went into Japanese shops, its name representing the binary numerals, one and zero, that encoded digital sound. Fifty CBS-Sony CDs were available, topped by Billy Joel's 52nd Street. 'There has never been an example as strong as the CD of how effective the combined power of the Sony Group can be,' exulted Ohga. Sony's CDP-101 cost $700 and CDs were twice the price of LPs. Aimed at the high end of the hi-fi hobby, the release sheet was geared to wealthy, middle-aged audiophiles. One fifth of the batch was classical.

Japanese stores ran out of stock in a week and supply was running nine months behind demand,[7] but the European launch went ahead in March 1983, with 100 Polygram releases, equally over-represented in classics. In Britain, 30,000 CDs sold in a month, and the reception was repeated in France, West Germany and Holland. In May, when CD reached Australia, EMI joined the format. 'We will do whatever the consumer wants,' grouched company spokesman Brian Southall. 'We'll press music on vinyl, tape or even banana leaves if that's what they will buy.'[8] By the time of the US launch in September, CD was the new world order. An in-car player arrived, followed in September 1984 by Walkman CD. Players fell to generally affordable prices but discs stayed high, fattening label profits. By 1986 CDs outsold LPs. US sales rose from a million in 1983 to 334 million by 1990, 943 million by 2000.

The desperate decade was over. Classical had a double-figure market share for the first time since before the Beatles. What's more, anything sold. Labels put out short-measure CDs. Tchaikovsky's fifth symphony, running forty minutes, occupied a whole disc on every label except Telarc. Customers who wanted the Bach cello suites paid for three discs on DG and EMI, but for only two on CBS and Decca.

Digital sound was stunningly transparent. A press demo of Tchaikovsky's 1812 Overture extruded carpentry noises from the Chicago cellos. On a third hearing, the sawing was traced to a microphone placed too close to the cellos. Early stereo and even mono recordings sounded more natural on CD than multi-miked modernities. Furtwängler, Ferrier, Beecham, Kreisler and Casals (though not harsh Toscanini) were outselling their successors. Worse still, the CD was indestructible. Once a consumer had bought a basic classical library he need never buy another record.

Although business boomed through the 1980s, the countdown to meltdown had begun. Not everyone liked digital. Nigel Kennedy, a quaintly counter-cultural British violinist with a 2 million-selling Four Seasons, had EMI record him on analogue machines. 'A lot of my favourite records were made on acetate,' he wrote, 'and I think that there would be far many more beautiful perform-ances if more performers could drag themselves away from the clinical and sterile technical standards provided for and expected by today's musical fashion.'[9] Unknown to Kennedy, as he played the Beethoven concerto with Klaus Tennstedt in Kiel, northern Germany, producers ran a digital tape as backup.[10]

'Anyone who cannot hear that CDs are incomparably superior to records, 9.7 to a perfect 10, has a tin ear and no business listening to music,' thundered Norio Ohga.[11] Karajan, equally emphatic, had 200 CDs out by his eightieth birthday, some of them in a 'special edition' with pastel covers by his wife, Eliette, who had taken up painting as a hobby. That year, Karajan accounted for a third of DG sales.[12] His influence, wrote *Gramophone*, was 'almost

incalculable . . . There can be few record collectors who are without at least one of his discs.'[13]

But Karajan was in torment. His health was broken and an
unexpectedly objective biography by an American sailing writer,
Roger Vaughan, exposed an ugly supremacism. 'I was born to
command,' said Karajan.[14] When Berlin players vetoed a female
clarinettist, Sabine Mayer, whose sound jarred against the rest of
the section, Karajan sulked in his tent for months before severing
ties with Berlin. Switching to Vienna, he demanded ever-higher
royalties to fund his video legacy. Within DG, his favourite producer Gunther Breest wanted to release the videodiscs but Holschneider argued they would be 'an expensive mistake'.[15] Karajan's
fourth recording of Tchaikovsky's Pathétique and Dvořák's New
World symphonies were mannered and insipid beside the controlled rigour of his prime; the cameras dwelled on his tightly
shut eyes and his fixed, face-lifted expression. CDs, meanwhile,
continued to grow and DG, said its rivals, 'was where we all
wanted to be'.[16]

Philips was the chief loser in the CD boom. Devastated by the
sudden death of disco, its Polygram subsidiary was $200 million in
debt by 1983. The Bee Gees launched a lawsuit, draining another
$70 million. Jan Timmer, a classically trained singer, took the helm,
moving Polygram HQ from sleepy Baarn to London and New
York, where he negotiated a merger with Warner. Yetnikoff,
terrified of competition, invoked anti-monopoly procedures and
stalled the deal at the Federal Trade Commission. Thwarted,
Timmer bought out Siemens' share, taking the whole of the music
and movie combine under Dutch control. In 1989 he floated
Polygram on the Amsterdam stock exchange with a valuation of
$5.6 billion.

The classical consequences were savage. Three autonomous
labels were geared to shareholder expectations and ordered to
obtain head office approval for all major outlays. Timmer meddled
in musical decisions. When he rose in 1990 to executive chairman
of the parent Philips group, his successor, Alain Levy, was 'the

kind of man who has to be in your face all the time or he's not doing his job'.[17] A thickset, square-spectacled, frizzy-haired executive of North African descent, Levy called himself 'a business-man, not a music man: I don't trust my ears'.[18] Classical chiefs quaked on his white carpet but found his ignorance easier to bear than Timmer's half-knowledge. 'For us, it was better with Levy,' said Holschneider, who was plotting the post-Karajan cartography.

Holschneider's model for the new DG was an Italian designer label, built around Claudio Abbado, once of La Scala and now of the Vienna Opera. In contrast to the reactionary Karajan, Abbado, intellectually chic and sexually charismatic, favoured living com-posers, left-wing causes and lean cuisine. Carlo-Maria Giulini would join him as elder statesman while Giuseppe Sinopoli, a physician and archaeologist who conducted the Philharmonia, would add an alternative dimension. Leonard Bernstein would be the label's international icon, guaranteed 'absolute star treatment',[19] his every whim fulfilled. 'I took a personal interest in the Abbado and Bernstein contracts,' said Holschneider. 'I had to make sure that if anything happened to Karajan we weren't left naked.'[20]

Sony, however, had ulterior plans. While Morita lectured Western leaders on how to run their economies, Ohga was circling CBS like an eagle at noon. 'I never knew when Ohga was going to be in New York, but he always came by,' said Joseph Dash. 'One day he says to me "Joe, I think Daniel Barenboim is going to be the next Karajan. You should sign him to do the Bruckner symphonies." I said, "Thanks very much, we'll look into it." ' James T. Wolfensohn, a CBS board director and future World Bank president who was Barenboim's close friend, had made a similar pitch. Dash was doubtful. 'I liked Barenboim, but I didn't think he'd sell enough records to support the kind of deal he wanted from us.'

He called Yetnikoff for a steer on dealing with his Japanese partner. 'The word came back: Ignore Ohga.'[21] This was the last time anyone at CBS was able to ignore Ohga. The company had been taken over by an asset stripper, Lawrence Tisch, and Yetnikoff was trying to sell its record division. He linked up with Ohga at a

Karajan Don Giovanni in Salzburg, only for his friend, in the middle of the second act, to be stretchered off following a heart attack. Morita agreed to the asking price but Tisch asked for more. Then came Black Monday of October 1987. Share values shrivelled and Tisch needed cash. Sony gulped down CBS Records before breakfast, adding Columbia Pictures for dessert. The bill was $6 billion but the yen was high and the shock value priceless. Sony had collared enough popular culture to feed its gadgets for ever. Matsushita and Toshiba followed suit with swoops on Universal Pictures, MCA Records and a bite of Time-Warner. Within months, much of Western entertainment was in Japanese hands and *Variety* was awash in despair.

To maintain confidence, Ohga left Sony Records in the hands of Yetnikoff, despite his escalating excesses. He was ordered into rehab. The Sony bosses, in his absence, pounced for their ultimate target. Karajan kept them waiting. 'He kept saying, I'll sign, I'll sign, just not today,' said Paul Burger, a Sony exec. On the morning of 16 July 1989 Ohga flew into Salzburg with Michael P. Schulhof, an American executive and physician, much liked by the maestro. 'I received a message that he wanted me to come to him straight from the airport,' said Ohga.[22] The Sony pair drove to Anif and were shown to the master's bedroom. Karajan had been suffering chest pains and cancelled the day's rehearsal. A cardiologist called to perform an ECG but was sent away. 'I have my most important friend here today,' said Karajan, 'and even the King of China cannot disturb our discussion.' Shortly before lunch, he asked for water. Schulhof brought a glass to his bed. 'He took a sip,' said Ohga, 'his face slumped to one side and he started to snort. Mickey Schulhof said: "My goodness, a heart attack!" I said, "Herbert, Herbert . . ." We called his wife – she was washing her hair – but he had already passed away.' Two days later, a devastated Ohga was rushed into open-heart surgery.

Karajan was buried at midnight in the Anif churchyard to avoid a media scrum. On the third night after his death, the widow Eliette went up to the grounds to commune with her loss. As she neared the grave, she sensed another presence.

'Who's there?' she cried, 'what do you want?'

'It's me, Carlos Kleiber,' wept the world's most elusive conductor. 'I had to come. He was the one I admired most.'

Eliette took Kleiber home and sat him down in the kitchen until dawn, trying to sign him up as director of the Easter Festival.[23] The monarch was dead, but the music went on. Karajan left a mountain of 950 recordings and a fortune of half a billion dollars, the estate swelled annually by royalties from such DG gimmicks as 'Karajan Express' and 'Karajan Adagio'. There was no limit to his recyclability. Eliette, loyal to his example, sued his last lawyer successfully for 3 million euros.

6. Madness

Until Sony came along, classics were a frugal operation. Pennies were counted and projects costed to the last double bass. 'We ran a tight ship,' said EMI's Peter Andry. 'We didn't go bananas,' said Joseph Dash.

All that altered with the advent of Ohga and his new head of classics, Gunther Breest, Karajan's DG producer. Breest was not a natural leader of men. A convivial colleague, he had spent too many years as Karajan's doormat to assume authority. 'If I have a personal motivation,' said Breest, 'it is that I don't want to disappoint Mr Ohga. He is a great visionary.'[1] Ohga announced that Sony would be 'the most important classical label by the end of the century'. Breest, blinkered by life at DG, remodelled the label along German lines, moving headquarters to Hamburg.

To CBS veterans it felt like a slap in the face with a Baltic flounder. Masterworks had been doing well in America, reclaiming a quarter of US classical sales and the top *Billboard* award in six of the past seven years. 'It's one of the most profitable entities within CBS Records,' said a Yetnikoff aide. Joseph Dash took Breest to the Met to hand Domingo a platinum disc for a million sales of Perhaps Love. Next day, Breest said there would be no more crossover on Sony Classical. In May 1990 he fired Dash and reduced New York to a remote branch office. CBS staffers, many of them Jewish, called Breest's team 'Nazis' and the Japanese 'Nips'. In Hamburg Andreas Holschneider told the evening newspaper that a 'yellow peril' was jeopardizing German music.[2] DG was under siege. Never before had one of its officers gone over to an enemy. The atmosphere turned acrid as old pals and drinking partners were forbidden to meet. Breest proceeded to outbid DG for Karajan's videos, paying $10 million and spending another $10 million on production and promotion costs. Knowing that Karajan on his own could not underpin a new laser disc format (known in Germany as Bildplatte, or picture disc), Breest shelled out another fortune to film concerts by Sergiu Celibidache, who had given up making records in 1948 on the grounds that listeners could not witness his input. 'Celi', nearing eighty, was a slightly wacky cult figure at the Munich Philharmonic. His oddity and scarcity value were not enough to save the Bildplatte, and DG nipped in to split Karajan sales by reeling out his 1970s operas on VHS. Sony's advanced format crashed shortly after takeoff.

Breest provocatively planted his tanks on DG's lawn, taking possession of a fin-de-siècle villa on the classy Nonnenstieg, complete with imperial staircase and decorated ceilings. He had Greek goddesses added to the décor of his private office and edged them in gold leaf. Money was no object and aesthetics no impediment. 'I still own an ashtray in the style of Hermès with a colour image of the villa,' said one employee.[3] Artists and agents arrived to witness the opulence. Many did a quick calculation and doubled their fees. The Berlin Philharmonic racked up its rates to 180,000 Deutschmarks ($125,000) for a three-session symphony, a cost base that required 40,000 sales to break even. The economics of classical recording parted company with market reality.

Breest's hirelings enjoyed a huge salary hike. A Decca man went from £40,000 a year to £100,000 overnight, then found he was the lowest paid producer at the water cooler. Olympia Gineri, Abbado's Vienna Opera assistant, was named head of artists and repertoire, with a brief to lure her boss away from DG. This was misplaced thinking since Abbado had developed a loathing for Gineri. Still, like other musicians, he could not resist Sony gold and when the Berlin Philharmonic elected him as Karajan's successor, ahead of Maazel and Levine, he signed over a small part of his work to Sony. Ohga proclaimed a 'joint interpretive venture with Abbado and the Berlin Philharmonic Orchestra' and Breest, snapping at DG's Italian strategy, signed Giulini and Muti. 'Look,' he told a visitor to his Salzburg festival office, decorated with maestro portraits, 'we have the greatest living Italian conductors on Sony Classical.'[4]

It may have looked good on the wall, but the detail defied belief. Abbado, who had won Berlin on the size of his DG contract, was not about to jeopardize his job. He gave DG first refusal on recordings and Sony the leftovers. While Breest bragged, Holschneider invited independent press witnesses, myself among them, to watch Abbado sign a new DG contract the morning after his inaugural concert in Berlin.

Breest switched to early music, Holschneider's heartland. Raiding Teldec, he hired Wolf Erichson, Harnoncourt's producer, to launch a new label, Vivarte. Erichson made a hundred recordings with the likes of Leonhardt, Kuijken, Bylsma and von Asperen, but he failed to sign Harnoncourt or any of the baroque big guns.

Gineri, her usefulness expired, was replaced by 'artist relations manager' Ervin Veg. Veg shared with Breest an affinity for fine cigars and wines. Some producers considered him a high-rolling braggart. 'You had only to say to Veg, lovely building and he'd reply, "I know the architect." Lovely meal: "I showed the chef how to scramble an egg." Good music: "I suggested to Wolfgang Amadeus that he compose this work."' Veg's friends called him 'a career diplomat, a man who spent a lot of his time unravelling other people's messes'.[5]

Breest snatched film composer John Williams and the Boston Pops from Philips. 'They were big earners for us,' said a rueful A&R chief.[6] He then swooped for a legend he had signed to DG in a deal brokered by a young publicist. Peter Gelb had been making a film about Vladimir Horowitz but got no interest at CBS or RCA. Breest brought the watery-eyed old master onto DG for six extraordinary recitals, recorded in his Manhattan living room by ex-CBS producer Thomas Frost. When Horowitz sat at the piano for the seventh disc on 20 October 1989 both he and Frost thought they were on DG, unaware that Breest and Gelb had switched them to Sony.[7] The sessions took twelve days, unusually fast for the fussy Horowitz. Four days after the final note, Horowitz died and Breest, for all his bluster, was left with a single release – one more for the trophy wall. He was getting a reputation for being unlucky and losing respect for the way he flashed his cash. 'Anything he wanted to do, he outbid the rest of us,' said EMI's Peter Alward.

The backlash took a different turn among conductors who, egos inflated with riches beyond reason, demanded extra rehearsals and star casts. If Breest refused, Abbado would phone Ohga, who longed to be loved by maestros. Ohga regularly overruled Breest, causing chaos on Sony Classical. Too many conductors were making too many records with no coherent purpose. Abbado's Mozart symphonies, Levine's Verdi and Maazel's Sibelius sounded anaemic beside their tightly focused earlier works. Other labels moved to higher ground. DG picked up the unwanted Pierre Boulez from Sony and recorded him with the perfectionist Cleveland Orchestra. Ray Minshull at Decca invested further in the Cleveland music director Christoph von Dohnanyi and guest conductor Vladimir Ashkenazy. At Philips, Erik Smith brought out the complete works of Mozart for the 1991 bicentennial. Holschneider, at DG, sniffed victory – pyrrhic though it might be – in a cautiously worded midpoint report: 'The past year, bringing a noticeable increase in competition, has in no way deterred DG from achieving its goals of stabilizing and maintaining its high international profile and further expanding its star artist roster.'[8]

The Sony splurge loosened budget constraints. As a matter of macho pride, Alain Levy urged his classical labels to spend more and win the war. Output on each of the majors rose to a hundred new releases a year, with no visible increase in demand. On the contrary, collectors finished replacing their old LPs and stopped buying CDs. 'The average classical collection in the US was around a hundred LPs,' noted a marketing man. 'In the '80s, people replaced them at a rate of eight to ten CDs a year; by the early nineties, it was three or four.'[9] 'Before CD, classics had six percent of the total market,' recalled one corporate chief. 'By 1987 it had doubled to twelve percent, by the end of the decade it was back down to six.'[10]

The boom was over. Black Monday and the end of communism set off a worldwide recession. The death of Bernstein, fourteen months after Karajan, eliminated the last household name maestro.

Consumers, confused by a glut of classical faces, stuck to the great and the dead. But as long as Sony poured forth, the others felt obliged to keep pace. A well-ordered economy ran riot. Breest, said EMI's Peter Alward, 'almost bankrupted the industry'.[11]

Ten years on, when the last ones to leave were turning out the lights, people asked each other why the glut had raged for so long; why Sony was allowed to blow $100 million before Ohga was called to account; why hardly anyone in the community of artists, producers, executives, critics, radio presenters and orchestral managers had denounced the absurdity of it all. Stores were swamped with unsold CDs but a pretence was maintained of prosperity and progress. *Gramophone* proclaimed a golden age of classical recording and faced stiff competition from *BBC Music* magazine, which mounted a free disc on the cover, dangerously devaluing the CD as a prestige item. The Classic FM radio franchise was founded on the same myth of classical resurgence. Gripped by self-delusion, the classical world ignored Euripides' warning: 'Those whom the gods wish to destroy they first make mad.'

Signs and wonders appeared in the heavens. On 7 July 1990, in the thick of a soccer World Cup, three tenors linked arms in a Roman arena and sang their way into the record books. Pavarotti and Domingo, sworn rivals, had come together out of compassion for José Carreras, a thinner vocalist who had survived leukaemia. Media giants dismissed their concert as a gimmick and Decca agreed to record it only on condition that the singers worked for a one-off fee. It seemed a fair deal – a million dollars for two hours' work. The tenors sang happily in the baths of Caracalla and a global television audience, numbed by goalless draws, rushed out to buy the disc in spectacular quantities. Fourteen million were sold, more than any single classical recording in history.

The tenors, incensed, demanded compensation. Pavarotti got an under-the-table extra $1 million from Decca – the secret broken in his manager's memoirs[12] – but the label owed no favours to the other two. Furious, Domingo and Carreras barred Decca from the 1994 World Cup replay. Warner won that auction for $16 million, needing to sell 6 million CDs to break even. They sold 8 million. The Three Tenors brand struck twice and, for pop executives, was proof positive that classical music could make big money.

It was not the only such omen. Nigel Kennedy's 1990 Four Seasons, its movements segmented into pop-sized three-minute tracks, was selling at a rate of two CDs a minute. Kennedy, who wore Aston Villa soccer shirts and Jimi Hendrix's headscarf, appealed more to grannies than to adolescents, but 2 million Four Seasons seemed to confirm the chimera of classical popularity.

Next came a symphony by a living composer that turned into the most sought-after CD on the high street – 'you know, the one where the girl's singing something and you can't tell what'. Henryk Mikolai Gorecki's third symphony achieved spiritual transcendence with a finale setting of a girl's poem, found scratched into a Gestapo prison wall. An antidote to Boulezian complexity, it had been dismissed as Holy Minimalism by curators of modernist correctness, but a million sales changed everyone's tune and contemporary classical music, previously a mass turn-off, was the new big thing. Minimalists John Adams and Einojuhani Rautavaara were chased down streets by chaps in suits. Gorecki, a Katowice craftsman, found himself at the centre of a bidding war between two music publishers. 'Marketing people who had been saying there's no money in classical music and modern music is the biggest loser of all, now said there's no money in classical music – but contemporary, that's huge,' recalled a BMG producer.[13]

From the distant past came the tonsured tenors. No one knows who proposed the remedy, but it seems that in order to cool motorists' belligerence during Madrid's murderous rush hour a radio station began playing Gregorian chant, sung by Benedictine monks of Santo Domingo de Silos, in the Burgos region. The recording was not new – the sessions dated from March 1973, March 1980 and June 1981 – but gridlocked Madrilenos stopped hitting each other at traffic lights and bought the disc in their thousands on EMI's Spanish subsidiary. On world release, the monks sold five and a half million CDs, their popularity boosted by hip-hop deejays who played chant at the end of all-night raves.

The canard of mass market potential filtered into other corporate areas when *Four Weddings and a Funeral*, a Polygram rom-com film, sold mountains of a soundtrack album that included Gershwin, Handel, Eisler and Parry, as well as original music by Richard Rodney Bennett and a W. H. Auden poem. The idea took root that classical music was intrinsically commercial and that a classical label was essential to any movie corporation. All the more reason to spend, spend, spend.

The stakes rose a notch when EMI's plainspeaking chairman Colin Southgate hired a diminutive American to run his labels. Jim Fifield, it was said, 'could enter a room and the temperature dropped ten degrees'. He introduced himself to EMI Classics with the words: 'Show me 10 per cent profit year on year and you won't have to see me again.' The threat was not even veiled.

Peter Andry sought reassurances from Fifield about his future as label chief. When none came, he took early retirement. 'Fifield never got rid of me,' said Andry, 'he just never got back to me.' Andry went off in October 1988 with banquets, bouquets and dry eyes. 'Remember,' he warned his successor, Richard Lyttelton, 'the artist is your enemy.'

A month later, Andry set up office on the other side of Baker Street as head of Warner Classics. 'It seemed a bit inappropriate,' said EMI men, but Andry was not another Breest, out to raid his old stable. Starting from scratch, he bought a batch of struggling mid-sized labels – Teldec in Germany, Erato in France, Elektra Nonesuch in New York, Finlandia in Helsinki and NVC Arts Video in Britain. A DG veteran, Hans Hirsch, became head of Teldec with Barenboim, Solti's Chicago successor, as his brand leader. Nonesuch had Gorecki; Erato signed Carreras.

Andry, still hungry, sussed out small labels. At Hyperion, Ted Perry had a complete edition of Schubert songs and a loyal customer base. One well-known literary agent swore he never bought a classical CD unless it was Hyperion. Andry took Perry to lunch. Over dessert, he pushed an open chequebook across the table.

'You fill in the price,' smiled Andry. The former cab driver pushed the cheque back untouched. 'What would I do with my life if I sold up?' demanded Ted Perry, independent to the death.

More contenders joined the classical merry-go-round. Rupert Murdoch contemplated a classical label and Virgin's Richard Branson hired an EMI man, Simon Foster, to start Virgin Classics. RCA, long in hibernation, bounced back under German owners, the Bertelsmann media group, and the leadership of Guenter Hensler, poached from Polygram. Hensler, like Andry, eschewed dawn raids. A man of fine intelligence who obtained degrees in conducting and economics before majoring in entertainment, Hensler reconstructed BMG classics niche by niche. He bought the German wing of Harmonia Mundi, specializing in earlier-than-early music, and commissioned Russian music on price-cutting Arte Nova. For contemporary classics with a sassy edge he hired the Pulitzer-winning music critic Tim Page, whose new label would, he assured Hensler, combine 'attributes of Nonesuch, the old Victrola label and the Modern Library'.[14] Page had a flush of hard, newsy ideas for BMG's Catalyst, ranging from a CD of Aids-stricken composers to a string quartet composed by Glenn Gould (Page was editor of Gould's writings), to a musical companion to Thomas Pynchon's cult novels.

'I wanted to make recordings that would be both of immediate interest *and* capable of standing the test of time,' said Page, when it was all over. 'Catalyst would be not only a new music label but a *smart* music label, something that would attract the same audience that attends a new Sondheim play or highly praised film, something that would reflect the diversity of sound that surrounds us and present some of the more engaging vantage points.'[15] Catalyst brought out the white-night symphonies of Rautavaara, the chili-pepper Mexican composer Silvestre Revueltas, the electronic explorer Alvin Curran – along with much else that was eclectic, unusual, ear-catching and nicely niche.

'Hensler ramped it up,' recalled James Glicker, who came in as marketing manager from packaged goods at Procter & Gamble but had studied music at college and shared the chairman's vocation.

'Guenter was an elder statesman, very good on artist relationships. He was prescient about conductors. He signed Yuri Temirkanov, Michael Tilson Thomas, Leonard Slatkin, Colin Davis. When everyone else tried to repeat the Three Tenors, he laid hands on some unreleased live Pavarottis that did very well for us.'[16]

Glicker analysed classical records by the criteria of yoghurt, his previous expertise. 'It was a well-liked product, but there was too much of it. The strength was also the weakness. Why did we keep repeating what we'd done better in the '60s with Reiner and Chicago? The mass market had no idea what to buy.' He proposed charging more for famous old recordings by Rubinstein and Horowitz than for hyped-up new ones by the flying-fingered Russian pianist, Evgeny Kissin – 'Kissin at eleven dollars, Rubinstein at sixteen – I didn't have much success persuading anyone.'

He wrestled with an industry hamstrung by habit and high on expenses where a classical executive could spend twenty-five grand on a world trip to find a location for the next sales conference but would veto a $5,000 sonata on grounds of cost. 'They spent ridiculous amounts buying an advertisement for my label in *Rolling Stone*,' said Tim Page, 'when I couldn't even afford an assistant.' Page was flown to Salzburg 'to meet with four BMG executives, three of whom were based in New York, a couple miles from my home'. He had spent the summer putting together 'a beautiful and hypnotic programme with the superb and acclaimed pianist Bruce Brubaker – music by Philip Glass, John Adams, Olivier Messiaen, Arvo Pärt, Alvin Curran and Mark-Anthony Turnage'. His meeting was a macabre classic of its kind:

The tape is never played. The glowing reviews are never read. Instead, Brubaker's press photo – a standard tux-and-piano number with a by-no-means-unattractive man at the centre – is passed around, to the marked furrowing of brows.

'It's so . . . *conservative*,' says the man in the gray suit.

'I don't like his haircut,' whines the whippet-thin trendoid with the coif, between sips of Diet-Pepsi. 'He should be wearing contacts instead of glasses,' says another executive, after a ruminative pause long enough to prove he'd given the matter thought.

I venture the obvious – that we can introduce Brubaker to a hair-stylist, replace his tuxedo with Day-Glo peacock feathers or whatever is deemed the hip thing that week (after all, BMG had wrapped the violinist Maria Bachmann in mosquito netting for her first cover), and buy him some contact lenses. What about the music, the mood, the artistry? No go.

'You don't understand, Tim,' it is explained patiently, as if to an idiot child. 'We want somebody with *attitude*. You can't fake attitude.'

Heads bob around the table.

And so, on the whim of the moment, one more long-planned, made-to-order, inexpensive to produce and presumably easy-to-sell project is shot down, for want of some mythical attitude. However, so the trip shouldn't be a total loss, as I prepare to leave (walking past the fancy posters, the giveaway knick-knacks on which BMG had spent a fortune) I am told the company has finally decided to 'look' for the funds to hire a $200-a-week assistant, so that I will no longer have to sort through hundreds of unsolicited tapes alone on my living room floor.[17]

It was small consolation. Hensler suffered a heart attack, retired early and died at sixty-three; Glicker got sent to Australia and Page resigned. Catalyst died. Virgin Classics was sold to EMI, and Erato, Teldec and other Warner subsidiaries were brought under. Homogeneity was the menace in waiting.

A dark cloud loomed from the east. A German trader in Hong Kong, active in record distribution, was asked for a package of popular classics to be sold door to door in South Korea. Spotting a drop in CD manufacturing costs, Klaus Heymann bought thirty orchestral tapes from a Slovak in Paris and pressed them for his client, who went bust. 'So there I was, stuck with thirty classical masters. I couldn't sell them at full price because these were unknown East European orchestras, although the performances were not too bad. I had to put them out on a budget label. That's how Naxos Records was born.'[18]

Priced at $6, Naxos were the cheapest classics by far, a third of the price of a premium DG. They sold across Asia in 1987, then in Woolworth's in Britain and in gas stations up and down Scandinavia, a slow-moving landmass where classical CDs had only ever been found before in smart city shops. Soon, Heymann was selling more classics in the north than all the majors put together. In three years he counted 4 million sales. By 1994, adding the US and Japan, he had 10 million with annual growth of 50 per cent. One in six classical records sold anywhere in the world was a Naxos.

'Basically a record collector who loves music,'[19] Heymann laid no claims to artistic vision. 'I sat down with a catalogue and marked everything that had more than ten recordings. That was our initial policy: record the hundred most recorded things in reasonably good quality, reasonably good sound, and make them available'.[20] In Slovakia and Slovenia, he paid orchestral players $100 a disc, for which they were duly thankful. Conductors and soloists got $500 or $1,000, no royalties, no frills. Every contract was for a single disc, no long-term exclusivities. The biggest name on the box was the composer's, followed by the work. Performers got small print at the back. Bucking the rules, Heymann reduced the artist to a cipher and sold entirely on piece and price. If one of his artists won an award, he refused to spend on publicity, arguing that the big labels had been ruined by the star system. Promoting an artist would only swell heads and increase fees. The Scrooge-like side of Heymann was balanced by a puritan work ethic and a complete lack of flam. Any money he made on records, Heymann would say, went back into repertoire – though there was enough left over to buy him a $10 million estate overlooking New Zealand's Mellon Bay, where he moved his family ahead of Hong Kong's return to China in July 1997. Artists, unaware of his prosperity, churned out Naxos CDs for $1,000 a go, reckoning that the volume of work would keep them occupied and in the public eye. A disc of Beethoven sonatas by the Hungarian pianist Jeno Jandó sold a quarter of a million. On any other label the royalties would have built Jandó a house in Budapest. On Naxos, publication was its own reward.

Heymann never argued with artists; he preferred not to meet them at all. Musicians, he said, 'have a certain charisma that lets them push you into doing things that don't make artistic or business sense'.[21] Performers who tried to obtain better conditions – the Franco-American conductor Antonio de Almeida, and the British cellist Raphael Wallfisch – were bluntly dismissed.

At Naxos' price, most things sold – abstruse Hindemith, in a performance by Franz-Paul Decker and the New Zealand Symphony Orchestra, cleared 18,000 in a year where, on DG or EMI with Abbado, it barely managed three figures. Naxos classical clips crept into such US television series as *ER*, *Sex in the City* and *The Sopranos*, paying Heymann hundreds of times with each episode's repetition around the world and nothing to the artists. Heymann, in one territory after another, bought out his distributors and acquired an overlordship of cottage labels that came to him for warehousing. If he saw an esoteric item selling well on Swedish BIS or German CPO, he would swiftly have it recorded for Naxos.

Pigtailed and sport-shirted in a wrinkle-proof business suit, Heymann was refreshingly transparent about the record business, quick to mock the vanity of artists and competitors whose designer items he replicated on the cheap. Musical likes and dislikes were luxuries that he kept out of the office. Scratch him hard and you would find a conventional German *Bildung* founded on the three Bs, but if the bottom ever dropped out of Beethoven Heymann would not scruple to scrap his output. Driven by opus numbers rather than any brilliance of interpretation, his catalogue bulged out into remote corners of repertoire, gaining Naxos anorak appeal. Each national office was given a licence to record local composers. There was a series of British music from Bournemouth and Glasgow, an American line from Nashville and Seattle, with conductors Marin Alsop, Paul Daniel and Dennis Russell Davies. 'The cost of recording an orchestra today is cheaper than it was in the beginning in Slovakia and Hungary,' exulted Heymann.[22] Early eastern Europe CDs were replaced with western versions and binned at two or three dollars under hypermarket labels of convenience.

Klaus Heymann was on a high, hitting the industry where it hurt most, in the slow-burning backlist. BMG tried to buy a stake in his company for $10 million. Tim Harrold, a Polygram executive, got on a plane to Hong Kong and presented himself to Heymann with two suitcases filled with high-denomination dollar bills. Richard Lyttelton, head of EMI Classics, offered $30 million. Heymann has a letter on file offering $100 million. In every case, the answer was No. 'I was having too much fun,' he laughed.[23] Jazz, nostalgia, talking books and educational CDs joined the Naxos roster. When the internet kicked in, he offered website access to the entire canon of Western classical music, threatening to corner the market in classical downloads.

The only thing that could have stopped him, he confessed, would have been a swift move by the majors to swamp the market with cheap reissues. Klemperer, Szell and Kubelik for six bucks would have killed stone dead the likes of Gunzenhauser, Wit and Halasz.[24] But the labels were in a war with Sony and could not afford to reduce revenues from their grateful dead. Alain Levy issued a prohibition on price-cutting. By the time he relented, the century was over and Heymann had a $50-million turnover and 2,500 masters in his vaults.

With merciless effrontery he proceeded to raid the recorded past for epics that had lapsed from circulation. Success with Kreisler, Casals and Rachmaninov emboldened him to nibble at the margins of mechanical copyright. Richard Lyttelton, on a New York trip, found a Naxos Callas recording on sale, copied from an EMI LP. After issuing a 'cease and desist' letter that Heymann ignored, EMI sued. Naxos won the first round but lost in the Court of Appeals at Albany, which vested all rights in the original producer. EMI demanded exemplary damages. Heymann took the case back to the lower court fighting, he said, on a matter of principle.[25] Months later he withdrew 150 historic titles from sale in the US 'as part of an amicable settlement'.[26] EMI claimed victory and other majors cheered a débâcle for Heymann, who turned seventy in October 2006. 'I wouldn't give five million for his catalogue now,' said Lyttelton scornfully,[27] but Heymann continued to prove that it was possible to succeed in classical recording without a dazzle of stars or a tower full of salary-guzzling executives.

The madness had to end; it was just a matter of who blinked first. Ohga was clearly not having as much fun as he had hoped. Classics was haemorrhaging cash and the rampaging Walter Yetnikoff was proving a painful embarrassment. On 29 June 1991 Ohga wrote to Yetnikoff: 'you are my old friend and we will stay as friends forever'.[28] Ten weeks later Yetnikoff was called to Ohga's New York office. 'I'm sorry,' said his old friend, 'but this hurts me more than it hurts you.' 'Please exit through the side door,' said the security guard.[29]

Yetnikoff's sacking was the signal for slim down. His successor was sharp-suited Tommy Mottola, an A&R hustler who had romanced Morita's goddaughter and left his wife for pop diva Mariah Carey. Ohga told Mottola he had to get approval on all new signings. Yetnikoff signed a no-attack confidentiality clause, which was supposed to ensure that he was never heard from again. He wound up serving soup at a homeless men's shelter on the Bowery. Schulhof followed him onto the scrapheap. Morita suffered a cerebral haemorrhage and Ohga, fearing that his time was short (he turned sixty in 1990), sought classical relief. He took up conducting – first in Japan, then with Maazel's Pittsburgh orchestra and Levine's at the Met, after giving each of them million-dollar gifts. 'I cannot find a successor,' he fretted in February 1992. 'If I find a good successor, I'll hand over to him and become a conductor, full time.'[30]

The enormity of his classical blunder could no longer be concealed. Breest had let Polygram reconquer the US charts and Sony Classical sorely needed an American sensibility. Peter Gelb's name came into contention. Gelb was making promo videos for Ronald Wilford's CAMI, the biggest artists agency, and running television sales for the Met. The son of an executive editor of the *New York Times*, he started out as a publicist at the Boston Symphony Orchestra and amazed *Times* critics by getting out-of-town Ozawa into their pages week after week. Wilford called him 'one of the most brilliant men I know'. Colleagues found him inarticulate and impossibly vain. 'I want you to be Peter's friend,' said Ozawa to one of his Boston interns. 'Why?' said the young man. 'Because he doesn't have one.'

On 14 July 1993 Wilford sold CAMI Video to Sony for $6 million, with Gelb thrown in. The new US vice-president of Sony Classical picked up a million-dollar salary and was welcomed as his deputy by the guileless Breest, who was having problems with Erwin Veg, his artist relations manager. Breest promoted Michael Haas, formerly of Decca, to head of A&R. Veg went into a huff and Tokyo sent in its head of human resources to sort out the fuss. During the kerfuffle, Gelb told Ohga of Breest's inadequacies. 'Gunther adored Peter Gelb, right up to the moment of his own execution,' said Haas.[31]

With Breest gone, Gelb moved the label back to New York, putting the Nonnenstieg folly up for sale. 'If Sony want to become more populist and American oriented, I can understand that,' Breest told a Hamburg newspaper, 'but I can't go along with it. I stand for something which cannot be achieved in an instant.'[32] Gelb scrapped Vivarte and put classics on ice. His revivalist plan was founded on the movies, for which he had a boyish fascination. 'One of the reasons I came to work for Sony,' he said, 'was that it gave me an opportunity to expand into feature film . . . [Sony] is interested in my continuing on film projects in future.'[33] Not very interested, it transpired. Gelb was allowed to make one feature film called *Voices*, a romantic life of the suicidal English composer Peter Warlock. It was never shown in cinemas and scuttled out ignominiously on video. Gelb continued to describe himself as a 'visionary, award-winning documentary filmmaker', though he never got to make another film.

Hollywood, however, did provide him with lift-off. Sony, practically on Gelb's first day, bought James Horner's soundtrack to James Cameron's *Titanic* with a theme song performed by Celine Dion. Mottola refused to have such mush on any of his pop labels and every other Sony boss turned it down. 'Gelb was the newest executive, the weakest,' said an insider. 'He couldn't refuse.'[34] *Titanic*, a three-hankie weepie, became the best-selling soundtrack of all time, racking up 25 million CDs and giving Gelb the aura of magician and the right to lecture his industry. 'It is neither commercially rewarding nor artistically relevant for us to make [classical] recordings that sell only a few thousand copies,' he would tell a 1997 Klassik Komm Conference in Hamburg. 'Rather than drift toward commercial oblivion with new recordings of old music that don't sell, we have started doing something about it.'[35]

The something was commissioning music for the middle of the road, music that suited both movies and concert play. The prototype was a score being written by John Corigliano, composer of a powerful Aids symphony (CD 82, p. 254), for a Canadian movie, *The Red Violin*, telling the tale of a valuable fiddle over three centuries. The fullness of Corigliano's score would be kitted out as a concerto for Sony star Joshua Bell to play on the symphony circuit, and ultimately in the BBC Proms. By marrying movies to the concert hall, Gelb aimed to revitalize classical recording. 'I am not afraid to admit that we are seeking success,' said Gelb. 'We are seeking artistic and commercial success. And we're doing it by commissioning new music and taking new musical initiatives. *We are attempting to redefine the meaning of classical music.*'

The rest of the industry looked on in awe and irritation as Gelb, with all the luck that Breest lacked, bulldozed his way to success. 'I'm not interested in crap like this,' he told an independent producer who brought in a $30,000 project. 'I'd rather lose a million on a movie than make peanuts on some pathetic symphony.'[36] 'I believe in great music,' he told a conference, 'I just don't want to record it.'

Gelb in hubris was a sight to behold. He lectured staff on his 'philosophy', accusing critics of 'negativism'. In the wake of the *Titanic* soundtrack he formed a cadre of easy-listening composers to furnish his output. They included Horner, Corigliano, John Williams, Elliot Goldenthal (partner of the Disney director Julie Taymor), Michael Kamen (*Band of Brothers*), Richard Danielpour and the Chinese immigrant, Tan Dun. Joshua Bell played Horner's soundtrack to Richard Eyre's biopic *Iris*. Yo Yo Ma, the finest cellist of his generation, soloed in Tan Dun's *Crouching Tiger, Hidden Dragon* and in Williams' score for *Seven Years in Tibet*.

Beyond movies, Gelb preached crossover. Ma led an orgy of genre bending with a hillbilly album, Appalachia Waltz, performed with country fiddler Mark O'Connor and double-bassist Edgar Meyer and promoted on bus stands around America. Ma followed with a set of Bach suites, paced to accompany a gardening video. Rising violinist Hilary Hahn played an Edgar Meyer concerto. Dreadlocked Bobby McFerrin caterwauled on classical tracks. An egregious pair of Operababes gave way to the still ghastlier Il Divo, a quartet of beefcake tenors.

Gelb discontinued all Sony conductors except the LA Philharmonic's Esa-Pekka Salonen, whom he persistently sought to offload on other labels. A Swiss-funded scheme to record the life's work of the avant-garde Hungarian composer György Ligeti was stopped in mid-flow and shunted on to Warner. This was music that required mental effort and it did not fit Gelb's fast-food methodology.

For a couple of years the formula worked like a dream and most of Gelb's chickens came to roost in the charts. But there is no success in music without imitators. Others got into the bidding for movie scores and the price went through the roof. Decca beat Gelb to Horner's *Braveheart*, selling one and a half million CDs. Decca also won Michael Nyman's *The Piano* and Gabriel Yared's *Mr Holland's Opus*. Gelb got lumbered with losers from Sony Pictures. Unable to repeat his *Titanic* fluke and without a flow of bread-and-butter classics, Gelb needed to find one big hit a year to stay solvent. With some ingenuity he reinvented Billy Joel, the middling pop singer, as a 'classical' composer of piano suites. Radiohead, a British rock group, appeared in 'classical' transcriptions. A little Welsh girl with a lovely warble was launched as an old-fashioned wunderkind, paraded before popes and presidents with pretty opera arias. But while Sony Classical claimed the credit for Charlotte Church, the profits went to another division, Sony Europe, since Gelb had refused to share the investment. That bad decision cost his label $3 million. As Charlotte Church went from winsome arias to teenage pop and sex scandal, Gelb's label lost its veneer of quality and became known as Sony Anything-but-Classical.

By the end of the century Gelb was glum and his business sinking. With Ohga in retirement, Gelb's 'brilliance' failed to convince hard-hat techno-Japs. Appalachia Waltz which became a Sony Classical number one, sold just four thousand a week, one-fiftieth of a pop hit. In the real world, Sony Classical amounted to a row of very few beans. 'How's business?' I asked Gelb in a lobby encounter at London's Savoy Hotel. 'Never been tougher,' grunted the failed messiah of classical recording.[37]

7. Meltdown

Ray Minshull was counting the days to retirement: 'Only fourteen hundred and thirty-seven to go.' By way of valediction he signed off a million-dollar Frau ohne Schatten for Solti, Berlioz's five-hour Les Troyens for Charles Dutoit in Montreal and, most lavishly of all, a Ring cycle for Dohnanyi in Cleveland. The logic was inscrutable. Frau was a slow seller, Solti's Ring was unsurpassable and while The Trojans had only Davis on Philips as competition, union rates in Montreal ruled out any possibility of profit. Minshull was playing himself out on a chord of luxury, flying first class between his favourite conductors in the company of a close personal friend. He gave Dutoit, a Swiss martinet who dressed like a business executive, a contract for twenty-five CDs over five years.

Still, it was assumed that Minshull knew what he was doing and the office ran like clockwork. 'Ray was very particular,' said a finance clerk. 'You could never send him a memo beginning "I'll be going tomorrow . . ." It would come back corrected to: "I will be going tomorrow." Everything had to be done properly.'[1]

When he reached sixty-five, Minshull slipped away into bucolic oblivion, never to be seen again. Holschneider retired that same year, handing over to Gianfranco Rebulla from DG's Italian office. 'It wasn't a bad choice,' he insisted, but his Italian redesign had been subsumed by the globality of the Sony war and DG was no longer to be defined in national colours. The marketing chief was Aman Pedersen, a Norwegian, and the head of A&R, Englishman Roger Wright. 'Apart from head of legal affairs,' said Wright, 'there wasn't a single German head of any department.'[2] Pedersen was a man of flair and impetuosity. When he fell for an artist, he fell big. The contract he gave Sinopoli was for eighty-eight CDs, John Eliot Gardiner was down for fifty-nine Bach cantata CDs, Cheryl Studer was his all-purpose soprano and Trevor Pinnock could do no wrong. Promoted to head of marketing, Pedersen faced a rude awakening. 'He'd predict 100,000 on the next Studer, and then he'd come back completely deflated with orders for a few hundred,' said colleagues. But Pedersen had a sharp eye for branding. He dressed up The Originals in Fifties livery and shiny black surfaces, selling 10 million units and putting a roar back into DG's stalled backlist.

Wright, nurturing talent, fell in love with the Hamburg atmosphere:

I was fascinated by recording, by capturing a particular moment, and at DG you are so conscious of the legacy. Andreas reinforced that on all of us. DG was the conductor's label par excellence, but it was also the label of pianists – Argerich, Pollini, Krystian Zimerman. We would ask ourselves: what are we looking for in a record? First, it should be artistically right, something we'd be proud of. Second, that it sustained the brand. And third, that it would sell. The sadness is that I arrived just at the point where we had to consider where the business was going, how to make fewer records. After a while we'd be saying to each other: why the hell are we doing this?

The day of reckoning had dawned.

Polygram's company report for 1996 proclaims a splendid record of expansion and achievement. Held up one way, the report is titled 'Creativity', held the other it is called 'Control'. Creativity features Brad Pitt, star of *Sleepers*, a film 'which took over a hundred million at the box-office'. Next page is Shania Twain with 'the best-selling female country album of all time'. Jackie Cheung is the 'Asian superstar', Richard Dreyfuss stars in *Mr Holland's Opus*, there is a scene from the British cult film *Trainspotting*, a still of the evergreen Elton John and an introductory shot of Italian popster Andrea Bocelli, 'a major success throughout the Benelux and Germany'. The only classical artists on show are the soprano Jessye Norman, who opened the year's Olympics, and Pavarotti, who parades with pop stars at a charity concert. Hanover, in the year reported, pressed its billionth CD. All was well in a never-ending Polyworld. 'The breadth of our repertoire, internationally and within each region, provides the strong base from which we believe future growth will come,' wrote president Alain Levy. 'Music as a whole remains an *important and growing* part of the total entertainment budget and has seen a decade of unprecedented growth, up 12 per cent per annum on a compound basis since 1986.'

'Important' and 'growing' were confident words. They applied to every aspect of the business except classical, where the adjective changed admonitorially to 'challenging'. Levy wrote of a need 'to expand the horizons of classical music'.[3] He had ordered 'a careful and comprehensive review' that would lead to 'a reduction in the overall number of recordings and releases, and the reorganisation of the recording studios'.

That kind of policy called for a hatchet man. Levy's eye fell on Chris Roberts, a sometime record-store assistant from Portland, Oregon, who had gone to Munich to write a doctoral thesis on cabaret and wound up writing jingles for German TV. Landing a Polygram job in 1989, Roberts proved the perfect corporation man, sensitive to his boss's wishes, ruthless to those below. In his mid-thirties, he dressed like a Roosevelt-era drugstore owner in sleeveless grey cardigan. He was head of Polygram Classics USA when Levy sent him to London to wield the axe.

'I looked at the situation,' said Roberts, 'and thought: people can't absorb all these records. A potential or occasional record buyer cannot differentiate one conductor from another, one interpretation or brand image from the next.'[4] He recast the three labels. DG would be core-classical, Decca vocal and crossover and Philips neutral, all to be ethically cleansed by willing executioners.

Roger Lewis was the Decca chopper. A fast riser, the ex head of music on BBC's Radio 1 pop station had moved to EMI UK, where his key classical signing was a half-Asian, half-British babe of fifteen whom he displayed on her debut album cover in a wet white swimsuit. Vanessa-Mae Nicolson sold 1.38 million CDs, earning Lewis widespread revulsion. 'The record was never aimed at the classical market anyway,' he shrugged.[5] To avert mutiny at

Decca, Roberts hired a traditional head of A&R – Evans Mirageas, artistic administrator of the Boston Symphony Orchestra and a close adviser of the soprano Renée Fleming. To strip down Philips, Roberts appointed Costa Pilavachi, a Greek-Canadian who had run the music programme at the National Arts Centre in Ottawa and was well connected to Ozawa and Gardiner. The new chiefs were given their cutting orders.

Roberts told them to start from the top – sack conductors. Paul Moseley, a Decca man, remembers coming into the office and seeing Lewis on one phone, Mirageas on another, simultaneously ending the record careers of Vladimir Ashkenazy and Christoph von Dohnanyi. 'Roger said I'll call Jasper (Parrott, Ashkenazy's agent), and you call Tom Morris (president of the Cleveland Orchestra). That was how they broke the news.'[6]

Ashkenazy had four contract years to run, Dohnanyi five.[7] Ashkenazy was only down to make one record a year, and once the Ring was cancelled, not much was saved by sacking Dohnanyi. The deed was done for exemplary reasons, to send a chill across the art. Despondency fell like a winter's fog, sowing mistrust between artists and producers, who were next for the scrapheap.

'The Decca Recording Centre was a money loser,' explained Mirageas. 'We had become obsolete in Research and Design . . . To carry an in-house staff of nearly forty engineers, editors, producers and technicians was simply no longer possible.' Skilled employees were flung onto the street. Many went straight to Naxos, where the sound improved exponentially. The last engineer left Decca on the final day of the century – Philip Siney, his name was – and that was the end of the celebrated Decca Sound.

'The toughest decisions,' said Mirageas, 'were how to prune the too-large artist roster and to close down the Decca Recording Centre . . . The market was shrinking and our very large investment in recordings was not recouping anything near the bare minimum to stay in business. I was charged with making those decisions and it was painful because every single artist was worthy of a contract in the best of times.

'If there is any pride involved in doing a hard job, I look back on this agonizing process with some pride. Polygram was prepared to be very generous with the departing employees. In the case of departing artists, most of it was accomplished by simply playing out existing contracts.'[8] That may have been the case with the seniorities, but many young artists were tossed, still twitching, onto a compost pile from which few rose again. The roll of Decca artists was slashed in 1997–8 from forty to sixteen. The number of recordings dropped from 120 in 1990 to 40 in 1998 and half as many in 2006.

At Philips, Pilavachi tried to let conductors down gently, dragging out contract talks until it became clear there would be no renewal. Muti, Previn, Marriner, Colin Davis and Brüggen were phased out. The only frontal confrontation was with Bernard Haitink, the label's prowhead for four decades. Haitink had persuaded Hans Kinzl, Pilavachi's predecessor, to let him record a second Mahler cycle with the Berlin Philharmonic, arguing that his interpretation had matured since his 1970s Amsterdam set. Three symphonies achieved negligible sales, five more were in the can. Pilavachi had to stop Haitink doing the eighth and ninth symphonies. A tetchy, graceless man, Haitink was living in London with his third wife, a popular member of the Royal Opera House orchestra. He was not the kind of artist to face adversity without retaliation. Dutch governments still flinched at the hoo-ha Haitink made when they tried to trim his Concertgebouw orchestra in the 1980s.

Pilavachi arranged to call on Haitink at his home, near Harrods, accompanied by the retired Kinzl and a producer, Clive Bennett. Haitink heard him out in total silence. 'Oh, so that's it,' he said, after a terrible pause. 'It's over.'

And so it was. Ten days before Harnoncourt was to record Bruckner's ninth symphony with the Vienna Philharmonic at Salzburg, a performance that included a keenly awaited restoration of the finale, Warner shut down Teldec and stopped all classical recording. The orchestra, eager to play Bruckner's last notes, agreed to be taped without fee and the Teldec crew recorded them unpaid. Harnoncourt had a card up his sleeve. He was due to conduct the Vienna New Year's Day concert, always a hit in Japan.

Labels, vying for that prize, were told that they had to buy the Bruckner if they wanted to waltz with Strauss. BMG placed a bid. Awed by the conductor's Habsburg aura, they took up his Teldec contract together with his technical crew.

This, however, was a rare act of mercy in the summer of wholesale slaughter. Sacking conductors was a symbolic parricide. The gods of the gramophone were shown to be made of tinfoil and tossed aside, like crumpled tissues. There was no discernible consumer reaction. The few who noticed the stoppage slackened their record buying habit, or gave up altogether.

Judgement day was delayed at DG, where Rebulla had fallen out with John Eliot Gardiner, whose girlfriend, Isabella de Sabata, was DG's head of press. The abrasive Englishman had a direct line to Chris Roberts, whom he had once conducted in an Oregon choir. Rebulla came under pressure to quit. 'He left in the disastrous summer when we were supposed to be telling all the artists we were going to drop,' grouched a colleague.

The DG baton passed to Karsten Witt of the Vienna Konzerthaus, a man without free-market experience. Jaws dropped when producers read his rose-tinted version of reality. 'Interest in classical music is growing,' Witt told *Billboard*. 'There are more festivals, promoters, venues, sponsorship – more people learning instruments. We are actually selling twice the number of recordings we sold during the time of the LP . . . There has been no decline.'[9]

Witt, it seemed, was keen to please all of the people all of the time. When Abbado, contracted to the Berlin Philharmonic, proposed to do Haydn symphonies with the Chamber Orchestra of Europe, Witt clapped his hands in delight. 'He couldn't say no to an artist, it was not in his nature,' said an associate. Finding that Witt was the wrong man to slash and burn, Roberts stepped in and did it himself. The massacre at DG was bloodier and costlier than any other. Giuseppe Sinopoli, one of the most civilized men ever to mount a podium, a philosopher of limitless curiosity, had his eighty-eight disc deal terminated with just thirty-five completed. Sinopoli, music director at Berlin's Deutsche Oper, sought satisfaction. It took four years and several million euros to settle his lawsuit. Weeks after the agreement, on 20 April 2001, Sinopoli dropped dead in mid-Aida. He was fifty-four years old and widely mourned, not least at DG where his dismissal was so expensively mishandled.

James Levine went, as did Ozawa. Trevor Pinnock's English Concert, financed by his DG deal, almost went bust and John Eliot Gardiner's Monteverdi Choir was plunged into crisis when plans for a 250th Bach anniversary cantata tour were undermined by DG's retraction. Gardiner's deal for fifty-nine Bach cantata CDs was cut to twelve. 'We were left stranded,' he raged,[10] reaching for lawyers. Matters were complicated by personal attachments. De Sabata was still on the DG payroll and Decca's Pilavachi was president of Gardiner's Monteverdi Choir. Prince Charles threw a fundraising dinner and Polygram pumped in £350,000 ($600,000) to save the Bach tour. 'It was a very generous settlement,' whispered an insider, but Gardiner was not appeased. With money raised from hundreds of fans, he set up his own label and recorded the cantatas with de Sabata as executive producer. They called the label Soli Dei Gloria (Purely for God's Glory), its spinal initials SDG. That, said friends, stood for 'Sod DG'. The first release won a *Gramophone* award as record of the year. 'Those records couldn't have been made at DG prices,' said an ally, 'not at the low level of sales that Jeggy [Gardiner] predicted.' Where SDG could break even on 5,000 CDs, DG would have had to sell ten times as many in order to sustain its corporate superstructure. Major labels stood exposed as bloated parasites, adding heavy overheads to artistic enterprise.

Demoralization set in. Karsten Witt talked to headhunters, who found him an even trickier job at London's South Bank Centre. Roger Wright joined the BBC as head of orchestras. 'I wish we'd had the time to do what Peter Alward was doing at EMI,' lamented Wright. Alward's EMI was the only label to conduct its cull with dignity, halving annual output from eighty-five to forty without shedding artists. Alward had managed to persuade Rattle, Jansons and others that the cuts were temporary.

Decca underwent its next decimation on the morning of 3 March 1997. 'All members of staff at the Chiswick site were called into the personnel office one at a time, at twenty-minute intervals, to be told their futures,' reported the entertainment trade union, Bectu. 'The twenty-nine staff who were sacked . . . were given no written confirmation of any details of their redundancy terms but were nevertheless escorted off the premises.'[11] One survivor was asked to draw up budgets for the next five years. She handed them to Mirageas, who thanked, and fired her. His own head rolled months later. 'It has been brutal and it has been bloody,' reflected Roger Lewis, 'but we had to go forward sensibly if we were to have a future.'[12]

At DG, instant dismissals were prohibited by German laws, which enforced a year's consultation. The atmosphere curdled. Many of the personnel were related by blood or marriage, some were third generation with the company. Roberts announced that the head office was moving to Berlin. Hamburg politicians thwarted that plan. To speed up natural wastage, Roberts sent in a new head of A&R, an American ex-soldier who spoke no German, had served in the Israeli army and had a daughter on a West Bank settlement. Michael Fine, a free-ranging producer with 500 cottage-label recordings to his credit, 'did not know a single DG artist'.[13] That, he came to realize, was the reason he had been hired. Fine moved to Hamburg with his wife in April 1997, just as the downturn went into slalom.

In 1996 the electronics giant Philips suffered a profits collapse. Jan Timmer went into retirement and Polygram was sold for $10 billion to Seagram, a Canadian liquor firm. The Seagram heir, Edgar J. Bronfman, had bought Universal Studios and was looking to save on 'synergies' between music and movies. Analysts were sent in, finding excess and decay. Two hundred rock bands and 3,000 staff were cashiered. Bronfman, who had once co-written a hit for Celine Dion, thought he knew the entertainment business. Alain Levy disagreed, and departed.

Roberts, orphaned, went to ground. 'Chris Roberts gave every impression of leaving the company and was virtually silent for months,' said Fine. 'The interregnum gave the DG management the opportunity to be somewhat autonomous as we took advantage of the power vacuum above us to conclude several deals that would never have been approved by Roberts.' The hiatus allowed Fine to form relationships with Abbado and Anne-Sophie Mutter, lining up projects of mutual interest.

Half a year later, the cardigan flounced back. Roberts, basking in Bronfman's approval, 'came to Hamburg with one subject on his agenda: restructuring, an American corporate euphemism for firing people . . . He noted darkly that the Universal corporate culture was "rougher" than Polygram's and that as German labour law made it difficult to remove people, we should make those reluctant to go miserable.'[14]

Fine, alarmed that Roberts was centralizing control of the three labels, formed a resistance group and plotted a management buyout. 'Somewhat indiscreetly I began to sound out colleagues . . . and with a small group of individuals began to look for money.' DG was valued at $350 million. Fine reckoned he could raise the money. The only drawback was that he had not asked Bronfman if he was prepared to sell. Roberts had forbidden him on pain of dismissal ever to contact the supreme boss. Fine was trying to find a way to reach Bronfman when, on a Lufthansa flight to London to hear the Welshman Bryn Terfel sing at Glyndebourne, he found himself sitting next to an American who showed an interest in his work. Fine set out his plan. The man gave him a lift into town in a red Jaguar and they exchanged business cards. Michael Adams, his name was. Only it wasn't. 'Adams' was a private detective, planted by Roberts with the collusion of a secretary in Fine's office. Spies, lies and secret cameras were the new accessories of classical recording. Music was just background.

Fine knew he was living on borrowed time. He had talked Anne-Sophie Mutter into doing Four Seasons for DG, a sure-fire hit, and went off to supervise the recording. Half an hour after the last chord was in the can, the phone rang. 'When I was called into Roberts' office to be fired,' wrote Fine, 'Mr Adams' dossier, an apparent transcript of our discussions, was the primary "evidence" against me.'

Roberts replaced Fine with Martin Engstroem, a Swedish agent who was once Sinopoli's manager. Engstroem ran a summer festival with SBS bank subsidy at the Swiss resort of Verbier which he promised to convert into a DG showcase. His artist signings were weak, however, and he was fired inside three years.

Roger Lewis, too, departed Decca after just twenty months, less successful than his PRs made out. 'He had Charlotte Church dancing on his coffee table at home and he couldn't see the point of her,' gloated a rival.[15] While negotiating his payoff, Lewis pitched for the BBC's Radio 3, missed out to Roger Wright and settled for a better-paid post as head of Classic FM. Costa Pilavachi succeeded him as head of Decca-Philips, under Chris Roberts' overlordship.

Higher up the food chain, Universal fell into the hands of Jean-Marie Messier, a media Napoleon who had turned a French water and sewage utility into the Vivendi entertainment empire. Chris Roberts went to ground again at the change, re-emerging at Messier's side at the 2001 Salzburg Festival, where the emperor went around telling people that music would soon be played through mobile phones. Messier met his Waterloo in a set of accounts that failed to add up. He was fired in June 2002. Colin Southgate flew to Hollywood to sell EMI to Warner, but Warner, after its AOL merger and the dotcom crash, was in freefall. Edgar Bronfman bought a stake in Warner and set about rebuilding his empire. Jim Fifield quit EMI, taking a $22 million payoff. His successor, Ken Berry, was soon paid $9 million to leave. 'EMI Chuck Berry' sang the headlines as the doors revolved once more – and back came Alain Levy, hey presto, as head of EMI in a game of musical chairs that was milking the music to death – for all but the little men in suits.

Classical recording continued to be condensed. DG, Decca and Philips made fewer records combined in 2001 than any single one of them had produced a decade before. The new 'classical' stars were triumphs of triviality. EMI put out a busty violinist from the

Helsinki opera orchestra who had appeared nude as Linda Brava in a *Playboy* centrefold. Decca countered with Bond, a girlie string quartet in skin-tight bodysuits. When sex failed, labels went for story – a pianist who raised wolves in Canada, another who wore electric-red socks. A sex-change prostitute, Jackie McAuliffe, who played the piano on a BBC docusoap, was signed by Decca. The blind pop singer Andrea Bocelli was redesignated classical and foisted on Valery Gergiev as a soloist in the Verdi Requiem, which he vocally murdered (see p. 294). The quality of music was strained along with the credulity of customers. Buying a classical CD was more a lottery than a mark of civilized taste. Universal issued an album of Classic Cuts, 'all the boring bits cut out'. BMG brought out a double disc, 'The Only Classical Album You'll Ever Need'. The record business was writing its obituary on the covers of its own products.

Technology, the source of recording, became its destroyer. With computers on every desktop and connectivity through the internet, information flowed with dangerous immediacy. Sales figures were no longer surmised in vague and wishful fashion: they were access-ible hour by hour. In March 1991 *Billboard* changed the way it tracked the weekly charts. Instead of relying on label output, it switched to data provided by Nielsen Soundscan, which monitored 85 per cent of all US tills where records were sold. 'Before Soundscan,' said Robert Hurwitz, head of esoteric Nonesuch, 'you spent $100,000 recording a Brahms symphony, you spent $25,000 mounting a promotional campaign and you shipped ten thousand copies. Two years later, seven thousand come back. But . . . you've released another two hundred records since the Brahms, so you really don't notice. Today . . . you look at Soundscan and you see: Week One, a hundred ten copies, Week Two, eighty-six . . . We're hit with hard, cold facts.'[16]

Soundscan responded cheerfully to press inquiries, revealing that Abbado's inaugural Brahms first symphony sold just 3,000 copies in five years. With Berlin recording rates necessitating 50,000 sales, it would not break even this side of the Second Coming. A DG

Abbado Edition shifted just sixty copies. Muti, Abbado's antipode, fared no better. Two of his Verdi operas on Sony failed to reach four figures. Simon Rattle's Sibelius on EMI managed 2,000 for the Second and Fifth, a few hundred for the rest. Haitink's Mahler Seventh trickled 400 in eighteen months. Barenboim scored 600 on a Bruckner Third. These were just US statistics, to be sure, and sales were healthier in Europe and Japan. But the pattern was consistent and the scale of disaster incontrovertible. America was by far the biggest classical market and its rejection of classics was an embarrassment that could no longer be concealed. 'This is not a transitory downturn,' said Gelb in one of his more lucid assessments, 'it's a disaster.'[17]

Retreat accelerated into rout. EMI axed plans for Jansons in Pittsburgh and Franz Welser-Möst in Cleveland. Warner quit the New York Philharmonic and Chicago. Concert attendances fell to record lows. In 1995–6 31 million Americans bought tickets to orchestral events; by 2004, one in ten had vanished.[18]

Maestros were reduced to hitting the phone and begging for work. Abbado lunched total strangers in an effort to drum up business in Berlin, where players derived half their income from recording. The best offer he got was to accompany a pair of troublesome EMI singers, Roberto Alagna and Angela Gheorghiu. Times were tough, so he took it.

Coping with the downturn deepened Abbado's millennial angst. Berlin players had been grumbling about his small-print rehearsals, so different from Karajan's broad sweep. New players were recruited from all over the globe except, slightingly, from the former East Germany and the eastern sector of Berlin. Abbado refused to play politics at auditions. In February 1998, after conducting a numinous Parsifal at the German National Opera, he refused a contract renewal, walking away from the world's finest orchestra. He had stomach cancer and was fighting adverse odds, but modern surgery worked wonders and he bounced back after a year's convalescence, directing youth orchestras in festival venues.

The Berlin players put two candidates on the ballot paper. In a close contest, the players chose forty-something Simon Rattle over

Daniel Barenboim, skipping a generation in a quest for renewal. Rattle's frizzy head plastered public hoardings in the German capital and EMI broke out the champagne. But the British Blairite – for all his social initiatives, which included chats with Turkish piece-workers and a Rite of Spring in deprived schools – failed to resolve the industrial crisis. Unable to make as many recordings in a year as Karajan would make in a month, he squeezed the city, billions in debt, to compensate his players for the earnings they had lost when the century of recording came to an end.

The coup de grâce was delivered by the rapid advance of the internet. BMG's James Glicker, back from Australia in 1997, 'went around the heads of all the labels and said what are you doing about the internet? They said: nothing, we've put the lawyers onto it.' There was no strategy for coping with illegal downloads except prosecution. Labels set about suing teenaged customers, earning disaffection and derision. The next wave of pop groups, led by Arctic Monkeys, were label-free artists. The men in suits hardly knew which way to turn. Classical music was scarcely affected by Napster-style file sharing but a mortal threat arose from live radio, springing up across the web, ever ready and often cleared for download.

Their only label remedy was classics-lite, led by Decca teen Hayley Westenra (a soundalike of Sixties sweetheart Mary Hopkin), Sony's Il Divo and Warner's Josh Groban, any of whom might have been mistaken for Mitch Miller's pop smoothies on 1950s Columbia. Beneath the setting yellow sun of Deutsche Grammophon, Swedish mezzo-soprano Anne Sofie von Otter crossed over with pop writer Elvis Costello. EMI Classics put out an oratorio by ex-Beatle Paul McCartney and a requiem by Karl Jenkins, a writer of advertising jingles. McCartney's opus was aptly described in the *Los Angeles Times* as 'a padded, vapid, recycled, cross-dressed, sentimental, pretty-pretty oratorio – the sort of thing that gives saccharine a bad name'.

Classics-lite created an illusion of vitality – 19 million US classical sales in 1997 jumped to 22 million in 2001[19] – but in 2004 when the novelty wore off the numbers slumped to 18.5 million and labels were left up slush creek without a paddle. 'We're still making records,' smiled bosses as they toasted one another at black-tie Brits and Grammy nights. Privately, they said, 'We keep busy, looking at artists, discussing them, and then not signing anyone.' A marketing man, newly sacked, said, 'I'd spend my whole day in meetings and come home at night wondering, what have I achieved?' Howard Stringer, the first Western head of Sony, told investors that he could not, with the best will in the world, justify the continuance of classical recordings in a field where all the best pieces had been recorded too many times and there were no new tunes on the block.

Peter Gelb, anticipating the chop, hit the social circuit with the look of a fortyish spinster at a debutantes' ball. Calling in his uptown connections, Gelb landed a plum job as head of the Metropolitan Opera after misogynists on the board rejected Deborah Borda of the Los Angeles Philharmonic on grounds of her femininity. 'My philosophy,' Gelb told the *New York Times*, swagger returning with every syllable, 'is that art can be both commercially successful and artistically successful.'[20] Had his assertion been put to the test it would have shown that his commercial successes at Sony were inartistic and his artistic successes invisible. 'Peter was very down about everything,' said an ally. 'He always said there was no money to be made in classical.'[21]

Days after Gelb pulled his parachute cord, Columbia merged with its historic rival Victor in a BMG-Sony deal designed to slash costs and shrink classics. That same week at Abbey Road musicians gathered for what executive producer Peter Alward designated 'the last-ever studio opera'. 'No one,' he said,[22] 'will put together anything like this again.' Domingo, in his sixties, was singing Tristan, a role he never tackled in the opera house. Isolde was Nina Stemme, a cast-iron Bayreuth heroine. The lesser parts were luxury cast: René Pape as King Marke, the lieder singer Olaf Bär as Kurwenal, the English ascetic Ian Bostridge as the shepherd and the hot Mexican prospect Rolando Villazón as the young sailor. The conductor was Antonio Pappano with the Covent Garden orchestra and chorus. It cost $1 million, but Alward had done his sums and figured that there were enough opera lovers who would pay to hear Domingo in a role they could not hope to see on stage. Only a line-up as extraordinary as this would now persuade people to sit through an opera at home and the classical boxed set was no longer much of a gift for a boring brother-in-law at Christmas. 'We have to face the realities of the twenty-first century,' sighed Alward.

One of nature's irrepressibles, red-topped and richly anecdotal, Alward had relished his decade as EMI's artistic director, developing an improbable alliance with Richard Lyttelton, the deceptively bluff label president. They were the Laurel and Hardy of the final days of classical recording. Alward was a trim aesthete, Lyttelton a roly-poly public schoolboy who ran a Sixties disco and racked up thirty Iron Maiden concerts. Alward's mother was a German refugee, Lyttelton's father a tenth earl. Alward could name every Wagner role, Lyttelton's knowledge stopped at eponyms. Neither, though, was quite what he seemed. Alward could tough out the best of maestros over a contract, while Lyttelton, for the love of art, blew a duke's ransom on six Bach suites, played rather too late in his career by the exuberant Mstislav Rostropovich. 'I had a million dollars in mind,' he said when the Russian cellist offered him the tapes, 'but I couldn't insult Slava with such an obvious offer, so I upped it to one and a quarter.' The suites were launched at a banquet for 200 at the second best restaurant in France and the recording, though weakly received, sold 700,000 sets – enough to cover Lyttelton's extravagance.

As president, Lyttelton protected Alward's purities from Alain Levy while pumping up the bottom line with crossover. Late in 2003, at a brainstorming session, the two men reached a joint conclusion that there was not much left for them to do. There was a hundred years of music in the vaults and it would last for ever, but there was no point in reiterating works that existed in epic interpretations and, while artists would always find an angle, the steady flow of classical records was no longer viable. EMI, a label whose origins predated all others bar Edison's, would survive. 'It is not a record label,' said Lyttelton determinedly. 'It's a music company.' The record was just a vehicle whose time was running out. Something else would turn up.

Once the two men shook hands in concord, the personal consequences were obvious. Alward, the last occupant of Gaisberg's seat, took an early pension at the age of fifty-three and went off to improve his piano playing. Shortly before Christmas 2004 a farewell dinner was thrown for him by Costa Pilavachi, his Decca competitor (who would depart a year later), with Lyttelton and the present author among the guests. There was no rancour and few regrets. Most around the table had done their bit to keep the art alive. Nobody wanted it to end this way, but all things in this life are finite and the act of closure is, of itself, cause for celebration. This is the way the world ends, as the poet said; not with a bang, perhaps, but with a dying cadence in the glow of candlelight, the closing of a circle.

A chance discovery, a tinkering of mechanics, an eruption of noise, had advanced human civilization and brought music into every home. Recording had been a mirror to music, its third dimension: the means by which a performer could stand back and assess sound objectively. It had served as a midwife to fame, a mainstay of the musical economy. There would be fear and uncertainty after it was gone and many fine performers would fail to make themselves heard. But somewhere in a garage or a back room another improviser would be at work, another wide-eyed Fred Gaisberg, another would-be David Sarnoff, and the spark would ignite again as it did in Leonardo da Vinci – the fusion of art and invention, vision and exploitation, that reshapes the world every century or so. The spark that was recording had lasted a whole century and that, as art forms go, was no brief encounter.

8. Post Mortem

Just as classical Greece lives on in legend and tourism, so classical recording survives in the imagination of diehards. At a seminar in Helsinki in October 2005, old-timers gathered to insist the earth was flat. An ex-Universal VP, Kevin Kleinmann, now with the Finnish cottage-label Ondine, talked deliriously of new business models. The editorial director of *Gramophone*, James Jolly, claimed that his magazine was reviewing more records than ever before. Both were telling a truth, of sorts. With the majors mired in classics-lite, fringe labels were bobbing along with low-circulation releases. Ondine had audaciously signed the Philadelphia Orchestra for three live recordings a year. No session fees, but the orchestra owned the product and the musicians were promised a profit share. 'The record company is like your stockbroker,' said Kleinmann. 'He manages your assets and keeps a fee, but you own your equity.'[1] The deal was paraded as Philadelphia's first record contract in a decade, but the releases, patchy and poorly edited, were no more convincing than other own-label CDs flowing from the Concertgebouw, the London Symphony and Bavarian Radio. To ensembles that had once depended on records for their wordly status, own-labels were no fame machine and the earnings put very little jam on the players' bread. LSO Live, with Haitink, Davis and Jansons, paid out under $500 in its fourth year to the players – less than they would have earned in an EMI morning at Abbey Road. Recording, as a buttress of the orchestral economy, was a thing of the past.

Many CDs reviewed in *Gramophone* and *BBC Music*, perhaps as many as half, were now self-promotions – paid for by performers, friends, governments or sponsors – a kind of vanity publishing that lacked editorial rigour and commercial rationale. The rest of the release sheet was made up of Naxos catalogue-fillers, mini-label bleatings and archival plunder. The body of classical recording was twitching spasmodically, giving false hope to those who waited by its life-support machine.

New media were sapping its strength. A 60Gb iPod, slippable into a shirt pocket, could accommodate the equivalent of 600 symphonic and opera CDs which, redundant, were sold off in thrift and charity shops for three bucks apiece. Classical recording had lost object value. All the music industry could do was rage against the dying of the light and pray for a download revival, though why consumers would take their music from record companies when they could receive it live from opera houses and concert halls was an unanswered question.

Either way, the classical record was dead. 'You want to know what killed it?' demanded Paul Burger, ex-president of Sony Europe. 'Wall Street killed it. People in the record business understood that classics was where we all came from, the basis of what we do. We were happy to carry on making records in that area, even losing a bit of money. But investors aren't like that. If they see sentiment, they make heads roll.'[2]

Corporatization had repressed creativity and fostered collusion. The big four – Universal, Sony-BMG, EMI, Warner – held 85 per cent of the US market,[3] a virtual monopoly. Charged with price fixing by forty-one state attorney-generals in September 2002, they paid a fine of $140 million, a modest settlement, according to former Federal Trade Commission chairman Robert Pitofsky who reckoned they had bilked consumers out of half a billion dollars in five years.[4]

Creatively, the oligopoly spread a homogeneous blur, one set of suits copying the others to justify their outrageous wages. Salaries had gone off the scale when Clive Davis argued that he could not negotiate with Bob Dylan when he was earning fifty grand a year and the singer 2 million. Davis, in the early 1970s, kept the big wage for himself. Yetnikoff spread it around middle management and sent label overheads sky-high. It was executive costs that made the break-even point for a classical release effectively unattainable.

Once the Liebersons, Culshaws, Schillers and Legges were gone, corporate bosses treated classics like a quaint maiden aunt, reducing its producers to ciphers. 'In the 1950s and 1960s,' said Nikolaus Harnoncourt, 'you dealt with real personalities, a producer who was responsible and took it on his shoulders. The next man above him was the head of the company. Later on, when the companies made battleships, the boss didn't even know that in a little corner somewhere classical music was being made. You had very nice people to negotiate with but they had no authority and you had no personal contact with the ones who decide.'[5] Weak producers gave conductors a chance to run riot. The worst records ever made were the product of an inflated ego and a timid production team.

Corporatization, inevitable when distribution is controlled by three or four chains, was the principal cause for the collapse of classical recording. The other factors, arranged here in binary Os and Is, accelerated its demise:

Overproduction began when Karajan upped his DG demands after Elsa Schiller's retirement. A pattern was established in which he, and rival maestros, recorded the same works over and over again. By 1994, there were seventy-nine Dvorak New World symphonies on sale. In 2006 a Swedish website listed 435 versions of Vivaldi's Four Seasons,[6] Etailer amazon.com offered 276 Beethoven Fifths, a mind-fuddling deterrent. Karajan, Marriner, Solti and Haitink accounted together for 2,000 releases. Put six impartial critics from different countries in a room and they would struggle to select a dozen indispensables from that disc mountain. Many of the rest should never have been made (the most otiose are listed in Part III). The compact disc boom carried their self-repetition way beyond the point of consumer saturation.

Indestructibility, the CD's unique selling point, spelled ruin for an industry that relied on consumers to replace records when they wore out. CD sound was as good as it was ever likely to get, equalizing quality across the board. Labels lost their sonic mystique when Naxos in Bratislava matched Berlin DG for clarity and Decca's studio best could be emulated by a spotty teen in a suburban back bedroom. As manufacturing costs fell, CDs were given away as promotional cover-mounts in newspapers and magazines.

A classical record, once an object of aspiration, lost its social value in a free shrinkwrap.

Norio **Ohga** rebooted Sony's overproduction by trying vainly to overtake DG. Tough as tinder at the board table, Ohga went mushy over classical music and broke the bank on records nobody needed. By the time his folly was stopped, music was going off the record and into a virtual vortex.

The **Internet** released music from jewel-cases to flow freely on websites. No studio line-up could match the excitement of a live download. Google and Amazon brought the whole of Western civilization to the world's fingertips. There was no further need to keep a home reference collection of classical recordings.

Other media made classics on record look stiff and outmoded. Modern homes had colour TVs with plasma screens and 200 satellite and cable channels, as well as a computer with its cornucopia of games. The packaged symphony and opera stood no chance against such diversions, even on DVD, the visual extension to audio CD.

Above all, a failure of **invention** sank the genre. When Heifetz, Menuhin, Horowitz and Rubinstein were in the ascendant they played music by living composers – Prokofiev, Rachmaninov, Sibelius, Bartók, Szymanowski. Even Toscanini, no modernist, put new works in his concerts as a matter of course. Stokowski, who died in 1977, gave some 800 world premieres. In their heyday, music was alive. Atonal modernism aroused audience mistrust. Stravinsky, who died in 1971, was the last household name composer, though few listened to his late serialisms. 'Ultimately, Classical was let down by the composer,' said ex-Sony producer Michael Haas. 'Without new music that intelligent sensitive consumers want to hear, there was no choice but to rehash and re-cook the past.'[7] Classical labels were stuck with dead, white, male, European composers and a regressive, ageing, heterogeneous audience. The failure to explore multicultural sounds was the final dereliction, the dying man losing touch with the world. A year or two past its centenary, classical recording sighed its last. Sic transit gloria mundi.

★

The end is a point from which history is viewed whole. As the earliest mass medium, two decades ahead of radio, recording brought music into everyday life. It invaded homes, schools and hospitals. Soldiers took records to war, missionaries into the heart of darkness. No place on earth was beyond reach of an aria. Music became a utility like running water, its ownership a mark of culture and refinement. There were practical consequences: the availability of music on tap, as it were, promoted musical passivity, eroded domestic performance and eradicated local distinctions. A musician crossing Germany in the 1920s would hear a different Beethoven sound in Bochum from the one he had experienced the night before in Bremen.[8] With the coming of records, orchestras came to sound much the same. There was also a concomitant improvement in playing standards. No audience today would tolerate the inaccuracies and disunity that prevailed in ensembles of the 1930s, plainly documented on unsparing CDs. Weak bands were driven out of business by the recording angel.

Soloists similarly reduced stylistic variety. Fritz Kreisler imposed a ubiquitous vibrato and Arthur Rubinstein fostered an irritating imbalance between piano and orchestra. Heifetz and Horowitz set impossible standards of note-perfection and the temptation to filch their effects proved irresistible. An upcoming Carnegie Hall contender would stock up with armloads of master-played Chopin at Tower Records or Sam Goody's, substituting imitation for interpretation. Conversely, records created a critical audience, alert to deviance and ineptitude. No twenty-first-century soloist could get away with Artur Schnabel's finger slips.

How much did classical recording affect our political destiny? The evidence is patchy. Lenin refused to listen to records in case Beethoven might melt his revolutionary zeal. Hitler inflicted interminable evenings of record playing, mainly Wagner and Lehár, on his acolytes; Churchill was partial to a spin of Gilbert and Sullivan. Poland's first prime minister was the formidably recorded pianist Ignacy Jan Paderewski. A German chancellor, Helmut Schmidt, played third piano in Mozart's three-piano concerto on EMI, with Christoph Eschenbach and Justus Franz.

One British premier, Edward Heath, conducted an Elgar overture, and another, Margaret Thatcher, narrated Copland's Lincoln's Portrait; former presidents of the US and Soviet Union, Clinton and Gorbachev, played parts in Peter and the Wolf for Naxos. A Norwegian prime minister wrote a scholarly note for the first Decca recording of a Grieg symphony. A King of Denmark, Frederick IX, made several records as a conductor. Classical records were well played in high places and occasionally reached a mass audience. Leonard Bernstein's recording of Mahler's Adagietto helped Americans address the death of John F. Kennedy. A perception of outer space was sounded by György Ligeti's Aventures in Stanley Kubrick's film *2001: A Space Odyssey* (CD 98, p. 274). Woody Allen used Gershwin as a metaphor for Manhattan. Webern signified terror in William Friedkin's *The Exorcist*.

The therapeutic usage of classical recording is empirically attested. A 1997 survey by the American Medical Association found that 'surgeons had lower blood pressure and pulse rates and performed better on non-surgical mental exercises while listening to music . . .' 'It has to be classical music,' stipulated a Loyola University Medical Center consultant. 'Anything else interferes with the rhythm of the operation.' A British transplant surgeon at St Mary's, Paddington, testified that he always put on a record in theatre – never the radio, which was liable to interruption and disruption – and always the same work, in his case a particular Mozart piano concerto.

Mozart on record was claimed to foster intelligence in pre-natal foetuses and ease pain in Swedish labour wards. Other remedial applications were attested in psychiatric and geriatric care. Classical records were part of school life until the 1960s; some believe that their withdrawal fostered rowdiness and lowered concentration spans. In Anthony Burgess's novel *A Clockwork Orange*, a recording of Beethoven's Ninth drove social outcasts to sadistic violence. Classical recordings are played at funeral services. Their use extends from before conception to beyond the grave.

Nevertheless, by comparison to pop music, their usage is minuscule. Ninety-two pop albums sold over 10 million US copies, led by The Eagles Greatest Hits (28 million) and followed by Michael Jackson's Thriller (26 million), Pink Floyd: The Wall (23 million), Led Zeppelin IV (22 million) and Billy Joel's Greatest Hits (21 million).

The figures for classical sales have been closely guarded, in the main because their modesty might have disarmed media hype. With nemesis approaching, labels came clean and cooperated in providing data for the following chart, the first verified sales list of the world's best-selling classical recordings. In all, twenty-five releases topped 1 million sales.

The all-time classical chart

1	Wagner: Ring – Solti (Decca)	1958–65	18 million
2	Three Tenors (Decca)	1990	14 million
3	Vivaldi: Four Seasons – I Musici/Ayo (Philips)	1959	9.5 million
4	Three Tenors 2 (Warner)	1994	7.8 million★
5	Canto Gregoriano (EMI)	1993	5.5 million
6	Andrea Bocelli Sacred Arias/Chung (Philips)	1999	5 million
7	Tchaikovsky: Piano concerto – Van Cliburn (RCA)	1959	3 million
8	Puccini: Tosca – Callas/Gobbi (EMI)	1953	3 million
9	O Holy Night – Pavarotti (Decca)	1976	3 million
10	Ramirez: Missa Criolla – Carreras (Philips)	1990	3 million
11	Vivaldi: Four Seasons – Kennedy (EMI)	1989	2.5 million
12	Elgar: Cello concerto – Du Pré (EMI)	1965	2.1 million
13	Orff: Carmina Burana – Levine (DG)	1989	2.1 million
14	Mozart: Horn concertos – Brain (EMI)	1953	2 million
15	O Sole Mio – Pavarotti (Decca)	2000	2 million★
16	Ave Maria – Kiri te Kanawa (Philips)	1985	2 million
17	Bach: Goldberg Variations – Gould (Columbia)	1955	1.8 million
18	Beethoven: Ninth symphony – BPO/Karajan	1962	1.5 million★★
19	Beethoven: Fifth symphony – VPO/Kleiber	1975	1.5 million★★
20	Three Tenors Christmas album (Sony)	2000	1.2 million★
21	Vivaldi Four Seasons – Nishizaki (Naxos)	1987	1.16 million

22	Gorecki: Third symphony (Warner)	1993	1.1 million
23	New Year's Concert – Ozawa/VPO (Philips)	2002	1.1 million
24	Gade: Jalousie Boston Pops/Arthur Fiedler (Victor)	1935	1 million
25	Caruso Arias (HMV/Victor)	1903	1 million

*Contains non-classical material.
**Deutsche Grammophon report sales 'above 1.5 million'; an independent source confirmed that the figure was below 2 million.

The chart excludes non-classical submissions. Sony Classical's top-seller, for example, was Titanic with 25 million, followed by Charlotte Church's 10 million; three Broadway shows also sold well into seven figures. The top classical entry, Glenn Gould's Goldberg Variations, came in at number 11. EMI's biggest 'classical' success after Gregorian chant was the pop violinist Vanessa-Mae with 3.5 million. On Decca, 'operatic megastar' Katherine Jenkins, who never set foot on an opera stage, sold more records in the UK than Callas. Bellowing Russell Watson, an old-fashioned, semi-trained belter, sold 1.7 million.

Such synthetic additives were not part of the classical narrative but symptoms of its terminal disease. The health of classical recording appears, from the chart above, to have depended heavily on Three Tenors and Four Seasons. But the chart is deceptive, for hundreds of classical records of great diversity sold upwards of half a million and thousands more made a decent profit. Classical recording was once a robust business, as testified by lifetime sales of its leading artists. The following figures are, for legal reasons, somewhat less precise than the album totals.

The top-selling classical artists (number of records sold)

1	Herbert von Karajan	200 million
2	Luciano Pavarotti	100 million
3	Georg Solti	50 million
4	Arthur Fiedler/Boston Pops	50 million*

5 Leonard Bernstein	30 million
5 Maria Callas	30 million
5 James Galway	30 million
5 Placido Domingo	30 million
5 Neville Marriner	30 million
10 José Carreras★	24 million
11 Andre Kostelanetz★	20 million
11 Eugene Ormandy	20 million
11 Arturo Toscanini	20 million
14 I Musici	12 million
15 Zubin Mehta (Three Tenors)	10 million
15 Seiji Ozawa	10 million
15 Daniel Barenboim	10 million
15 Nikolaus Harnoncourt	10 million
19 Bernard Haitink	7–8 million

★Contains non-classical additives.

No other artist comes close. Cecilia Bartoli, the next biggest diva after Callas, has sold 4 million units in fifteen years.

Adding up the top-selling artists and extrapolating their totals across overall output figures, one arrives at a total classical sale of somewhere between 1 and 1.3 billion records. Pop comparison proves unexpectedly instructive. Fifteen pop artists topped 200 million sales, and fifty-eight made 100 million. The all-time leaders[9] are the Beatles with EMI estimates of 1 to 1.3 billion sales – exactly the same as the entirety of classical recording. The Beatles affected modern times more than any politician, scientist, writer or film maker. If classical recording as a cultural artefact achieved a similar impact over the century, it can safely be described as a world changing medium, life enhancing and incontrovertibly worthwhile.

So what remains? At the back of the store and out in cyberspace, an indelible heritage of thousands of recordings, some of them defining milestones in musical history. The end, however, was nigh. Hyperion, after Ted Perry's death, lost a million-pound lawsuit and was pushed to the brink, Chandos cut staff by two-thirds and Dorian Records went bankrupt. Naxos was named *Gramophone*'s Label of the Year 2005, the only company to sustain full classical production. That summer in Aspen, Colorado, Warner's chairman Edgar J. Bronfman urged artists to join his internet-only label 'to develop in a supportive lower-risk environment'. If this did not quite mean the end of the record, the next sentence did. 'We are excited by the power of digital distribution now available to every potential artist.'[10] But if distribution was now available to every potential artist, who needed big labels? Peer to peer, musician to listener, was the new way for music to flow, by-passing established channels. Arctic Monkeys rose without a label. Music companies were out of the loop. Their last resort was to file another 2,000 lawsuits against home downloaders, criminalizing their customers.

In a fluid environment, radio revived. Free to air and hot to trot, stations in Europe and the US stored their programmes online, enabling listeners to catch music they had missed and, on occasion, to download it. In May 2005 the BBC took a leap into the unknown. Roger Wright, once DG's artistic pilot and now head of Radio 3, put a Beethoven cycle from Manchester on the web for a week. The orchestra was the BBC Philharmonic, which was paid for by every UK household, and the conductor Gianandrea Noseda. Wright argued that licence-payers had a right to own the music for free, and if others abroad took advantage, that could only enhance the prestige of the BBC and the British nation, 'growing the brand' in cyberspace terminology.

At launch point, there was no agreed assessment of likely interest. A few thousand maybe, was the expectation. When the totals arrived, quiet reserve turned to frank astonishment at 1.4 million downloads. Many of the takers were classical first-timers, as shown by the numbers who took symphonies one and two (150,000 each) as starter choices in preference to the much-performed and historically important Eroica (90,000), a title that would be recognized by anyone with a classical background. Even more encouragingly, the freeloaders were spread across twenty-six different countries. The largest contingents, two-fifths of the total, were in the UK and US. But there were 17,000 downloads in Vietnam, 15,000 in Thailand, 13,000 in Taiwan. There was, it appeared, an appetite for classical masterpieces in countries where the record industry, even in its heyday, never trod. Wright was ecstatic. 'We hope this will encourage new audiences to explore online classical music,' he told the BBC website.

The remnants of the record industry turned apoplectic, filing complaints in Parliament and a restraint on further downloads. 'They are stealing our market,' said label chiefs, oblivious to their own latter-day withdrawal from Beethoven. Wright offered to share his download database. Few took the opportunity, since they were no longer in the market for selling Beethoven. Helplessly, the record industry watched public feet walking past racks of recorded music in high street shops and public fingers seeking out the live and unpredictable online. This was a seminal moment in mass behaviour – the last spin of the musical disc. In the following months, the collapse of Tower Records left many major cities without a classical outlet, Warner ended classical output and Sony-RMG – Columbia and Victor combined – sacked classical president Gilbert Hetherwick and much of his division. The game was over: an art form had come to its end.

Notes to Part I

Unless noted below, all quotations in the text are taken from personal interviews or conversations.

1. Matinee

1. The recording, Kempff's first, was issued by Deutsche Grammophon with the serial number 62400 and became a sought-after rarity.
2. Artur Schnabel, *My Life and Music*, Gerrards Cross: Colin Smythe, 1970, p. 98.
3. Wilhelm Kempff, *Wass ich hörte, wass ich sah*, Munich: R. Piper & Co., 1981.
4. Schnabel, *My Life and Music*, p. 98.
5. *Musical America*, February 1952, p. 31.
6. Jerrold Northrop Moore, *Sound Revolutions: A Biography of Fred Gaisberg, Founding Father of Commercial Recording*, London: Sanctuary, 1999, p. 17.
7. E.g. Andreas Holschneider, president of DG, and Peter Andry, EMI head; author interviews, July 2005.
8. Luciano Pavarotti (with William Wright), *My Own Story*, London: Sidgwick & Jackson, 1981, p. 284.
9. Northrop Moore, *Sound Revolutions*, p. 159.
10. F. W. Gaisberg, *Music on Record*, London: Robert Hale, 1947, p. 81.
11. Quoted in Wolfgang Stresemann (ed.), *Das Berliner Philharmonische Orchester*, Stuttgart: DVA, 1987, reproduced in notes to DG 423 527-2.
12. BIRS lecture of 19 May 1972, quoted in Peter Martland, *Since Records Began – EMI, the First 100 Years*, London: B. T. Batsford, 1997, p. 167.
13. BIRS lecture of 19 May 1972, quoted in Northrop Moore, *Sound Revolutions*, pp. 287–8.
14. Northrop Moore, *Sound Revolutions*, p. 329.

15. Harvey Sachs, *The Letters of Arturo Toscanini*, London: Faber and Faber, 2002, p. 183.

16. Charles O'Connell, *The Other Side of the Record*, New York: Alfred Knopf, 1947, p. 137.

17. William Primrose, *Walk on the North Side*, Provo, Utah: Brigham Young University Press, 1978, pp. 97–8.

18. Milton Katims writing in *International Classical Record Collector*, Winter 1998, p. 66.

19. *New York Herald Tribune*, reviews of 17 May 1942 and n.d. 1943.

20. O'Connell, *The Other Side of the Record*, p. 129.

21. Wilhelm Furtwängler (tr. Shaun Whiteside), *Notebooks*, London: Quartet Books, 1989, p. 169.

2. Middlemen

1. See Chairman Alfred Clark's address to EMI AGM, 1938, in Peter Martland, *Since Records Began – EMI, the First 100 Years*, London: B. T. Batsford, 1997.

2. Don Hunstein, conversation, May 2005.

3. Schuyler Chapin, *Musical Chairs*, New York: Putnams, 1977, p. 134.

4. Robert Metz, *CBS: Reflections in a Bloodshot Eye*, Chicago: Playboy Press, 1975, p. 147.

5. Ibid., p. 151.

6. Quoted in *Audiofile*, no. 10, 1997.

7. Martland, *Since Records Began*, p. 154.

8. Statement by EMI chairman Sir Louis Sterling, ibid.

9. George Martin (with Jeremy Hornsby), *All You Need Is Ears*, London: Macmillan, 1979, p. 51.

10. Elisabeth Schwarzkopf, *On and Off the Record*, London: Faber and Faber, 1982, p. 15.

11. Ibid., p. 107.

12. After divorcing the English mezzo Nancy Evans, a stalwart of the Britten circle, to whom he was married when he and Schwarzkopf met.

13. Peter Andry, interview, August 2005.

14. As recounted by Peter Andry, ibid.

15. Richard Osborne, *Herbert von Karajan: A Life in Music*, London: Chatto & Windus, 1998, p. 434.

16. Related in Brian Hunt, 'Memories of the Maestro', *Daily Telegraph*, 25 October 1995; and Jon Tolansky, 'Furtwängler', *Classical Record Collector*, Winter 2004.

17. Sam H. Shirakawa, *The Devil's Music Master*, New York: Oxford University Press, 1992, p. 382.

18. Alan Jefferson, communication to the author.

19. John Culshaw, *Putting the Record Straight: The Autobiography of John Culshaw*, London: Secker & Warburg, 1981, p. 180.

20. *Time* magazine, 19 December 1955.

21. Recalled by Paul Myers, email to the author, 21 April 2005.

22. Jack Law, interview in *Hampstead and Highgate Express*, 20 November 1981.

23. Michael Haas, email to the author, 16 April 2005.

24. Memoir by Charles Gerhardt, *International Classical Record Collector*, Winter 1997, pp. 46–51.

25. James Mallinson, email to the author, 24 July 2005.

26. Peter Andry, interview, 26 July 2005.

27. Nella Marcus, interview, May 2005.

28. Sarah Dimenstein, telephone interview, 27 May 2005.

29. Information from Denham Ford, Beecham's assistant.

30. William Westbrook Burton, *The Decca Boys*, BBC Radio 3, 2005.

31. Georg Solti, interview, July 1997.

32. Solti archive held at the Solti family home, London.

33. Peter Andry, interview, 26 July 2005.

34. *The Decca Boys*.

35. Undated letter in Solti archive, apparently 1958.

36. Confidential interview.

37. Christopher Raeburn, telephone interview, July 2005.

38. Confidential interview.

39. Peter Andry, interview, May 2005.

40. Pali Meller Marcovicz (ed.), *Deutsche Grammophon Gesellschaft: eine Chronologie*, Hamburg: DGG GmbH, 1998, p. 16.

41. Andreas Holschneider, telephone interview, 3 July 2005.

42. See Tom Bower, *Blind Eye to Murder*, London: André Deutsch, 1981.

43. Wilfried Feldenkirchen, *Siemens, 1918–1945*, Munich: Siemens, 1995, p 285. I am grateful to Marek Jaros of the Wiener Library, London, for indicating this source.

44. Interview on CD, Fricsay erzähltes leben, DG 474 383–2.

45. Ibid.
46. Dietrich Fischer-Dieskau, *Echoes of a Lifetime*, London: Macmillan, 1989, pp. 68–9.
47. By marketing consultant Hans Domizlaff.
48. Fricsay erzähltes leben, DG 474 383–2.
49. Siegmund Nissel, interview, May 2005.
50. Martin Lovett, interview, May 2005.
51. Neville Marriner, interview, May 2004.
52. The founders, in 1949, were James Grayson, Michael Naida and Henry Gage.
53. See Petula Clark at the Paris Olympia, Silva Screen records, 2004; Silva 1169.
54. Peter Heyworth and John Lucas, *Otto Klemperer: His Life and Times*, vol. II, Cambridge: Cambridge University Press, 1996, p. 236.
55. Related to the author by Klemperer's daughter, Lotte, 1997.

3. Midpoint

1. Brian Southall, *Abbey Road*, London 1997, p. 56.
2. A barely fictionalized report of these machinations can be found in Brown Meggs's bitter novel of the classical recording industry, *Aria*, London: Hamish Hamilton, 1978, pp. 132–40.
3. John G. Deacon, email to the author, 30 May 2005.
4. Donald Clarke, *The Rise and Fall of Popular Music*, London: Penguin, 1995.
5. Paul Myers, email to author, 2005.
6. Don Hunstein, conversation, May 2005.
7. Andreas Holschneider interview, July 2005.
8. Peter Alward interview, October 2004.
9. Interview on The Originals, DG 449 725–2; author's translation from the German.
10. Interview with Susan Elliott for *Audio Magazine*, late 1992, http://www.classicrecs.com/jackint1.htm.
11. Related to the author by Lotte Klemperer, 1997.
12. Michael Stegemann, 'Half a Century of Immortality: Glenn Gould's first recording of the Goldberg Variations,' essay accompanying Sony-BMG anniversary reissue 82876698352.

13. Jörg Demus and Rosalyn Tureck had attempted the cycle on small labels.

14. Otto Friedrich, *Glenn Gould: A Life and Variations*, London: Lime Tree, 1990, p. 50.

15. Stegemann, 'Half a Century of Immortality'.

16. Paul Myers, email to the author, 10 June 2005.

17. Schuyler Chapin, *Musical Chairs*, New York: Putnams, 1977, p. 208.

18. Ibid., p. 213.

19. Ibid., pp. 216–17.

20. Article in *High Fidelity* magazine for the cycle's completion, September 1967.

21. Confirmed by Paul Myers in William Westbrook Burton, *Conversations about Bernstein*, New York: Oxford University Press, 1995, p. 59, and comments to the author.

22. Statistics confirmed by Peter Munves, Masterworks marketing director, telephone interview, July 2005.

23. Paul Myers, email to the author, 6 June 2005.

24. Comment to the author by his friend, the conductor José Serebrier, August 2005.

25. Nella Marcus, email to the author, 19 May 2005.

26. James Lock, Decca chief engineer, note to Decca Legends series.

27. John Culshaw, *Ring Resounding: The Recording in Stereo of 'Der Ring Des Nibelungen'*, London: Secker & Warburg, 1967, p. 79.

28. Culshaw to Solti, n.d., Solti archive held at the Solti family home, London.

29. Solti archive, n.d.

30. Syracuse WONO, 4 February 1967.

31. Nella Marcus, interview, May 2005.

32. Paul Myers, email to the author, 10 June 2005.

33. Richard Osborne, *Herbert von Karajan: A Life in Music*, London: Chatto & Windus, 1998, p. 490.

34. Sleeve notes to German edition of Deutsche Grammophon Beethoven cycle.

35. Ibid.

36. John Culshaw, *Putting the Record Straight: The Autobiography of John Culshaw*, London: Secker & Warburg, 1981, p. 195.

37. The letter is dated 15 November 1962.

38. Martin Lovett, interview, May 2005.

39. Pali Meller Marcovicz (ed.), *Deutsche Grammophon Gesellschaft: eine Chronologie*, Hamburg: DGG GmbH, 1998, p. 22.

4. Millionaires

1. Ringo Starr, for Pete Best.
2. *Evening Standard*, 4 March 1966.
3. The *Guardian*, 22 October 1996.
4. Frederic Dannen, *Hit Men*, London: Muller, 1990, p. 65.
5. Peter Andry, interview, 1995.
6. Suvi Raj Grubb, *Music Makers on Record*, London: Hamish Hamilton, 1986, p. 42.
7. Paul Myers, email to the author, 21 April 2005.
8. Andrew Keener writing in *Gramophone*, October 2005, p. 56.
9. Peter Munves, telephone interview, June 2005.
10. Ibid.
11. Edward Greenfield, conversation, Salzburg, August 1987.
12. From Arthur Jacobs (ed.), *The Music Yearbook, 1973–4*, London: Macmillan, 1974, pp. 371–81.
13. National Public Radio interview, July 2002.
14. Nikolaus Harnoncourt, interview, Amsterdam, 27 October 2005.
15. Andreas Holschneider, telephone interview, 3 July 2005.
16. Quoted in 'Remembering Karl Richter', Unitel catalogue, 2004.
17. Nikolaus Harnoncourt, interview, Amsterdam, 27 October 2005.
18. Nikolaus Harnoncourt, interview, Graz, October 2000.
19. Nikolaus Harnoncourt, interview, Amsterdam, 27 October 2005.
20. Nikolaus Harnoncourt, interview, Graz, October 2000.
21. Gustav Leonhardt, interview, 2005.
22. Nikolaus Harnoncourt, interview, Amsterdam, 27 October 2005.
23. Richard Adeney, interview, July 2005.
24. Interview with Anthony Kirkby, www.scena.org, 1 June 2000.
25. Erik Smith, *Mostly Mozart*, Winchester: privately published, 2005, p. 174.
26. Quotes here and below from Neville Marriner, interviews, May 2004 and in *Sunday Times* magazine, 23 September 1984.
27. *Gramophone*, September 1970, p. 437.
28. Smith, *Mostly Mozart*, p. 173.
29. Christopher Raeburn, telephone interview, July 2005.

30. Anna Barry writing in *Gramophone*, October 2005, p. 57.

31. Erik Smith, interview with Alan Blyth, *Gramophone*, December 1972.

32. Paul Myers, email to the author, 21 April 2005.

33. Don Hunstein, conversation, May 2005.

34. Dannen, *Hit Men*, p. 115.

35. The cocktail rather than the tool. Interview with Walter Yetnikoff, www.blogcritics.org, 4 March 2004.

36. Ralph Mace, RCA executive, email to the author, 25 August 2005.

37. Confidential interview.

38. Georg Solti with Harvey Sachs, *Solti on Solti: A Memoir*, London: Chatto & Windus, 1997. p. 114.

39. Stephen Rubin, telephone interview, 22 July 2005.

40. Herbert Breslin and Anne Midgette, *The King and I*, New York: Doubleday, 2004, p. 41.

41. Ibid., p. 39.

42. *Gramophone*, April 1988, Deutsche Grammophon advertising supplement.

43. Richard Osborne, *Herbert von Karajan: A Life in Music*, London: Chatto & Windus, 1998, p. 558.

44. Quotes here and below from Peter Andry, interview, 26 July 2005.

45. Ibid.

46. John Mordler, telephone interview, 29 July 2005.

47. Note to EMI CD see CD 71, p. 242.

48. Norman Lebrecht, *The Maestro Myth*, London: Simon & Schuster, 1991, p. 241.

49. See Osborne, *Herbert von Karajan*, pp. 575–90.

50. Conversations with Peter Alward, 2002–5.

51. Panel discussion, Bavarian TV, 2005.

52. Claim: Osborne, *Herbert von Karajan*, p. 439; denial: Sarah Dimenstein, telephone interview, June 2005.

53. Bruno Montsaigneon (tr. Stewart Spencer), *Sviatoslav Richter, Notebooks and Conversations*, London: Faber and Faber, 2001, pp. 118–19.

54. Interview with Tully Potter, *International Classical Record Collector*, Winter 1997, pp. 36–40.

55. Information from James Mallinson, Michael Haas, emails to author, May 2005.

56. Valerie Solti, interview, May 2005.
57. Obituary, Sir Edward Lewis, *Music Week*, January 1980.
58. John Best, email to the author, 27 May 2005.
59. Tokyo, May 1970, quoted in Osborne, *Herbert von Karajan*, p. 591.
60. Kees A. Schouhamer Immink, 'The Compact Disc Story', *Journal of the Audio Engineering Society*, vol. 46, no. 5, May 1998.
61. For a detailed account see John Nathan, *Sony: The Private Life*, London: HarperCollins, 1999, pp. 141–3.
62. Raymond Cooke, telephone interview, December 1982.
63. *Gramophone*, April 1978, p. 1784.
64. Personal recollection.
65. Andreas Holschneider, telephone interview, 3 July 2005.

5. Miracles on Miracles

1. Sleeve note to Shura Gehrman, Schwanengesang; with Nina Walker (piano), Nimbus 5022.
2. Paul Burger, chief executive, Sony Music (Europe), interview, December 2005.
3. Quotes here and below from Paul Myers, email to author, 10 June 2005, and Joseph Dash, telephone interview, July 2005.
4. Neville Marriner, interview, May 2004.
5. Michael Haas, email to the author, 16 April 2005.
6. Andreas Holschneider, telephone interview, 3 July 2005.
7. 'Why Britain Is off the Record', *Sunday Times*, 9 January 1983.
8. Brian Southall, telephone interview, April 1983.
9. Sleeve note to Beethoven violin concerto, NDR Symphony Orchestra, cond. Klaus Tennstedt, CDC 7 54574 2.
10. Observed by the author, June 1992.
11. John Nathan, *Sony: The Private Life*, London: HarperCollins, 1999, p. 145.
12. Confirmed to the author by Andreas Holschneider.
13. *Gramophone*, April 1988, p. 1393.
14. Roger Vaughan, *Herbert von Karajan: A Biographical Portrait*, London: Weidenfeld & Nicolson, 1986.
15. Andreas Holschneider, comment to the author, July 2005.
16. Paul Burger interview, December 2005.
17. Confidential interview.

18. *Fortune*, 1 September 1992.
19. Deutsche Grammophon press release.
20. Andreas Holschneider, telephone interview, 3 July 2005.
21. Joseph Dash, telephone interview, July 2005.
22. Norio Ohga, interview, Tokyo, February 1992.
23. Information obtained from a family friend.

6. Madness

1. Gunther Breest, interview, Salzburg, August 1991.
2. Norman Lebrecht, *When the Music Stops*, London: Simon & Schuster, 1996, p. 380.
3. Medi Gasteiner, email to the author, 31 July 2005.
4. Gunther Breest, interview, July 1991.
5. Confidential interview.
6. Costa Pilavachi, interview, August 2005.
7. See Harold Schonberg, *Horowitz*, London: Simon & Schuster, 1992, pp. 308–9.
8. Press statement, November 1990.
9. James Glicker, telephone interview, 29 July 2005.
10. Paul Burger, interview, December 2005.
11. Peter Alward, interview, September 2004.
12. Herbert Breslin and Anne Midgette, *The King and I*, New York: Doubleday, 2004, p. 218.
13. Tim Page, telephone interview, 11 September 2005.
14. Tim Page, conversation with the author, July 2005.
15. Tim Page, unpublished article for Tower Records magazine, n.d.
16. James Glicker, telephone interview, 29 July 2005.
17. Page, unpublished article for Tower Records magazine.
18. Klaus Heymann, interview 1995; in Lebrecht *When the Music Stops*, p. 313.
19. Andrew Clark, 'Buccaneer of Classical Music', *Financial Times*, 19 May 1997.
20. Michael Shmith, 'King of Naxos and His 2,400 Subjects,' the *Age* (Melbourne), 12 July 2002.
21. In Lebrecht *When the Music Stops*, p. 313.
22. Interview, *Classical Music*, 13 August 2005, p. 25.
23. Klaus Heymann, interview, April 2002.

24. Ibid.
25. Klaus Heymann, emails to the author, 7 and 14 April 2005.
26. Klaus Heymann, email to the author, 16 November 2005.
27. Richard Lyttelton, comment to the author, June 2005.
28. John Nathan, *Sony: The Private Life*, London: HarperCollins, 1999, p. 244.
29. Walter Yetnikoff, *Howling for the Moon*, New York: Random House, 2003, pp. 260–61.
30. Norio Ohga, interview, Tokyo, February 1992.
31. Michael Haas, email to author, 31 August 2005.
32. Quoted by the author in the *Daily Telegraph*, 3 April 1995, p. 15.
33. Ibid.
34. Confidential interview.
35. Peter Gelb, 'One Label's Strategy: Make It New but Make It Pay, *New York Times*, Arts & Leisure Section, 22 March 1998.
36. Confidential interview.
37. Conversation with the author and another, 1993.

7. Meltdown

1. Confidential interview.
2. Roger Wright, interview, July 2005.
3. Polygram annual report, 1996, p. 7, emphasis added.
4. Alain Levy, interview 1 April 1997, in *Daily Telegraph*, 3 April 1997, p. 19.
5. Malcolm Hayes, 'How to Rock the Classical World', *Independent*, 1 May 1996, pp. 14, 15.
6. Paul Moseley, interview, July 2005.
7. To March 2001 and August 2002, respectively.
8. Evans Mirageas, email to author, 23 April 2005.
9. Interview with Heidi Waleson, *Billboard*, 22 March 1997.
10. Interview with John Eliot Gardiner, *Guardian*, 10 January 2005.
11. Sue Harris of Bectu, press release, 27 March 1997.
12. Interview with Simon Tait, *The Times*, 26 November 1997.
13. Fine's memoir of his DG period can be found online at www.finesoundproductions.com.
14. Ibid.
15. Confidential interview.

16. Robert Hurwitz, interview in Alan Kozinn, 'A Once Proud Industry Fends off Extinction', *New York Times*, 8 December 1996.

17. Norman Lebrecht, 'A Record of Disaster', *Daily Telegraph*, 5 February 1997.

18. ASOL figures, quoted by Alan Bostick in the *Tennessean*, 9 April 2005.

19. Data from Soundscan.

20. Peter Gelb, interview with Allan Kozinn, 7 November 2004.

21. Chris Craker, interview, June 2005.

22. Over lunch with the author, September 2003.

8. Post Mortem

1. *City Paper*, Philadelphia, 12 May 2005.

2. Paul Burger, interview, December 2005.

3. Report to Merrill Lynch Media and Entertainment Conference, 14 September 2005.

4. *USA Today*, 30 September 2002.

5. Nikolaus Harnoncourt, interview, Amsterdam, 27 October 2005.

6. See www.svalander.se.

7. Michael Haas, email to author, 31 August 2005.

8. Berthold Goldschmidt, comment to the author, January 1993.

9. Elvis Presley is the only other artist to reach 1 billion; the next highest is Abba, with 260 million.

10. Edgar J. Bronfman speaking in Aspen, Colorado, 22 August 2005.

PART II

Masterpieces: 100 Milestones of the Recorded Century

Charting the summits of classical recording is no different from cataloguing the major works of English literature. The process falls into three categories – the unarguable, the either/or, and the otherwise influential.

The first group is self-selecting: *Canterbury Tales*, *King Lear*, *Paradise Lost*, *Oliver Twist*, *The Great Gatsby*, *1984*, John Updike's Rabbit tetralogy – works which shaped the world we inhabit.

The second is comprised of tough choices – *Hamlet* or *Othello*; *Mill on the Floss* or *The Woman in White*; *Tale of Two Cities* or *Great Expectations*; Edith Wharton or Katherine Mansfield; Philip Roth's *American Pastoral* or *The Plot Against America*; Salman Rushdie or not. The challenge is to ensure that the titles included are both unarguably important and representative of an author at peak form.

The third section is the most difficult and potentially the most contentious. It contains works that define a genre or epoch but are not of enduring literary merit; obscure works and undervalued authors; slight and unpretentious texts; choices that seem quirky yet, in relation to the whole, add a dimension of completeness. On these terms Thomas Wolfe's *Bonfire of the Vanities* might perhaps get the vote over Ian McEwan's *A Child in Time*, its exact contemporary; Jerzy Kosinski's *The Painted Bird* overrides his better-known *Being There* and Bruce Chatwin's *Utz* makes the grade in a class of its own. There is a guiding logic, and a great deal of fun, in the act of compilation and the ultimate satisfaction is to reflect an art as a single, continuous artefact.

The tripwire is to play safe and include the obvious. Edgar Allan Poe is undoubtedly a grand master, but is any of his works an unqualified masterpiece? It would take a brave compiler to omit Poe altogether from an anthology of literature in English, but if the compendium is to maintain interest and credibility it must display the confidence and conviction to omit some celebrity names and include at least a couple of contenders from the outer periphery of consensual wisdom.

These are the rules I have generally observed in choosing the hundred most important classical recordings. I make no claim that the final list contains the 'best' classical recordings of all time, for it is inadvisable ever to apply value judgements to works of art. The criteria I applied are not concerned primarily with intensity of performance and clarity of sound, critical as such qualities may be to followers of the art. Rather, I have been guided by the influence these recordings exerted on the public imagination and on the development of recording itself as an accessory to civilized society. Just as *Oliver Twist* introduced social conscience to the canon of English literature so the box of LPs that established stereo as a domestic necessity is a milestone in recording. If that set happened also to be the biggest selling classical record of all time, its presence would be imperative regardless of the calibre of artists and performance (which, as it happens, are pretty close to immaculate in concept and execution).

At the opposite end of the scale, the 181st recording of Vivaldi's Four Seasons would not warrant prolonged consideration for inclusion – unless it was played in a little-known transcription for nose flutes, in which case it would stand a good chance of getting into Part III's alternative list of twenty horrors. Between these two poles lie thousands of recordings that I have listened to, discussed endlessly with musicians, producers and experts, and in many instances over three decades attended the sessions or live performances in which they were made. A set of perceptual criteria emerged from these experiences, helping me to sift wheat from chaff while reinforcing my already robust critical detachment from the intrinsically commercial priorities of the music industry.

Onto these personal impressions I sought and grafted the views of more than a thousand readers from many countries who responded to the series as it appeared weekly in the London *Evening Standard* and on the Canadian-based www.scena.org website (the present text is based on those articles, but greatly expanded with detailed musical analysis). These reader suggestions, heated and voluminous, occasionally apoplectic, recommended me to around 8,000 records, some so esoteric as to be practically unobtainable (or even, in one instance, unrecorded) and others so trenchantly proposed that I was obliged to revise my original scheme and reconsider an artist or a record in light of fresh evidence and advocacy.

A pair of fiery appeals from different continents on behalf of Miles Davis's Sketches of Spain had to be turned down with regret, both on account of the work's non-classical genre and of my prior choice of Rodrigo's Concierto de Aranjuez, the basis for Davis's masterpiece. Several respondents recommended Chopin recordings by Ivan Moravec, a wonderfully thoughtful Czech pianist, but not one who contributed meaningfully to the history of the gramophone. Others spoke for the guitarist Augustin Barrios, arguably the first classical composer to record his own work, and for Wanda Wilkomirska's Connoisseur Society performance of Prokofiev sonatas, a trailblazer in its day. There were several petitions on behalf of Lawrence Foster's illuminating EMI recording of Georges Enescu's opera Oedipe, a set which, for all its mellifluousness, failed to penetrate the repertoire of major opera houses and could not therefore qualify as a cultural turning point. On the other hand, Antonio de Almeida's set of Halévy's discarded La Juive did just that.

I tracked down most reader suggestions and relished the pursuit of rarities almost as much as the critical assessment. Some of my own initial choices fell by the wayside on grounds of inaccessibility. The early recordings of Béla Bartók, the first composer to use recording as a working tool, turned out to exist mostly in private collections and, while the state label Hungaroton issued a compilation, it took a search by three state officials to find me a copy, on which the quality of sound eliminated prolonged contemplation. By contrast, George Gershwin's two recordings of Rhapsody in Blue with orchestra are unaccountably scarce and inadequately sound-engineered; even so, their authorial immediacy and the ready availability of parallel piano-roll CDs was sufficient to warrant inclusion.

Many readers were smitten by cult worship of Glenn Gould, Wilhelm Furtwängler, Maria Callas or Carlos Kleiber and some will surely complain that their hero or heroine is under-represented. To assuage their hurt, I would point out that several titans of the record studio are not represented at all. Despite strong recommendations, no record by the prolific conductors Carlo-Maria Giulini or Karl Böhm made the cut, and this despite my personal regard for the Schubert symphonies that both maestros recorded, Böhm rustic and humorous, Giulini gently affectionate. Neither man, however, changed the course of recording or left a footprint large enough in recorded sand to command inclusion except (in Böhm's case) as an accompanist. Nor, by the same token, was there room for conductors as eminent and industrious as Serge Koussevitsky, Rudolf Kempe, Eugen Jochum, Bernard Haitink, Charles Munch, Ernest Ansermet, Kurt Masur and Gennady Rozhdestvensky.

In compiling the list I scrupulously avoided the sin of pro-portionality – judging an artist by length of discography. A list of '100 Greatest Recordings' published in the 1,000th issue of *Gramophone* magazine (December 2005) was founded on no fewer than nine performances by Herbert von Karajan, apparently in tribute to the vast number of records he churned out over half a century. Whatever one feels about Karajan, no single artist can surely be held to represent almost 10 per cent of recorded history and, while Karajan made and sold a lot of records, he was but one maestro among many in a milieu of shifting tastes and reputations, a canon enriched by human idiosyncrasy and impoverished in its decline by the corporate imposition of ephemeral homogeneity.

Just how pernicious was this drive for soundalike performances was brought home to me one evening in Germany when, after spending the day listening to an overhyped young violinist work his way through the Beethoven concerto, I repaired for a beer with the recording team to a bar where, this being Germany, classical music was playing as background. The Mendelssohn concerto we recognized automatically but we couldn't identify the soloist, so we went through a specialist process of elimination by ear: not Kreisler, not Heifetz, not Menuhin, not Stern, not Milstein, not Oistrakh, not Perlman, not Kremer, not Haendel, not Mutter. After ruling out twenty of the best, we summoned the bar owner and demanded to see the CD sleeve. To our dismay, the violinist coming through the speakers was the one we had been working with all day. His playing was so dull, so lacking in colour and individuality, that some of the best ears in studio world failed to pick him out in a blind audition. That, for me, was a scales-falling moment, a revelation of how ruthlessly corporate pressures were pushing music into a corridor of conformity whose narrowness was choking off its life force. It was also a moment that reinforced my appreciation of all the rich humanity that had run before, a panoply of performers and producers who, unafraid of risk, engraved records that continue to evoke wonderment.

The century of recording yielded a kaleidoscope of personalities whose performances amount to an indelible history of interpretation. Within that legacy there are summits and troughs, as well as miles upon miles of meandering flatlands. My task here has been to pick out the peaks on a contour map and arrange them in chronological order. No one is expected to agree with all of my selections, but the list as a whole is a faithful representation of a century of achievement and, at the very least, the starting point for an infinity of web debate.

1. Caruso: The First Recordings
Enrico Caruso
Gramophone and Typewriter Co. Ltd: Milan (Grande Hotel),
11 April 1902

The history of recording begins not with Edison the inventor, nor with Emil Berliner who patented the flat disc, but with a short, fat Neapolitan who, for a hundred pounds sterling in a Milan hotel room, pierced the clatter of mechanical noise with a richly baritonal tenor. Enrico Caruso was the voice of choice for Italian verismo composers. He had just premiered Franchetti's ephemeral Germania at La Scala and insisted on incorporating two of its arias in his debut recording. The first – Studenti! Udite! – so excited the producer Fred Gaisberg that he wrote on the wax a matrix number already given to a visiting soprano. Gaisberg's Italian partner, Alfred Michaelis, left a more sober account of the session:

Dressed like a dandy and twirling a cane, Caruso sauntered down Via Manzoni and – to the delight of those worshippers of tenors, the waiters – entered the Grande Hotel where we were waiting for him. We barred from the room his escort of braves with the exception of his accompanist, Maestro Cottone . . . Caruso wanted to get the job over quickly as he was anxious to earn that £100 and have his lunch [but] he forgot all this when he started on the job[1].

The remaining eight tracks were prime Verdi – Celeste Aida and Rigoletto's Questa o quella; a pair of Boitos; a Tosca showstopper; Donizetti's Una furtive lagrima from L'Elisir d'amore; a spot of ephemeral Mascagni and a Massenet aria. Salvatore Cottone's piano tinkles somewhere in the back of the room and a loud cough punctures one song: no one ever devised a way of editing on wax.

1. Quoted in Jerrold Northrop Moore, *Sound Revolutions: A Biography of Fred Gaisberg, Founding Father of Commercial Recording*, London: Sanctuary, 1999, p. 94.

The discs were instant bestsellers, winning Caruso his first engagements at Covent Garden and the Met, the stages of his greatest fame. Jovial, uncomplicated, musical by instinct and never knowingly underpaid, he died young but wealthy, supporting a vast number of Neapolitan cousins on his record royalties. More significantly, he is the role model for every well-regarded tenor on record.

What, exactly, was the extra quality that Caruso brought to the party? First of all, stability: a voice that sat deeper than tenor and did not wobble under stress. Beyond that, he possessed an exuberance whose infectiousness transcended sonic limitations and gave listeners the impression that here was a man who was full of life and enjoyed his work, whether he was singing tragedy or comedy. The great racking groan he gives at the end of E lucevan le stelle could only have come from a man who had loved and, irresistibly, suffered loss.

2. Gershwin: Rhapsody in Blue
George Gershwin, Paul Whiteman band
Columbia: New York, 10 June 1924

In his early twenties, and the century's, George Gershwin was one of the happiest, busiest men on earth. Too young to go to war, he had risen from street-corner song-plugger to writing shows for Broadway and songs – Swanee, Somebody Loves Me, Fascinatin' Rhythm – that were on everyone's lips. Prolific? He invented the word. In a matter of two and a half weeks in January 1924 Gershwin dashed off A Rhapsody in Blue which, orchestrated by the bandsman Ferdé Grofé, became a hot jazz sensation and the first all-American piano concerto. Among the curiosity seekers at the Aeolian Hall premiere were Rachmaninov, Stokowski, Kreisler and Jascha Heifetz.

Gershwin recorded the Rhapsody twice with Whiteman – acoustically in June 1924 and three years later in superior electrical sound. The first band had exactly the same players as the premiere;

the second was augmented by Tommy Dorsey and Bix Beider-becke and marred by serious clashes between Gershwin and the bandmaster. His playing on both occasions is headlong and propulsive yet imbued with an introspection, and possibly a sadness, that isolates him from the ambient hubbub. The jittery jazz era was both a reaction to the war and a denial; Gershwin in these recordings manages to evoke that ambivalence. For unfathomable reasons, these performances are scarce and seldom reissued. Gershwin's piano rolls constitute an adequate replacement, the more introspective for being played alone (attempts to overlay them with modern orchestras are too oxymoronic to warrant discussion). Otherwise, the most authentic evocations are those by Earl Wild, who played the concerto with both Whiteman and Toscanini, and Leonard Bernstein's, directed from the piano by an empathetic composer-pianist of similar background.

3. *Beethoven: Violin Concerto*
Fritz Kreisler, Berlin State Opera Orchestra/Leo Blech
EMI: Berlin (Singakademie), 14–16 December 1926

There was only one Fritz Kreisler. Honey-toned and twinkling with good humour beneath handsomely coiffed hair, Kreisler exerted a hypnotic fascination not only on audiences but on the rest of his profession for generations to come. He continues to be revered by violinists as diverse as Nigel Kennedy and Maxim Vengerov.

As the foremost soloist of the early recording era he used the medium to change the way the violin was played, applying an obligatory vibrato in softer passages to mask the inadequacies of sound reproduction. His cadenza for the Beethoven concerto – the section where soloists are supposed to let their hair down – was taken up by the overwhelming majority of concert soloists, unwilling to pit their imagination against so magnetic a personality. Its synoptic ascending chords have become as standard to the repertoire as the concerto itself.

Viennese by birth and of sunny disposition, Kreisler adopted a pronounced austerity in the Beethoven concerto, as if conscious of its immensity. His attack is measured and unostentatious, every note assiduously and beautifully articulated. His playing transcends the possibility of difficulty and yields nothing but pleasure. As for the cadenzas, they do what they are meant to: they reflect back on what has just been played and project forward to what is yet to come. Kreisler's is the benchmark account of this concerto beyond all comparison. Although he re-recorded it with better sound in London ten years later, his Berlin performance is unsurpassably intense. No other violinist has ever made a high trill sound organically like a nightingale's song, or the concerto resound so evocatively with pre-romantic rural simplicities. (Among dozens of successors, only Menuhin/Furtwängler, Oistrakh/Klemperer, Haendel/Kubelik, Krebbers/Haitink and Tetzlaff/Zinman successfully suggest an alternate sound world.)

Reputedly the highest paid fiddler of his day, Kreisler spent much of his leisure time raising funds for less fortunate citizens. As soon as he finished these sessions he set up a fund for needy students at the University of Berlin and received a medal from the Austrian ambassador for helping hungry children in his homeland. Humanity was inextricable from the way that Fritz Kreisler made his music.

4. Mendelssohn/Schumann: Trios in D Minor
Alfred Cortot, Jacques Thibaud, Pablo (Pau) Casals
EMI: London (Queen's Hall), 20–21 June 1927 and
15–18 November 1928

The recorded century yielded three paramount piano trios. The Beaux Arts lasted longest: three students who met at the Tanglewood Festival in 1955 and played on, with personnel changes, for half a century. The Million Dollar Trio were the richest – Jascha Heifetz, Arthur Rubinstein and Gregor Piatigorsky conjoined by a 1940s RCA Hollywood pay deal. But the trio that established the form on record and exemplified its delicate balance between piano, violin and cello came about quite by chance. In 1905 the Catalan cellist Pau Casals, new in Paris, met the pianist Alfred Cortot and violinist Jacques Thibaud, who were living in the same neighbourhood. They played trios for fun, in between sets of tennis; then they moved on for rising fees to private salons and finally they emerged on record in the thick of international careers.

Schubert's B-flat trio was their warhorse, performed fifty times with tremendous brio. More eloquent, though, was the fireside intimacy they brought out in the mature, mood-swinging Mendelssohn trio, written paradoxically at the height of his fame and personal happiness, just before the second symphony, yet rippling with discontent and premonitions of mortality. The conversation between the three instruments turns alternately social and philosophical, pleasantries interspersed with reflections on the meaning of life, nowhere more so than in Cortot's breathtaking introduction to the Andante. In the Schumann, fervent and fractious by turn, it is strings that lead the search through romantic irresolution towards a brotherly harmony.

Casals quit the trio in 1934, preoccupied with the Spanish Civil War and his hatred of fascism. The other two stayed in France, where Cortot served as Commissioner for Fine Arts in the Vichy government and gave recitals with Wilhelm Kempff at a Paris exhibition of heroic sculptures by Hitler's favourite, Arno Breker. Perversely, Casals forgave him after the war, but he refused to answer letters from the relatively uncorrupted Thibaud, or to meet him ever again. Music meant everything to these men, but it was no healer.

1. Music on the move: A crowd in Queen's Park, Manchester, *c.* 1907, listening to a gigantic Auxeto gramophone playing Caruso and Scotti singing Solenne in Quest'ora from La Forza del Destino.

2. Making the record: Fred Gaisberg (*centre*), the first professional producer, turning pages in a 1920s Berlin studio for violinist Fritz Kreisler (*left*) and his accompanist Franz Rupp.

3. Music at home: young Norwegians sample the latest releases, *c.* 1930.

4. The maestro: Arturo Toscanini in full cry at the 1937 Salzburg Festival.

5. Prophet before profit: Artur Schnabel, the pianist who said no, then maybe.

6. Her master's voice: American contralto Marian Anderson glued to her own aural image, early 1940s.

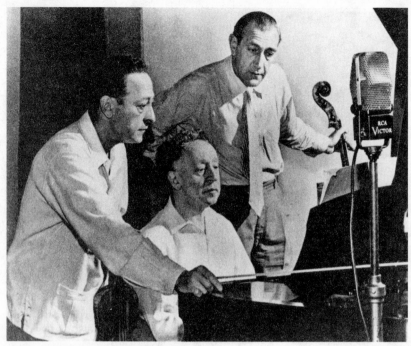

7. Breaking the record: The Million Dollar Trio of Gregor Piatigorsky (cello), Jascha Heifetz (violin) and Arthur Rubinstein (piano), Hollywood, 1949.

8. The matriarch: Professor Elsa Schiller, former concentration camp victim, reinvented Deutsche Grammophon in the yellow colour of her Nazi abjection.

9. The mega-maestro: Herbert von Karajan (*left*), 'like a cat who has collared the cream', at lunch in Berlin, 1955, with critic Hans Heinz Stuckenschmidt (*centre*) and Berlin Philharmonic manager Gerhart von Westermann.

10. The pianist who refused to play live: Glenn Gould with Leonard Bernstein and the New York Philharmonic Orchestra, New York, March 1961.

11. The man who signed himself God: Goddard Lieberson, mastermind of stage musicals and president of Columbia Records.

12. Faust and Mephisto: Herbert von Karajan and Walter Legge (*centre*) at Abbey Road, March 1960, but which sold more of his soul?

13. The brotherhood of Decca: Sir Georg Solti (*left*) with his symbiotic producer John Culshaw in the Sofiensaal, Vienna, Spring 1966, during a recording of Strauss's Elektra.

14. 'Like a bunch of monkeys': (*left to right*) Herbert von Karajan with Sviatoslav Richter, Mstislav Rostropovich and David Oistrakh after their flawed recording of the Beethoven triple concerto, Berlin, 1970.

15. Power players: Herbert von Karajan and Sony Chairman Akio Morita announcing the building of a CD plant on Karajan's land at Anif, near Salzburg, March 1986.

16. The self-made recording machine: Neville Marriner in rehearsal, 1990s.

5. Rachmaninov: Second Piano Concerto in C Minor
Sergei Rachmaninov, Philadelphia Orchestra/Leopold Stokowski
RCA (Sony-BMG): Philadelphia, 10 and 13 April 1929

Famously conceived after a nervous breakdown that followed the disastrous premiere of his first symphony, the concerto was Rachmaninov's chief calling card as a soloist. Exiled by the Russian Revolution, he first recorded it in 1924 with Leopold Stokowski and his formidable Philadelphians, but the five-disc acoustic set was made obsolete by the arrival of electrical recording and did little to relieve his poverty.

Perpetually on tour, Rachmaninov endured another bout of depression, brought on by a yearning for endless Russian vistas. His fourth concerto flopped. Stokowski secured a repeat recording of the second, but infuriated him by making cuts in the score in an attempt to squeeze it onto four discs. Rachmaninov, who put up with truncations to all his other works, especially the symphonies, absolutely refused to reduce the C minor by so much as one note. He played the Philadelphia performances complete and unabridged in a state of bristling tension that can still be heard on the record, as if conductor and orchestra were dancing on eggshells around him. For so large and lumbering a man, Rachmaninov had a gossamer touch at the keyboard, defying the weight of his own fingers in the sustained quiet passages of the Adagio while Stokowski struggled to rein back his bucking steed of a band. It is conflict, as much as any artistry, that makes this performance unforgettable.

This 1929 recording of the second concerto has never gone out of print, though an error at RCA in 1952 resulted in some passages being substituted by rejected out-takes, an anomaly that persisted unnoticed for thirty-six years until the CD reissue alerted scholars to the peculiarity. Apart from being the definitive guide to playing the century's most popular concerto, this is one of very few recordings that exists, like a Rodin sculpture, in alternative, user-friendly casts.

6. Rachmaninov: Third Piano Concerto in D Minor
Vladimir Horowitz, London Symphony Orchestra/Albert Coates
EMI: London (Kingsway Hall), 29–30 December 1930

Rachmaninov was unfailingly generous to talented young pianists, always willing to coach them in his works regardless of the rivalry they might represent to his own highly-paid solo career. In the early months of the Great Depression he heard rumours of a young Russian émigré who played his music better than anyone alive. He ran into Vladimir Horowitz by chance in the basement of Steinway's New York showroom on 57th Street and accompanied him, stool by stool, in a four-handed run-through of the D minor concerto. 'Horowitz,' exclaimed Rachmaninov afterwards, 'swallowed it whole . . . he had the courage, intensity, the daring.'

The D-minor concerto launched Horowitz's phenomenal career. Ahead of this recording, he played it in Chicago, Cincinnati, New York, Philadelphia, Boston, Berlin, Amsterdam and finally London, where he took it into the studio with a British conductor who had run the opera house in pre-revolutionary St Petersburg.

Unlike the composer's effusive and fairly sunny recording, Horowitz took the music to an edge of darkness where Rachmaninov, himself depressive, dared not venture. He made child's play of tricky fingerwork and zipped through prestissimi at double speed, braking precipitately into a sombre adagio. Sheer velocity makes this account of the work irresistible, but there is also a dangerous current of mental imbalance – of the kind that would make David Helfgott's performance in the 1996 movie *Shine* so riveting. Horowitz was twice hospitalized after nervous breakdowns. The concerto became his trademark work, re-recorded each time he emerged from isolation as if to assert his unchallenged mastery (Rachmaninov himself left a luminous account, as did the British pianist Stephen Hough, using the composer's markings). Horowitz, though, had the stamp of authority. After his 1942 open-air performance in the Hollywood Bowl, the dying composer trundled onto the stage and announced that this was exactly how he had always dreamed the D–minor concerto should sound.

7. *Beethoven: The 32 Piano Sonatas*
Artur Schnabel
EMI: London, 1932–5

Of all pianists, the philosopher Artur Schnabel held out longest against the recording machine. It was, he argued, unmusical to perform without an audience and it ran against the art's essential ephemerality to fix an interpretation for all time when making music was something that changed according to the artist's mood, the weather, or something he had just read in the morning paper.

Schnabel finally acquiesced after the Wall Street crash, agreeing to record the thirty-two Beethoven sonatas in an edition he had edited and performed integrally in Berlin. His condition was that the records were sold on subscription only, so that he knew the names of everyone who listened and had some perception of the audience at his fingertips. This delighted the record label, which took money in advance from subscribers and did not invest a penny of its own in the project.

'Memories of my first year of making records in London belong to the most painful of my life,' recalled Schnabel. 'I suffered agonies and was in a state of despair each time I recorded. I felt as if I were harried to death – and most unhappy. Everything was artificial – the light, the air, the sound – and it took me quite a long time to get the company to adjust their equipment to music [*sic*] and even longer to adjust myself to the equipment, however much improved it was.'[2]

'Tempted by a nice fat guarantee, he eventually agreed that it was possible to reconcile his ideals with the machinery,' noted producer Fred Gaisberg. 'I supervised every one of our twenty

2. Artur Schnabel, *My Life and Music*, Gerrards Cross: Colin Smythe, p. 98.

sessions per annum during the next ten years and rate the experience of hearing his performances and listening to his impromptu lectures as a most liberal allowance of instruction combined with entertainment.'[3]

There was perpetual dialogue in these recordings – between pianist and composer, and in every possible break between Schnabel and the recording crew on a range of topics from theology to sex scandal. As much as actual performance – tender in the middle sonatas, titanic in the late – the cycle is propelled by good conversation, a flow of narrative incident that keeps it eternally fresh. The tempo that he sets in the very first sonata, opus 2/1, sounds simply incontrovertible – fast, to be sure, but not so much to show off virtuosity as a display of Beethoven's teenaged exuberance. When he opens the Moonlight, which any half-trained child can play, Schnabel avoids flashing his cuffs and playing with artificial portentousness; instead, he achieves a Rembrandt shade of nocturnality that no other artist has matched. He treats each sonata with individual respect, its character teased out with subtlety that often has nothing to do with the published title. The Appassionata, for instance, is exuberant and somewhat glib, less life-or-death passion than kiss-and-run one-night stand.

Small of hand as he was broad of mind, Schnabel can be heard struggling to reach tops and bottoms in the mountainous spans of the Hammerklavier Sonata, opus 106, at a tempo the wrong side of suicidal. Reckless in his reckoning of Beethoven's intent, he scatters wrong notes like confetti – and, in so doing, reflects the unattainable, the distant beloved, the shimmer of utopia that is the composer's eternal goal. Start to finish, this is a road map to Beethoven's mind and, through Schnabel's guidance, to love, life and our place on earth.

3. F. W. Gaisberg, *Music on Record*, London: Robert Hale, 1947, pp. 193–4.

8. Debussy: La Mer/Elgar: Enigma Variations
BBC Symphony Orchestra/Arturo Toscanini
EMI: London (Queen's Hall), 3 and 12 June 1935, released 1987

Two maestros mistrusted recording. Wilhelm Furtwängler deplored its fixity while Arturo Toscanini declared the sound to be
unmusical. 'Our last two experiences with Toscanini have been
such as to discourage any further attempts to record him,' wrote
RCA producer Charles O'Connell in 1933. 'Furthermore, having
spent in the neighbourhood of $10,000 in these attempts we are
fairly well cured of that ambition.'[4] As far as America was concerned at the time, the Italian was history.

Two years later, during a BBC Summer Music Festival, EMI's
Fred Gaisberg sneaked state-of-art machines into two concerts.
Toscanini was having an unusually happy time with the BBC's
orchestra (founded by Adrian Boult in 1930), admiring its principal
players and seldom raising his voice in rehearsal. The Debussy suite,
which he played with many green-pencilled alterations, shimmered
like the English Channel at Eastbourne on a summer's day, a
pointillist's paradise. There is nothing literal in the depiction of
dawn or waves, just a glowing impression of nature at ease, the
storm threat faintly veiled.

The Elgar was rather more contentious. Toscanini set off at a
cracking pace, startling British critics who were accustomed to the
late composer's lugubrious tempi. 'It is lovely music and it must
be alive,' Toscanini told principal viola Bernard Shore, who played
a soaring, faintly satirical solo in the sixth variation. The performance had an overwhelming, aching, unsurpassable beauty. 'He
creates the illusion that nothing comes between you and the music,'
noted the young conductor John Barbirolli.

Gaisberg found the recordings 'outstanding from the technical
point of view', but Toscanini refused to listen. He was heading

---

4. Letter in EMI archive, Hayes, Middlesex, quoted in sleeve note to this
recording by Tony Harrison.

back to America where NBC had promised him a super-orchestra. The boxy-sounding studio recordings he went on to make in New York fulfilled his worst fears about the medium and, after playback, he never listened to his work again. The Queen's Hall sessions are the only recordings of Toscanini at his peak in the best sound of his lifetime, unaware that he was being preserved for posterity. The recordings were held in vaults for half a century until EMI was legally entitled to bring them to light.

9. *Sibelius: Violin Concerto*
Jascha Heifetz, London Philharmonic Orchestra/
Thomas Beecham
EMI: London (Abbey Road), 26 November and
14 December 1935

Jean Sibelius wrote his only concerto in 1903 and conducted it a year later in Helsinki with Viktor Nováček, a Czech conservatoire teacher, as soloist. Next morning his biggest fan, the Finnish critic Karl Flodin, dismissed the work as 'a mistake', its leaps and bounds inimical to the composer's free-flowing nature. Sibelius revised the score and presented a second version in Berlin, with another Czech soloist, Carl Halir, and Richard Strauss as conductor. This time the reviews were merely indifferent. One violinist after another tried it out over the next three decades and gave it up as musically and physically unrewarding. As late as 1937, the (London) *Times'* chief critic called the concerto 'a poor work'.

Along came Jascha Heifetz, a player whose technique outshone all others. Heifetz had learned the piece as a boy in St Petersburg. After fleeing the 1917 Revolution he made his name in America with fiery showpieces and did not get round to playing the Sibelius concerto until 1934. An RCA recording, planned in Philadelphia, crashed after a disagreement over tempi between Heifetz and conductor Leopold Stokowski. In London the next year Heifetz linked up with Sir Thomas Beecham, the most ardent of Sibelius interpreters, and together they gave the concerto the benefit of unblinking conviction. Heifetz, often accused of aloofness, played with ferocious advocacy, hitting each note on the head and driving the piece forward as if it were a Tchaikovsky crowd pleaser.

Heifetz had made minute cuts in the score for improved coherence, but the Sibelian tone prevails throughout and the affinities to his symphonies are pronounced. That said, there is a mysteriously Jewish hint of Kol Nidrei towards the end of the Adagio and Beecham's structural shaping gives the piece a touch of Palladian grace. Once the enigma had been cracked others rushed in. Seventy recordings appeared over half a century, more than any other concerto. Somehow, it became mostly associated on record with women soloists – Ginette Neveu, Ida Haendel, Kyung Wha Chung, Viktoria Mullova, Anne-Sophie Mutter, Sarah Chang.

10. *Mahler: Ninth Symphony*
Vienna Philharmonic Orchestra/Bruno Walter
EMI: Vienna (Musikvereinsaal), 16 January 1938

On 16 January 1938 Bruno Walter conducted the Vienna Philharmonic in Gustav Mahler's ninth symphony, a work they had premiered together twenty-five years before, some months after the composer's death. Mahler's brother-in-law, Arnold Rosé, still led the orchestra as concertmaster, but Mahler's music had been racially banned in Germany and rejected for its unbuttoned emotion in stiff-lipped English-speaking countries. With Adolf Hitler hammering at the gates, a nervous audience knew they might be hearing this music for the last time in their lives. In the front rows sat Mahler's widow, Alma, and the Austrian chancellor, Kurt Schuschnigg, who, weeks later, would surrender his country to the Third Reich. Many in the hall, and six in the orchestra, would die in Nazi concentration camps. As a presentiment of doom, this disc has few parallels in Western civilization since the writing on the wall at Belshazzar's biblical feast.

As a musical performance, it is more prescient still. The opening is ominously solemn yet without fear, stately and unhurried. As the tempo picks up it asserts a bold defiance, an otherwordly detachment that ignores the tramping jackboots of political events. The second movement's ironies are caustically pointed and in the rondo-burlesque the orchestra stays barely on the right side of reckless. The taut finale avoids the temptation of consolation, opting to face an unavoidably grim future without compromise. Rosé's valedictory solo is unbearably moving, his line firm and unflustered. Weeks later he was roughed up by uniformed thugs and forced to flee to London, where he died penniless at the end of the war, knowing that his violinist daughter, Alma, had been murdered in Auschwitz.

Fred Gaisberg took away this first recording of Mahler's last completed symphony aware that its tiny potential market was diminishing by the day. By the time he had finished a rough edit, Walter was a homeless refugee in Holland, seeking a visa to Britain or the US. The conductor criticized some roughness in the string playing but decided that the performance ought to be released regardless. It came out just before the war and a few copies reached Nazi-occupied Europe. In Prague, young composers gathered in Viktor Ullmann's flat to draw strength from this prohibited music. Ullmann, who had dedicated his only piano sonata to the memory of Gustav Mahler, was listed with most of his friends for deportation to Theresienstadt and ultimately gassed in Auschwitz.

11. *Bach: Cello Suites*
Pablo (Pau) Casals
EMI: London, 23 November 1936; Paris 2–3 June 1939
and 13 June 1939

The six Bach suites for unaccompanied cello were practically unknown until a waif picked them up in a Barcelona store in 1890 and chose them as his morning exercises, played before breakfast every day for the rest of his long life. The kid was Pau Casals and his record success brought the suites into general circulation.

Eyes tightly shut on stage, Casals endowed the music with a spiritual dimension that was probably never intended by its composer. In the thick of the Spanish Civil War he played the cycle for workers and fighters on the Republican side. The happiest day of his life, he said, was performing the E-flat suite before an audience of 8,000. When the Republic fell, he recast the suites as a lament and a reproach, refusing to re-enter his native land so long as it was under fascist rule.

He recorded the D minor and C major in London during the war, the other four in Paris when all was lost. His interpretations at this stage are brisk and unfussy, though decorated with a highly personal vibrato, which he called 'expressive intonation'. This freedom is more than just metaphorical. It lifts a symmetrical passage in the Allemande of the G-major suite out of its baroque casing and into a vivid, infinitely flexible modernity. This was Casals' way of making old music sound newly relevant, and it seldom fails right the way through the cycle. The Sarabande of the C-major suite is taken at a leisurely pace that no one could conceivably dance to, but it is promptly counterweighted by two Bourrées that simply leap from the speakers; the concluding Gigue turns reflectively inwards, a final dance alone with his thoughts.

Casals can sometimes sound heavy-handed in comparison to such elegantly recorded successors as the Frenchmen Pierre Fournier, Paul Tortelier and Maurice Gendron, but he gives this utilitarian music grandeur, dignity and, above all, hope. This is as much a testament as a performance, a blueprint for the cello future.

12. *Tchaikovsky: First Piano Concerto in B-Flat Minor (with Brahms: Second Piano Concerto)*

Vladimir Horowitz, NBC Symphony Orchestra/Arturo Toscanini

RCA (Sony-BMG)/Naxos Historical: New York (Carnegie Hall), 6 and 14 May 1941 (and 9 May 1940)

The father/son-in-law relationship is fraught enough without the father being an Italian martinet and the son-in-law Jewish, gay and schizophrenic. Such is the price of celebrity that Arturo Toscanini and Vladimir Horowitz were obliged to work together in public and on record. They neither looked nor sounded comfortable in collusion but at their finest hour, a 1943 Carnegie Hall performance of the Tchaikovsky concerto, they raised $10,190,045 in war bond sales and won a thank-you from President Roosevelt.

This is an earlier encounter, edgy and confrontational. From the great banging chords of the opening theme, the pianist is pulling away from the baton rhythm, off on a riff of his own in a thrillingly trance-like state of anarchy. The conductor does his best to maintain an illusion of social control but in the second-movement Andantino the pianist gleefully overrides the accompanying wood-wind and runs off again with the band panting behind him. The ending is a heaved sigh of catharsis, as if family relations have been briefly restored.

This was not the first time Tchaikovsky had been used as a boxing ring, or the last. Horowitz left Thomas Beecham flounder-ing in the work in their joint New York debut, and two East Europeans, Sviatoslav Richter and Krystian Zimerman, made public mincemeat of Herbert von Karajan on record. The bombast in the music lends itself to interpersonal conflict.

Not so the Brahms B-flat major. Of the present recording Horowitz said: 'I never liked the concerto very much, and I played it so badly, and my ideas about music were so different from Toscanini's.' Both men set out so fast they seemed to be looking for a knockout in the third movement, neither showing any mercy for the score. It's an inimitable record of human disharmony, treasurable in its headstrong perversity.

13. *Strauss conducts Strauss: Don Juan; Don Quixote; Ein Heldenleben; Till Eulenspiegel; Japanische Festmusik; etc.*

Berlin Philharmonic Orchestra, Staatskapelle Berlin, Bayerische Staatsorchester/Richard Strauss

DG: Berlin and Munich, 1927–41

Richard Strauss was the oldest composer of consequence to record his own music. Like Mahler, Strauss was one of the world's leading opera conductors, music director in Berlin (1898–1918) and Vienna (1919–24). Impassive on the podium, he scorned as sweaty amateurs men who jumped about and waved their arms. His grip was exercised with the flicker of an eyebrow, an increased noise by the faint raising of an elbow. There was nothing haughty about his attitude to music or musicians. 'Kindly play as it is written,' was his severest reproof. An observer noted: 'His tone of voice is light and he orders matters so smoothly that he meets with neither objections nor restrictions; instead there is a free flowing exchange of explanations, questions and answers.' In lunch breaks he played cards with players, who deemed it an honour to lose their hard-earned to a legendary composer.

The subtlety of his tempo shifts can be heard here in his great tone poems, along with sudden explosions of orchestral power. Eroticism flowed unblushingly in Salome's strip dance and A Hero's Life. In Till Eulenspiegel, the sense of fun is irrepressible. Strauss must have enjoyed making records; he certainly loved the money they brought in. His 1941 recording of the Rosenkavalier waltz, a piece whose profits built him a house, is rich with the odour of self-satisfaction.

By now, Strauss was politically compromised and in mounting distress. He had initially accepted a cultural post from the Nazis but got caught making anti-Hitler remarks in letters to his former librettist, Stefan Zweig. His daughter-in-law was Jewish, her mother was deported and his grandsons could have been seized at any time. Under these gathering clouds, Strauss in 1941 composed and conducted a political offering – a festive work for the 2,600th anniversary of the Japanese monarchy, replete with ersatz orientalisms in a pottage of schmaltz. The performance here is as proficient – and historic – as any other. Whatever Strauss put into his music, his expression never betrayed a scintilla of emotion.

14. *Blow the Wind Southerly*
Kathleen Ferrier
Decca: London (West Hampstead studios),
10–11 February 1949

The brief flame that was Ferrier is musically matchless. Devoid of beauty, brilliance or sexual appeal, she inspired a fierce ardour in countless adherents. Utterly English in style and ethic, she entranced Bruno Walter as the paramount Mahler singer and made a powerful recording with the Vienna Philharmonic of Das Lied von der Erde. Her late Brahms had ethereal beauty, her Britten a stoic grandeur (she was a less than credible victim in the first Rape of Lucretia). The colour of her voice was Victorian contralto, belonging to another time, and that was probably its chief attraction.

A telephone operator from Blackburn, Lancashire, Ferrier enjoyed ten brief years of glory, from her mid-Blitz debut at a National Gallery lunchtime concert to her death of cancer in 1953, aged 41, having bravely sung Eurydice at Covent Garden with a broken hip, leaning on a stage wall to prop her up to the end. She was the embodiment of an England that would never say die.

Away from the recital hall and opera house, Ferrier was keenly aware of her roots in a dying culture, a world of folksong that was being overwhelmed by popular music on radio and records. While Britten and his contemporaries sought to conserve folksongs in symphonic museum settings, Ferrier persisted in singing the people's music straight from the source in a manner that evoked an Arcadian, pre-industrial idyll. Many of her favourites were fishing songs, arising from that peculiar blend of danger and boredom that accompanies those who go down to the sea in boats.

Utterly without nostalgia, partnered at the piano by unfussy Phyllis Spurr, she sang out her girlhood in Decca's bleak West Hampstead studio, preserving a flourish of love, longing and lament that would exist for ever more on record but would never again be heard in its natural context, on quaysides and village squares. The title song endures as her epitaph, but it is in simple love songs like Ma Bonny Lad, or My Boy Willie, and in the mourning of young love lost Down by the Salley Gardens, that Ferrier's artistry shines eternal.

15. *Chopin: Waltzes*
Dinu Lipatti
EMI: Geneva (Radio Geneva studios), June 1950

The Romanian pianist Dinu Lipatti, just thirty-three when he died, made his precious few recordings while suffering from leukaemia and searching with increasing desperation for emergent cures. Despite his condition, there is nothing of the sickbed about his performances. A student of the iconoclastic Alfred Cortot, who did much to advance his career by word of recommendation, Lipatti's crisp, witty articulation overturns the image of Chopin himself as a morbid melancholic, not long for this world. There is a devilment to Lipatti's playing, an almost improvisatory approach that is derived in part from Cortot and in part from his private passion for trying out hot jazz with close friends.

A powerfully built man of wealthy parentage, Lipatti spent the late 1930s in Paris but wound up with his wife starving in Switzerland. The Geneva Conservatoire eventually gave him a job and EMI gave him a record contract. The first London sessions were rapturously received and plans were in hand for a US tour when the cancer struck. The discovery of the drug cortisone gave him an illusory remission in the summer of 1950 and EMI's men shot over to Geneva to capture the Chopin waltzes. Lipatti's energy and optimism made even the gloomier waltzes in minor keys sparkle and sway. The run of B minor, E minor and A minor in the middle of the series amounts in his hands to a kaleidoscope of subtly shifting moods within a Chekovian stage set, dramatic and irresoluble.

Lipatti went on after the recording to play a concerto in Lucerne and a solo recital in Besançon, but the respite was short lived and he was gone by Christmas. The few discs he left behind – Mozart and Schumann concertos with Karajan; a recital of Bach, Mozart, Schubert and Chopin; and the Chopin waltzes and nocturnes – reveal a pianist of expressive genius who nonetheless allowed the music to speak for itself. Although Rubinstein and Horowitz were more celebrated in Chopin, Lipatti was the pianists' Chopin pianist.

16. Barber: Knoxville: Summer of 1915
Eleanor Steber, Dumbarton Oaks Orchestra/William Strickland
CBS: New York (30th Street studio), 7 November 1950

The most performed concert work by any American composer is Samuel Barber's Adagio for Strings, a reinstrumentation of the second movement of his B minor string quartet that became, at President Roosevelt's funeral, the nation's music of commemoration, and, in Oliver Stone's film *Platoon*, its lament for the Vietnam War.

Barber (1910–81) was an outmoded romantic who belonged in patrician style and gesture to an American pastoral that preceded two world wars and the onset of modernism. Unstintingly melodic, he wrote in long, arching lines that contradicted the jagged urban rhythms of Copland and Bernstein, his close contemporaries, let alone the austerities of atonalism.

Brought up within earshot of his aunt, the famed contralto Louise Homer, Barber wrote fluently for female voices. Knoxville, to a text by James Agee (scriptwriter of *The African Queen*), was unapologetically nostalgic, a snapshot of a quiet evening in a Tennessee small town, a bored small boy lying on the rough wet grass listening to 'a streetcar raising its iron moan'. The soprano

Eleanor Steber, who commissioned the work, said 'that was exactly my childhood' and sang the 1948 premiere in Boston. She went on to make the first recording as the march of time quickened and 'parents on porches' were to be seen no more. Curatorially, this warmly engaging, crisply articulated recording is prime American heritage, as precious as the Liberty Bell.

17. *Opera Duets*
Jussi Björling with Robert Merrill (baritone), RCA Victor
Orchestra/Renato Cellini
RCA: New York (NBC studios), 3 January 1951

The 'Swedish Caruso' died, like his namesake, some months short of his fiftieth birthday, the victim of aggressive alcohol abuse. Decca producer John Culshaw, visiting him early one morning at his Rome hotel during sessions for Un Ballo in Maschera, found Björling halfway through a second whisky bottle. Culshaw promptly replaced him with Carlo Bergonzi.

Astonishingly, though his health was wrecked by the addiction, his voice was unimpaired. At Covent Garden the summer before he died he suffered a heart attack on stage but insisted, after a half-hour delay, on resuming the role. His secret was a phenomenal breathing technique and the patience to wait until his prime before tackling the biggest roles.

Trained by his tenor father and touring with three brothers as a family quartet, his career was stalled by the Second World War and when his fame took off in the 1950s he tried to make up for lost time by grabbing money gigs and spending wildly. At work on the opera stage, though, he was consummately professional, impressing colleagues as sceptical as Maria Callas with his sensitive phrasing. Some of the best tracks he cut were duets. Paired with the Met baritone Robert Merrill, Björling recorded a Pearl Fishers duet that has never been equalled, along with twosomes from Forza and Bohème – and the marbled heavens oath scene from Otello, a summit role that he was planning to sing for the first time in the season of his premature death. The power of these duets is not so much in the singing as in the listening. Björling, for all his fame and power, is audibly intent upon his partner's every half-breath, as if joined in the act of love.

18. Beethoven: Ninth Symphony
NBC Symphony Orchestra/Arturo Toscanini
RCA: New York (Carnegie Hall), 31 March and 1 April 1952

There have been many historic Ninths on record. There was Leonard Bernstein, at the fall of the Berlin Wall, substituting the cry of Freiheit (freedom) for Freude (joy). Karajan's 1962 Berlin LP, just after the Wall went up, is the all-time best-selling Ninth. Wilhelm Furtwängler gave a momentous performance for the post-war reopening of Bayreuth. Felix Weingartner, a friend of Brahms, engraved a truly authentic style in two recordings of 1926 and 1935.

But of all recorded Ninths, and there are around sixty, one takes precedence for its furious energy and faith in human goodness. Toscanini had been conducting the Ninth for exactly half a century when he entered Carnegie Hall for what he intended as a significant valediction. When he first conducted the work in Milan in 1902, the city had heard it only three times before. Now the Ninth was not only the most familiar of masterpieces but also the most meaningful, a signal of hope after the ravages of war. Toscanini had played it at the reconsecration of La Scala in 1946; here he presented it as a cultural jewel to be passed to future generations.

The first two movements are breathtakingly fast, the Adagio engagingly taut and gloriously warm-toned. The Robert Shaw Chorus and all-American quartet in the finale – Eileen Farrell, Nan Merriman, Jan Peerce and Norman Scott – err on the side of might, threatening to burst their lungs, but the pacing is supple and the heat intense. Amid the bombast, one hears islands of intimacy and calm. Taped in Carnegie Hall in preference to NBC's cramped studio, the sound is vivid. 'I am almost satisfied,' said

Toscanini at playback, adding after a moment's reflection, 'I still don't understand that music.'

19. Suk: Asrael Symphony
Czech Philharmonic Orchestra/Vaclav Talich
Supraphon: Prague (Dvořák Hall, Rudolfinum),
22–29 May 1952

For a small nation the Czechs are notably over-endowed with great composers, but the symphony that stirs them most comes from a minor master. Joseph Suk was a violinist who married Dvořák's daughter, Otilie. When his father-in-law died in May 1904, Suk dutifully started a requiem, naming it after the angel, Asrael, who accompanies souls to paradise. In the middle of the fourth movement, Otilie fell sick; she died in July 1905. He tore up the Adagio and wrote a new one: To Otilka.

Asrael is a double lament, an entombment of hope. Muted in grief, restrained in rage, the symphony would embody for Czechs all that they were unable to express during two world wars and foreign occupations. In the Nazi camp of Theresienstadt and the Soviet labour camps, oppressed composers quoted themes from Asrael to sustain the doomed souls around them.

The glory of the work is that it refuses to become mired in misery and escapes quickly into the uplands of recovery. A successful soloist and chamber musician, Suk knew the classical repertoire well enough to quote deftly from Verdi, Beethoven, Brahms and, inevitably, Dvořák. But the piece avoids patchwork and its finale, a loving portrait of Otilie, reworks Brucknerian textures in wholly original ways.

Vaclav Talich, Suk's close friend, conducted the Czech Philharmonic from 1919 to 1941. Like Wilhelm Furtwängler in Berlin, he stayed put during the Hitler years and suffered for it afterwards. The communists banished him to Bratislava, where he founded the Slovak Philharmonic. In the Stalinist darkness of 1952 he was brought back to Prague to conduct Asrael. Arrests were rife and men were hanged on trumped-up treason charges. Underplaying the work's emotions, Talich unfolded a noble account of national suffering and hope, a performance that captures a terrible moment and preserves its solemn dignity for all time.

20. *Wagner: Tristan und Isolde*
Kirsten Flagstad, Ludwig Suthaus, Blanche Thebom,
Philharmonia Orchestra/Wilhelm Furtwängler
EMI: London (Kingsway Hall), 10–23 June 1952

This landmark recording was almost never made. Furtwängler, its conductor, told EMI that he would never work again with the scheming producer Walter Legge, whom he accused of sabotaging his career to promote Herbert von Karajan. Flagstad, the great Isolde, told the record company that she would not make the recording without Furtwängler, whom she trusted implicitly, or without Legge, whom she relied upon discreetly to substitute her missing two top Cs in Act Two with the voice of his wife, Elisabeth Schwarzkopf. The impasse was insuperable and time was ticking loudly away. Flagstad was fifty-seven years old and had announced her retirement.

A compromise was found. Legge apologized to Furtwängler in writing for any hurt caused by 'alleged' remarks. The conductor, for his part, acknowledged the excellence of Legge's London orchestra and waived his demands for a Berlin or Bayreuth record-ing. Casting was quickly settled. The Tristan and Brangäne were second choices – Lauritz Melchior was found to be past it for Tristan and Martha Mödl was about to sing Isolde for the unmen-tionable Karajan. Furtwängler inserted Suthaus, whom he had conducted as Tristan in 1947, and Flagstad recommended Thebom, an American of Swedish extraction whom she had taken under her wing. Both acquitted themselves well; Josef Greindl and Dietrich Fischer-Dieskau sang a fine King Mark and Kurwenal, but the limelight belonged to soprano and conductor.

Flagstad sang an Isolde to melt an iceberg, tender rather than erotic, her love for Tristan deepened by maturity. Her sound fills space like floodwater, leaving no room for disbelief. Furtwängler, intellectually uncomfortable with the business of recording, had never conducted an opera in studio before. He disliked the basement-level hall and the noise of Central Line trains running beside it, but his performance was imbued with calm assurance and inspirational risk; his health was failing and he was anxious to leave an interpretative legacy.

When all was over, he put an arm round Legge's shoulder and said: 'My name will be remembered for this, but yours should be.' Legge griped privately that this was the only compliment he ever got in forty recordings they made together. There were two hours left at the end of the final session and Legge suggested that Furtwängler should make use of the orchestra and hall to record Mahler's Songs of a Wayfarer with Fischer-Dieskau. The conductor turned on him brusquely and said: 'I promised you *Tristan*, and that's all you're getting.' They never worked together again.

21. *Verdi: Aida*
Renata Tebaldi, Mario del Monaco, Ebe Stignani, Santa Cecilia
Academy Chorus and Orchestra/Alberto Erede
Decca: Rome (Santa Cecilia), August 1952

Renata Tebaldi was Nature's antidote to Maria Callas. Restrained where the Greek raged, pure toned where Callas shrieked, she was adored by cognoscenti but never obtained equivalent celebrity. Thirty years old in this recording, Tebaldi had made her US debut as Aida in San Francisco in 1950 but was not called to New York for another five years, after which she became a Met fixture, the jewel in its crown after Rudolf Bing fired her tempestuous rival. While Callas was the media darling, Tebaldi was queen of the footlights, the serene ruler of illusion.

A year older than Callas, she never married nor slept with millionaires, she turned up on time at rehearsal and sang with relish. Her only obduracy was a refusal to sing non-Italian roles or eat foreign food, deeming lesser tongues and cuisines to be uncultured.

Callas made headlines of their rivalry, asking journalists if they did not prefer her champagne to the Met's Coca-Cola. Tebaldi replied that she found champagne rather sour. They carved up the opera summits. While Callas ruled La Scala, Tebaldi played Florence and Rome. Callas occupied Covent Garden, which Tebaldi boycotted as 'a Callas house'. Beyond the hostility lay a sincere mutual respect.

This Aida was Tebaldi's launchpad, a year ahead of the coming of Callas. It was also the first recording of the opera to sound like the real thing. Although constricted by mono sound, the Santa Cecilia hall gave a cavernous dimension to Verdi's Egyptian desert and a choking claustrophobia to the climactic entombment. Despite forty degrees of heat and no air conditioning, Tebaldi sang without strain, soaring above huge choruses and dropping alternately to a whisper. She sang softer than any living spinto and although the huge Mario del Monaco was not an ideal vocal partner, the conductor, Alberto Erede, was the best balancer of singing voices. Many claim to prefer Tebaldi's stereo Aida with Bergonzi and Karajan, but this performance has the virtues of freshness and daring. Nothing is held back and Stignani, often a foil to Callas, finds an altogether more credible persona opposite the luminous Tebaldi. Half a century later there was still no Aida (bar Tebaldi's Karajan retake) to match this set.

22. Strauss: Four Last Songs
Lisa della Casa, Vienna Philharmonic Orchestra/Karl Böhm
Decca: Vienna (Musikverein, Grosser Saal), June 1953

The four last songs of Richard Strauss – a fifth turned up after the edition went to print – were premiered at the Royal Albert Hall on 22 May 1950, eight months after the composer's death, by the phenomenal Kirsten Flagstad, conducted by Wilhelm Furtwängler (a radio tape can be found on the Norwegian label, Simax). Confusion and controversy set in. Flagstad had sung the songs in the order Strauss wrote them, as falling leaves from a wintry oak. Boosey & Hawkes, the publishers, shuffled the order to open with upbeat Frühling (Springtime).

Sena Jurinac sang the first commercial recording for EMI (Fritz Busch conducting in Stockholm) following the published order and with some interpretative uncertainty. Decca's was the second recording, and it had extra merits. The orchestra was once Strauss's own and the Swiss soprano Lisa della Casa possessed a vocal serenity which, more than Flagstad's steely magnificence, evoked the singing voice of Strauss's wife, Pauline, his lifelong inspiration. The conductor was Karl Böhm, a card-playing chum of the composer's, and the mood was more sunny than commemorative. Tempi were brisk, the breathing natural.

Most conspicuously of all, the order in which the songs were sung differed both from Flagstad and from Boosey, beginning logically with Beim Schlafengehen (On Going to Sleep), a farewell by an uncomplicated artist looking back on a life he had relished to the full and was ready to relinquish with a smile. September came next, followed by Frühling and finally Im Abendrot (At Dusk). Della Casa sang without operatic affectation, as if she were privately recalling a beloved grandfather, and the solos of the Vienna concertmaster, Wolfgang Schneiderhahn, have the sweetness of fond regret. The Decca producer was Victor Olof, on the verge of a scandalous defection to EMI, and his balancing was exemplary for a late mono recording. Many singers have subsequently shone in this cycle – Schwarzkopf (Szell), Lucia Popp (Tennstedt), Jessye Norman (Masur), Karita Mattila (Abbado) – but Della Casa was first on record to give the songs credence and joy.

23. *Puccini: Tosca*
Maria Callas, Tito Gobbi, Giuseppe di Stefano, Chorus and
Orchestra of La Scala/Victor De Sabata
EMI: Milan (La Scala), 10–21 August 1953

It may be the most perennial of operas but in the public mind there is only one Tosca. Never the sweetest of voices or natures, Maria Callas brought veracity to a grubby plot and ferocity to its apotheosis. Groped by the sleazebag Scarpia, who has arrested and tortured her artist husband, Tosca grabs a fruit knife and stabs him dead. Callas, on stage, would strike so hard with the plastic prop knife that she drew blood from Gobbi, her regular partner, and gasps from the audience, who thought she had really killed him.

Their recording, with Giuseppe di Stefano a heroic Cavaradossi and the La Scala team under its austere music director Victor de Sabata, was made early enough in her career for Callas to take guidance from a conductor. De Sabata drilled her for half an hour in the end aria of the second act, making her sing the final line thirty times until she emitted a low growl that lay far beneath her register, a sound so ominous it chills the marrow. The Te Deum scene took six hours before De Sabata expressed satisfaction. EMI's Walter Legge sat back and let events take their course, selecting the best takes from miles of tape when the musicians had dispersed.

The Callas voice, never conventionally beautiful, possessed a theatrical dimension that was felt more on record than on stage. Her Vissi d'arte, on her knees before Scarpia, goes squally with stress but the listener is made to believe in her agony more than in the tonal perfection of other heroines. Callas on record always lives out her characters. The portrait may not be lovely, but it is brutally real.

Tosca was the last role that she sang on stage before retiring in 1965, hurt in pride and heart when the Greek shipowner Aristotle Onassis left her to marry Jacqueline Kennedy. No artist would ever match her recorded appeal. In the twenty-first century, three decades after her death, Callas stills sells more records than any living soprano.

24. Brahms: First Piano Concerto (D Minor)
Arthur Rubinstein, Chicago Symphony Orchestra/Fritz Reiner
RCA: Chicago (Orchestra Hall), 17 April 1954

Beaten by CBS to the LP, RCA got in first with stereo. After experimental sessions in New York with the audio-aware Leopold Stokowski, the engineers went to Boston to tape a Berlioz Damnation of Faust with Charles Munch. The results were spacious but swoony beside good mono sound. The engineers moved on to Chicago, where the orchestra had a tough new music director in Fritz Reiner, and the label's top-selling pianist, Arthur Rubinstein, was down to play the first Brahms concerto.

Conductor and soloist had a blazing row over Reiner's casual remark that Chopin was an effeminate composer and probably gay, an insult that Rubinstein took personally and nationally, being Polish by birth. In a frigid atmosphere the two professionals set about performing the warmest of concertos, a richly coloured tapestry of romantic sound. Rubinstein reined in his usual exuberance and played with limpid precision, the piano set realistically centre-left, instead of far to the front as he preferred. Reiner summoned gorgeously lyrical playing from the orchestra, opening the Adagio with velvety strings and tartly spiced winds and maintaining the tightest imaginable control of line throughout three-quarters of a very short hour. Recordings by Curzon, Solomon, Brendel and Gilels will all have their advocates, but the tempering of a wilful soloist by a strong-minded conductor provides a taut backdrop for music of sublime beauty and awesome structure.

The producers Richard Mohr and Jack Pfeiffer, with engineers Lewis Layton and Leslie Chase (all legendary names to audiophiles), limited themselves to three microphones, each wired to a separate channel, giving a precise image of left and right and an overview of centre. This was stereo's coming-of-age recording, the session where it proved its worth, and the team returned jubilantly to base. Much to their dismay, the record was not issued for another four years, while labels wrangled over a unified stereo format and the public was persuaded to invest in new systems.

25. Bach: Goldberg Variations
Glenn Gould
Columbia (Sony-BMG): New York (30th Street studio),
10 and 14–16 June 1955

The Canadian pianist made his first major-label recording in a goldfish bowl of a studio, his every eccentricity gawked at by media. 'Gould spurns the sandwiches sent in to the recording crew, subsisting instead on arrowroot biscuits washed down with his special spring water or skimmed milk,' reported the *Herald Tribune*. Few legends have been observed so intently in the making.

Gould was a feature writer's dream. In hot sunshine, he turned up in coat, beret, muffler and gloves, carrying his own piano stool. He soaked his arms in boiling water before playing and popped any number of pills for migraine, eczema or ennui. He sang as he played, in a grumbling basso, and insisted on as many retakes as it took – eighteen in the twelfth variation – before he signed off. 'Let him sing,' said producer Howard H. Scott. 'He played like a god.'

The record was issued in a cover consisting of thirty tiny photographs of the pianist in action, one for each variation. 'We couldn't agree which was best,' said Scott, 'so we compromised and used them all.' The playing was like nothing on earth. It brought a delirious freshness to an austere work, playing excitable riffs on music that had never been made to smile. Unbothered by the occasional wrong note, Gould searched for mood and metre. This, he said, was music that 'rests lightly on the wings of the unchecked wind'.

His personal sound is flinty, slightly brittle, but from the opening phrases he does for the Goldbergs what Casals did for the cello suites, diverting them from Bach's intended purpose – to lull an insomniac count to sleep – into a realm of rapt spirituality. Gould's touch commands attention, evoking a numinous parallel world into which he alone possesses the password. From start to finish, the playing is unexpected, sometimes helter-skelter (second variation), sometimes so slow and quiet (twenty-sixth) that one wonders whether his mind has not drifted momentarily elsewhere until the sheer concentrated effort of communication surges through. No one on record had ever treated a piano, or a piece of music, in any comparable way. Gould burst onto the scene like a fiery angel, a comet from another constellation.

Nine years later he gave up public appearances to spend the rest of his working life in a record studio, usually at night, working obsessively over an eclectic range of music that embraced Arnold Schoenberg, Richard Strauss and several Canadians of no great merit. The Goldbergs were central to his artistic make-up. In 1981 he had a second stab at the set, more comprehensively but less revealingly. A year later, he was dead, aged 50.

26. Mozart: The Marriage of Figaro
Vienna Philharmonic Orchestra/Erich Kleiber
Decca: Vienna (Redoutensaal), June 1955

This was fantasy casting. Vienna, in the decade after the Second World War, had an unmatchable Mozart ensemble with the likes of Hilde Gueden (Countess), Lisa della Casa (Susanna) and Alfred Poell (Count Almaviva) on the payroll of the bombed-out State Opera, which was being rebuilt from rubble by public subscription. For the bicentenary of Mozart's birth, the British company Decca (which had the Vienna Philharmonic Orchestra on exclusive contract) set about recording the three Da Ponte operas with idiomatic Austrians – Don Giovanni under Josef Krips, Così fan Tutte with Karl Böhm and Figaro in the most experienced of hands, conducted by a man who had fled Hitler's Europe to South America and was now back as the continent's most sought-after guest conductor.

Erich Kleiber, as a boy, had heard Mahler conduct Mozart in Vienna. He went on to lead the Berlin State Opera into the modern era, giving the world premiere of Berg's Wozzeck after more than 120 sectional rehearsals. After the war he lifted Covent Garden onto a higher plane of performance and confined himself in late middle age to conducting the pieces he felt really mattered. Before approaching Figaro he spent months in Vienna scouring early manuscripts and texts. At his insistence, all recitatives (or spoken parts) were to be recorded for the first time.

The working habits of the Vienna Philharmonic were perpetually chaotic, with players coming and going to better-paid gigs. But Kleiber stamped his authority on the opening of the overture with a tempo that felt so organically correct that musicians and singers were riveted to his baton through more than a fortnight of sessions. Much as Kleiber consulted Mozart's ur-texts, the drama plays out at a contemporary, convincing twentieth-century pace.

The singing is unobtrusively beautiful. Two Italians, Cesare Siepi and Fernando Corena, were brought in to sing Figaro and Bartolo while a Belgian, Suzanne Danco, was Cherubino. But the atmosphere is indubitably Viennese and the mischief stems from Mozart himself. One aria after another – Porgi amor, Voi che sapete, Venite – rolls out from Della Casa, Danco and Gueden like a string of pearls, not a flaw to be heard under the recording microscope. This, felt junior producer Peter Andry, had to be as good as it gets.[5]

The release was timed for November 1955 to coincide with the reopening of the Vienna Opera. Böhm resigned as director before the opening and Herbert von Karajan was waiting in the wings. Kleiber was invited to participate in the reconsecration with a Verdi Requiem but, amid Viennese intrigue, was landed with inferior soloists. Hurt and depressed, he resumed his wanderings. On 27 January 1956, 200 years to the day after Mozart's birth, he was found dead in a bath in a Swiss hotel.

5. Comment to the author, June 2005.

27. Bartók: Concerto for Orchestra
Chicago Symphony Orchestra/Fritz Reiner
RCA (Sony-BMG): Chicago (Orchestra Hall),
22 October 1955

In 1943 the wealthy Boston conductor Serge Koussevitsky gave Bartók $1,000 for an orchestral piece at a time when the self-exiled Hungarian was sick with leukaemia and struggling to pay medical bills ('We live from half-year to half-year,' he told friends). Few were aware that the commission had been discreetly stimulated by Fritz Reiner, the Pittsburgh music director, who had known the great composer since college days in Budapest. It had been Reiner who signed the affidavit that gained Bartók and his wife entry to the United States.

The result of the commission exceeded all expectations – not just a new work but an entirely original form, a score in which every instrument of the orchestra gets a chance to shine, within a vigorous Socractic dialogue that served as a working model for the United Nations, a forum in which every country, no matter how small, would have its right to a say.

Koussevitsky conducted a celebrated premiere in December 1944, nationally broadcast and gaining the work instant masterpiece status. Reiner directed the second performance soon after in Pittsburgh. Over the next decade the Concerto for Orchestra was played 200 times, more than any other contemporary orchestral work. On record, though, it remained elusive. Koussevitsky gave a literal rendition on RCA, colourful and bombastic; Eduard van Beinum traversed the score in Amsterdam with an excess of elegance; others over-enthused.

It took Reiner to bring out the waspish wit, the scurrilous parody on Shostakovich's seventh symphony (seen as a Soviet triumph) and the yearning for a Hungary that neither man would see again. With a superior orchestra in Chicago, Reiner went for precision at wild speed – the Pesante section of the finale leaves a mere listener breathless – but also for tenderness and towering emotion. In Reiner's hands the work comes together as a structural unity rather than a run of cameos. You hardly need to know that Bartók is paying respectful tribute to the instruments of the orchestra. The music is simply monumental.

28. Tchaikovsky: Symphonies 4–6
Leningrad Philharmonic Orchestra/Kurt Sanderling, Evgeny Mravinsky
DG: Vienna (Musikvereinsaal), June 1956

Under communism, the world was denied the sight and sound of Russia's top ensembles. When the travel ban was slightly eased in the year that Khrushchev denounced Stalin's crimes, Vienna received a visit from the Leningrad Philharmonic under its gaunt chief conductor, Evgeny Mravinsky, and his German-exile deputy, Kurt Sanderling.

Undernourished, shadowed by spies and fearful for their families back home, the players had no unmonitored contact with Viennese musicians or audiences and dared not smile at concertgoers in the lobby for fear of being hauled in and interrogated by the organs of state. Their only means of communication was music, and that was blazingly expressive. The plangent edge to the woodwind confirmed a tradition stretching back to Tchaikovsky, whose major works this orchestra had premiered. Its swagger of ownership was unmistakable in these performances, turning the corners in the score without needing to mind the kerb.

Sanderling opened with an imposing Fourth, unfolded with reduced bombast and skilled story-telling. Mravinsky, previously unheard in western Europe, directed the ominous Fifth and mournful Pathétique symphonies with grave humanity, hinting at a suffering that was shared by all on earth. The bassoon solos in the Fifth underlined the cultural difference between Russian and Viennese sorrow; the finale of the Pathétique was wrenchingly tragic. Nothing of this sort had been heard on record and Deutsche Grammophon's Elsa Schiller took a flight to Moscow to negotiate a licence for release in the gently thawing international climate. But the thaw was short-lived, and so was the release. Four months later Soviet forces crushed the Hungarian uprising and the Cold War froze over once more.

Four years passed before the Kremlin allowed Mravinsky and the Leningraders to fly to London and re-record the symphonies in stereo. The sessions were held at Wembley Town Hall, away from the heart of the city, and the playing lacked the same urgency. The Vienna concerts had the thrill of revelation.

29. Grieg, Schumann: Piano Concertos
Solomon, Philharmonia Orchestra/Herbert Menges
EMI/Testament: London (Abbey Road), 1956

Early in the LP era, some bright spark in a pin-striped suit noticed that Grieg and Schumann each wrote one piano concerto and that both were in the same key, A minor, and of similar length. The enterprising fellow slapped them on either side of a black disc and they have been inseparable ever since, despite their uneven temperament. The Grieg is a splashy song of Norway with lots of noise and little emotional subtlety while the Schumann plumbs depths of torment and madness. Few artists succeed in balancing these discrepancies. Solomon achieved a coherent fusion.

A plainspoken East End tailor's son who made his name giving wartime concerts for the armed forces, Solomon Cutner (he dropped the surname) was, with Clifford Curzon, the foremost British pianist of his generation. Impassive on stage, tubby and prematurely bald, his reserve was a welcome antidote to the show-manship of most piano stars. With Solomon, thoughtfulness pre-vailed, reducing music to a germinal idea. He had a direct line to one composer – his teacher, Mathilde Verne, had studied with Clara Schumann – and a tactful affinity with the other. His per-formances sound just right: tuneful, masterfully narrated and with just enough suspense to hold the ear unerringly to the speaker.

He never had a chance to shine on the international stage for, weeks after making this recording, he suffered a brain haemorrhage at the age of fifty-one. He made a good recovery, had the use of all limbs and faculties and played a full game of tennis but, though he lived until 1988, Solomon never touched the keyboard again.

30. Weill: Berlin and American Theatre Songs
Lotte Lenya
Columbia (Sony-BMG): Hamburg (Friedrich Ebert Halle),
5–7 July 1955; New York (30th Street studio),
5–9 August 1957

There was only one Lotte Lenya and without her there could have been no Kurt Weill. Mad as she drove the little bald composer with her vanities and infidelities, Lenya's was the voice that drove Weill to the edge of aural possibility, to the point where singing and speaking became indistinguishable (a terrain that Schoenberg sought less successfully in Sprechgesang).

Lenya's was not so much a voice as an urban rumble, traffic heard from the twenty-fourth storey of a tower block. Weill was a small-town technician, disturbed by city lights. They had been on the point of getting divorced in Berlin while he composed The Rise and Fall of the City of Mahagonny, in which Lenya epitomized the abrasive nervousness of pre-Hitler Germany. Reunited in exile, they found a new language as Weill wrote for Broadway and Lenya toned down her man-eating delivery.

Although her singing was never beautiful, her rhythms were impeccable and her roles unrivalled. As Pirate Jenny she was any man's. In Surabaya Jonny she teased and taunted. As Macky's knife she slashed. There is more sex in one of her demisemiquavers than in the collected works of Madonna. Many, Madonna included, tried to replicate her edginess – Mary Martin, Ute Lemper, Teresa Stratas, Julia Migenes, Anne Sofie von Otter – but Lenya is inimitably daring, an art in her own right. In the Broadway rep, she is unrepentantly provocative. Weill might have pitched at Middle America in Knickerbocker Holiday, but carrot-topped Lenya is nobody's housewife and when she sings It Never Was You every man knows that he cannot be sure of her. On Weill's death in 1950 she performed the supreme act of love by recording these songs, retrieving his work from looming oblivion.

31. Ravel: Daphnis et Chloé
London Symphony Orchestra/Pierre Monteux
Decca: London (Kingsway Hall), 27–28 April 1959

Never a podium peacock, Pierre Monteux was one of the quiet makers of music. Among the premieres he gave were Stravinsky's Petrushka and Rite of Spring and Debussy's Jeux; among the symphony orchestras he directed were Boston (1919–24), Paris (1929–38) and San Francisco (1936–52).

At the age of eighty-three, despairing of inconsistent French orchestras, Monteux took on a challenge in London where three strong bands were competing for record dates with the fiery brilliance of EMI's Philharmonia. Monteux struck up a rapport with the LSO and agreed in the summer of 1958 to become its principal conductor – on a twenty-five-year contract, with an option for renewal. His optimism was as unquenchable as his French accent was irresistible. Against the monolithic structuralism of Otto Klemperer at the Philharmonia, Monteux introduced a sensibility for grace and gesture, for refined detail within the magnificence of a musical edifice.

Ravel's great love ballet was a work he had brought into existence for Diaghilev back in 1912. He drew a Debussian shimmer from the seductive strings and a seductive twinkle from the woodwinds. The awakening at the start of the third scene is, in Monteux's interpretation, the antithesis of Wagner: a dawn of defining translucence that could never have been seen by anyone other than a Mediterranean Frenchman.

Playing always felt like fun when Monteux was around and several players went to private lessons in conducting. The principal horn, Barry Tuckwell, and leader of the second violins, Neville

Marriner, went on to successful baton careers. The LSO's next chief, Andre Previn, was another pupil. Monteux's influence on record was far greater than the few records he made.

Decca had agreed to take the uncommercial Daphnis on condition he squeezed the entire ballet onto one LP. Monteux, unflustered, brought the work in at just over fifty minutes, leaving room for a Pavane pour une infante défunte. He was, said producer John Culshaw, the antithesis of 'the orgasm-a-minute school of conducting'.

32. Shostakovich: Violin and Cello Concertos
David Oistrakh, Mstislav Rostropovich
CBS (Sony-BMG): New York (Carnegie Hall), 2 January 1956;
Philadelphia (Broadwood Hotel), 8 November 1959

Dmitri Shostakovich was fortunate in his soloists. Two violin concertos were written for David Oistrakh, close friend and inspired artist; both cello concertos were done for Mstislav Rostropovich, equally eloquent in his advocacy. On both occasions, the first concerto was superior to the second.

After Stalin's death de-iced the Cold War, America was agog to hear Soviet artists and record companies keen to capture them in new works. Oistrakh brought the violin concerto to Carnegie Hall ten weeks after giving its first performance in Leningrad. He described it as 'one of the composer's deepest conceptions' and played it with explicitly nervous energy, hinting at the Great Terror, at the years it lay in a bottom drawer before Shostakovich dared show him the manuscript. The conductor, Dmitri Mitropoulos, had just given the tenth symphony its US premiere and seemed to have an intuitive understanding of the composer's coded messages. The concerto is written without trumpets or trombones, a denial of Kremlin bombast. It plays up the plaintive lone voice of the violin against a grumbling backdrop before, in the second and fourth movements, dancing ironic rings around puffed-up tyrannies.

Rostropovich introduced the mellower cello concerto with Eugene Ormandy and the Philadelphia Orchestra three years later in front of invited delegations of US and Soviet composers intent on simulating big power harmony. His interpretation revelled in romantic tunefulness. Once again the concerto was wet on the page, a month after its Moscow premiere. Rostropovich charms his way through some of the more intractable passages; his most fervent moments come in the second-movement Moderato, where the pain is deep seated. Shostakovich sat in the hall, and later in the recording booth. Don Hunstein's session photographs show him vivacious and relaxed, almost dancing onto the stage to take bows with soloist and conductor. Rostropovich would later explain that this concerto is suffused 'with the suffering of the whole Russian people'.

33. Schubert: Death and the Maiden
Amadeus Quartet
DG: Hanover (Beethovensaal), 3–6 April 1959

Three Austro-German Jewish refugees met in a British detention camp early in the Second World War. On release, they met a British student of Jewish extraction and formed a string quartet, taking Mozart's middle name. Their debut, in London's Wigmore Hall in January 1948, was paid for by Imogen Holst, the composer's daughter. The Amadeus Quartet went on to give 4,000 concerts over the next four decades and their disbandment, after the death of viola player Peter Schidlof, made the top of the front page of the *New York Times* on 11 August 1987.

The group's fame was founded on records. After a brief spell with EMI they transferred to Deutsche Grammophon for long runs of Mozart, Haydn, Beethoven, Schubert, Brahms. Mistrustful of modernity – they played no Schoenberg, Janáček or Shostakovich – the Amadeus were nonetheless sympathetic to Benjamin Britten, who wrote his deathbed third quartet for them.

Their success was founded on incessant tension. Voluble in their disagreements, the players refused to share the same train compartment when travelling and wore their individuality grumpily on stage, so that each performance was a contest of wills. They softened over the years but recordings from their prime sound, for all the intensity of rehearsal, almost impetuous in their attack. This Schubert session was their turning point, their debut on DG. The opening attack is functionally brisk and not particularly beautiful, but as the players unfold the story it acquires a searing edge of quest and loss, funereally sad in the Andante, furiously resentful in the finale, and propelled throughout by four vehement, stubborn personalities. There was nothing comfortable or domestic in their music making.

34. *Bizet: Symphony in C Major, L'Arlésienne Suites*
French National Radio Orchestra, Royal Philharmonic
Orchestra/Thomas Beecham
EMI: Paris (Salle Wagram), October–November 1959; London
(Abbey Road), 21 November 1956

Sir Thomas Beecham scorned all English composers except Delius and conducted French scores with the finesse of a Michelin-starred chef. Where other English-speaking conductors encountered nothing but recalcitrance and sour winds from Paris orchestras, for Beecham they sparkled like the Eiffel Tower on Christmas Eve. A patent medicine heir who squandered his Beecham Pills fortune on bringing music to ungrateful compatriots, he spent his last years as a tax exile in France, complaining that socialism had made England a place where 'it is impossible to live and no one can afford to die'. The French danced to his beat with verve and daring and Beecham brought some of their frothier treasures to world attention.

Bizet's symphony in C, written at age seventeen, was discovered only in 1935 in an archive of the Paris Conservatoire. The aged Felix Weingartner gave the world premiere and Walter Legge offered it to Beecham for recording, but he was not much interested and it was given to a session conductor, Walter Goehr. It took a couple of decades for Beecham to discover the delights of this tuneful score, an early anticipation, and then he loved it so much that he recorded it twice – first mono, then stereo. There is no discernible depth to this college exercise, even in the woodwindy, winsome Adagio, but Beecham made it so much his own that, after his death in 1961, it practically vanished from the repertoire.

The Arlésienne suites, commissioned as entr'actes for an Alphonse Daudet play, are a trivial patchwork of indigenous themes that Beecham treats with childlike wonder – D'you hear that tune, m'boy? – and a lashing of leathery, sceptical wit. There is a passage at the opening of the first suite that he makes sound like the retired section of a Lancashire brass band, a private joke that few but this son of the English industrial north would possibly appreciate. For mischief and malice, pleasure and pomp, there was no greater entertainer in music – or, indeed, no finer interpreter of froth.

35. *Bartók: Piano Concertos 1–3*
Géza Anda, Berlin Radio Symphony Orchestra/Ferenc Fricsay
DG: Berlin (Jesus-Christus-Kirche), September 1959 and
October 1960

Musical life in post-war West Berlin was rebuilt by the Hungarian Ferenc Fricsay (1914–63), music director of the opera house and radio orchestra. Before Karajan came along, he was Deutsche Grammophon's chief conductor, delivering thrilling performances of the Dvořák and Verdi requiems, the Mozart operas and much else, especially modern music. In Bartók, his own teacher, the intensity redoubled.

Géza Anda, another graduate of the Liszt Academy in Budapest, played the Salzburg Festival every year from 1952 until his death in 1976, a longer run than any other pianist; his pupils included the future DG boss Andreas Holschneider. Between them, Fricsay and Anda exerted a principled influence on the course of classical recording.

Together in Bartók they were beyond compare, giving more than sixty performances of the second concerto alone. Much as they revered the composer, both men took an alarmingly flexible approach to the music, stretching each other's tempi, one darting ahead while the other dauntingly dallied. This angularity, Hungarian to a fault, was balanced by a serene tenderness in the slow movements, languid as a summer's night in Szeged. Contrast and conflict keep the attention on a knife's edge. At the opening of the first concerto, while Anda sets out his theme, Fricsay distracts the ear with orchestral commentaries in a typically Bartókian way, allowing nocturnal savageries to invade our safety. The second concerto feels even more dangerous and the third, though classically ingratiating, ripples with dark corners and fears. Beyond the public presentation, secrets are being shared in an impenetrable expatriate dialect.

Intimately as they knew the works and each other, Fricsay and Anda took nine full sessions to record the last two concertos, striving for unattainable resolutions. Fricsay knew he was mortally ill with cancer and that these might be his last works. Each collaboration, said Anda, marked 'the renewal of an almost brotherly friendship'.[6] The discs won a sheaf of awards and fixed Bartók, never the easiest of composers, permanently at the heart of concerto repertoire.

36. Bach: St Matthew Passion
Philharmonia Orchestra/Otto Klemperer
EMI: London (Kingsway Hall), 1960–61

When Otto Klemperer got around to recording Bach's great oratorio, he was in his mid-seventies and slowing down – beating so slowly, in fact, that soloists had trouble sustaining breath. In a

6. Sleeve note.

coffee-break huddle they agreed that one of them had to speak up. Dietrich Fischer-Dieskau drew the short straw.

'Dr Klemperer,' ventured the respectful baritone.

'Ja, Fischer?'

'Dr Klemperer, I had a dream last night, and in my dream Johann Sebastian Bach thanked me for singing the Passion, but he said, "Why so slow?"'

Klemperer scowled, tapped his stand and resumed conducting at exactly half the tempo. The singers were almost deoxygenated when he rasped: 'Fischer?'

'Yes, Dr Klemperer.'

'I, too, had a dream last night. And in my dream, Johann Sebastian Bach thanked me for conducting his Passion, but he said, "Tell me, Dr Klemperer – *who is this Fischer*?"'

Slow it was, but never has Bach sounded so monumentally assured, performed in an imperious, archaic style that echoed Mendelssohn's approach when he performed this work to revive Bach's dormant reputation in 1830. Within the stately magnificence of the narrative there is subtle flexibility in Klemperer's beat, allowing constant surprise and challenge in the shaping of a phrase. Anathema to the lickety-split early-music moguls, the performance feels faithful in a spiritual sense to its creator's intentions.

The soloists were Elisabeth Schwarzkopf, Christa Ludwig, Nicolai Gedda, Peter Pears, Walter Berry, Helen Watts, Geraint Evans and Ottakar Kraus, a fantasy pack assembled by the perfectionist producer Walter Legge. The orchestra was London's finest and some of the solo passages verge on the celestial. Fischer-Dieskau would dine out ever after on the Klemperer story, but one of the soloists refused to accept the conductor's writ. Peter Pears, Britten's partner, insisted that his recitatives had to be taken at a snappier pace. Using his lover's clout, Pears sneaked in his changes after the conductor had approved the final take.

37. Bach: Concerto for Two Violins and String Ensemble
David and Igor Oistrakh, Royal Philharmonic Orchestra/
Eugene Goossens
DG: London (Wembley Town Hall), February 1961

David Oistrakh (1908–74) was a legend among violinists from the day he won the Queen Elisabeth competition in Brussels in 1937. For almost two decades he was kept behind the Iron Curtain. His son Igor was among the first Soviets allowed out after Stalin's death, playing in London for the impresarios Lilian and Victor Hochhauser and paving the way for his father's emergence. David Oistrakh joined the Hochhauser bill in 1954, flying on to a Carnegie Hall debut fixed by Sol Hurok in November 1955. Menuhin and Isaac Stern led the acclaim for his unflappable technique and lightly worn profundity. Heifetz refused to greet him, fearing (he said) that he might suffer McCarthyite persecution for mingling with Commies.

David Oistrakh's playing owed nothing to self-promotion. He took a more leisurely tempo than flashy virtuosi and played with a smile that concealed the stress of living under terror. He was initially refused permission to travel with his son for fear one of them might defect (an option he discussed with Hochhauser). When DG paid the Moscow authorities hard currency for a double recording, the pair were suffused with joy at sharing each other's company in a strange land.

In a draughty London hall in dreary midwinter, the rules of musical collaboration and baroque performance were suddenly suspended as father and son entered a dialogue that they could not freely engage in at home. Instead of being formal and well rehearsed, the performance was spontaneous, contradictory and mutually respectful. There was no reluctance on either side to interrupt but the reciprocal affection, most intensely expressed in the gentle Largo, melts all differences of age and outlook. This is a paragon of musical communication, a disc to be played in moments of grief and isolation. It tells us that no man is an island, that we can always find a music to touch the ones we know and love, that understanding is but a bow-stroke away.

38. Prokofiev: Piano Sonata No. 8 (with Debussy: Estampes, Preludes; Scriabin: Fifth Sonata)
Sviatoslav Richter
DG: London (Wembley Town Hall), July 1961

Richter was the last of the Russian legends to be let out. A cultured Odessa pianist of Swedish-German parentage, furnished with an inimitable timbre and encyclopaedic musical knowledge, he had voted as a juror for the American Van Cliburn at the 1958 Tchaikovsky international piano competition and was made to wait another two years before the Kremlin granted him a passport under a US–Soviet cultural exchange.

Nervous in North America, shadowed by minders and alarmed by material wealth, he cut a big-selling Brahms second concerto in Chicago which he deplored as 'one of my worst records . . . I've lost count of the number of times I've listened to it in attempt to find something good in it.' On record he was elusive, his best performances confined to scrappy-sounding Russian pressings, until, landing in London in July 1961, he gave five public performances in ten days, interspersed with recordings – the two Liszt concertos with the LSO and Kirill Kondrashin for Philips, followed by an exhilarating solo recital of Debussy and Prokofiev for DG.

French Impressionism brought out Richter's phenomenal range of colours. His Prokofiev was both intuitive and remarkably unpresumptuous, avoiding any show of personal acquaintance with the composer, whose seventh sonata he had premiered during the blackest months of war. The Eighth had gone to his rival, Emil Gilels, and Richter considered it the richest of the cycle, 'like a tree whose branches have to bear the weight of its fruit'. This performance is rapt, possessive and emotionally detached, as much a discovery for the artist as for his listeners, with harmonies that are quite off the scale of human cognizance, a sound like no other and a landmark in piano lore. Richter said the sonata contained 'a complete human life, with all its contradictions and anomalies'. Repeated hearing confirms its massiveness, as well as the genius of its soloist. 'I don't play for an audience,' Richter used to say, 'I play for myself. If I derive any satisfaction then the audience, too, is content.'

39. Copland: Clarinet Concerto (with Bernstein: Prelude, Fugue and Riffs)
Benny Goodman, Columbia Symphony Strings/Aaron Copland
Columbia (Sony-BMG): New York (Manhattan Center),
20 February 1963

Copland, in 1947, was famous for Appalachian Spring, El Salon Mexico and Fanfare for the Common Man. A shy, ugly, gay Jewish socialist from Brooklyn, he made music that reflected America to itself as a simple, honest, manly, pastoral land. The paradox was ignored by everyone except Senator McCarthy, who had Copland high on his list.

Low on spirits and funds, Copland took $2,000 for a clarinet concerto from the jazzman Benny Goodman, who forgot all about it until a two-year deadline passed and other soloists showed interest. Goodman hastily organized a national radio premiere for the new work on 6 November 1950, conducted by Fritz Reiner. Soloist and conductor differed, the reviews were tepid and the reception did not improve with a series of further performances.

The turnaround came when Copland, a novice conductor and unpushy man, asked to direct the recording. He took the opening movement at half pace to settle Goodman's nerves and this version 'really launched the concerto'. A decade later the two men played it again in what Goodman promised would be a reconsidered approach. This time he tapped into Copland's language, finding swing in classical structure.

The concerto opens with a phrase from Mahler's ninth symphony, which it twists from bleak tragedy to pastel elegy. The dialogue of soloist and strings (plus harp and piano) – sociable, mildly astringent, warmly cocooned – acquires a Brazilian under-beat, an awareness of other American cultures. The conclusion is upbeat, happy-smiley beneath a glass showcase. 'I think it will make everyone weep,' said Copland.

40. *Ives: Fourth Symphony*
American Symphony Orchestra/Leopold Stokowski
CBS: New York (Carnegie Hall), 25 April 1965

Charles Ives was an American original. A self-made insurance millionaire, he wrote orchestral music that veered from the ama-teurishly banal to the unplayably complex and kept much of it in a drawer for decades, fearing rejection. After his death in 1954 Leopold Stokowski, with an eye to the spectacular, made two attempts in Houston to premiere the massive fourth symphony, which is furnished with chorus, separate chamber ensemble and a percussion section including bells and gongs – and which opens with the kind of backwoods chapel hymn ('Watchman, tell us of the night') that gets sung in B-westerns just before the baddies wheel into town. Integrating unadorned simplicity with the tonal complexity of succeeding passages based on his thorny piano sonata is just one of the challenges of this frustratingly elusive piece.

Twice Stokowski gave up, despairing of inadequate part-writing and contradictory polyrhythms that threw the orchestra into cacophonous confusion. Getting all the bits and bands to play together was beyond the wit of one man. Things got worse. The second movement tramps with the Pilgrim Fathers through swamps and jungles (and the discordances of Ives's second sonata) before reaching redemption in the Fourth of July and some inti-mations of early jazz. The fugue is based partly on Ives's string quartet and the finale, glossingly, on Nearer My God to Thee.

Stoki decided to crack the nut by employing two extra conduc-tors – David Katz and José Serebrier – to beat the cross-rhythms.

Suddenly everything fell into place and Ives was revealed as the source of America's greatest symphony, a rambling, wildly energetic, unpreachy and none-too-scrupulous evocation of the national momentum. For the conductor, in his eighties, it was the apotheosis of his commitment to modern music and his record label recorded the occasion live, fearing the work might never be repeated, for reasons of cost and complexity. No subsequent recording captures the same shock of discovering a musical continent.

41. Schubert: Piano Duets
Benjamin Britten, Sviatoslav Richter
Decca: Aldeburgh (Parish Church and Jubilee Hall), 20 June 1964 and 22 June 1965

In musical conversations one player or other always tries to take the lead, play louder, push the pace. And when a famous composer sits at one end of the piano, protocol demands that any performer at the other end yields precedence. There is no such thing as equality in a duet. This record is a rare exception.

In June 1964 the Russian pianist Sviatoslav Richter arrived with his wife at the Aldeburgh Festival as guests of its founder, Benjamin Britten. Hardly had he checked in to the simple East Anglian hotel than Richter demanded to play for Britten's public. The composer found him a dead mid-morning slot and slipped unannounced onto the piano stool beside him. Privately, Britten considered him 'the best pianist ever'.

Listen as closely as you like to this recording and you will not be able to tell which of the two performers played primo and which secondo in the Schubert A flat major Variations, such was their mutual respect and sensitivity. Critics craned their necks to see who had his feet on the pedals, but it hardly mattered, for this was a Parnassian dialogue in which neither man moderated his momentum or gave ground to the other, yet together they found an elevated plane of discourse. At one level, this was Hausmusik, a domestic recreation played by two family members in candlelight between dinner and bed. But the ebb and flow of the variations reveals shadows on the composer's mind, anxieties of illness and death that are brought out even more troublingly in the Britten–Richter performance the following year of the ominous F-minor Fantasy, a work of the composer's final flowering. The two recitals were aired on the BBC and released by Decca. There is nothing like them on record.

42. *Bernstein: Chichester Psalms*
John Bogart (alto), Camerata Singers, New York Philharmonic Orchestra/Leonard Bernstein
Columbia (Sony-BMG): New York (Manhattan Center), July 1965

Apart from Bruckner and Scriabin, Leonard Bernstein recorded practically all the major symphonists, classical and contemporary, some of them twice over, as well as every worthwhile American composer alive or dead. Exhilarating on the podium, leaping higher than any maestro outside the Olympics, Bernstein's enthusiasms were dulled on record by over-bright sound in his CBS heyday, while his second coming on Deutsche Grammophon was often wayward in tempo and expression, the line of argument bent towards his current fancy. For clarity and precision on record, Bernstein was usually outshone by Karajan, Haitink and Solti, his European rivals.

In American music, though, he was unarguably supreme. No maestro did more to elucidate the crabby genius of Charles Ives (whom he called the Grandma Moses of music), the vivid timbres of Aaron Copland, the Norman Rockwell landscapes of Roy Harris, the consolations of Samuel Barber – above all, the swinging rhythms of George Gershwin, with whom he powerfully empathized.

His own symphonic music suffered the backlash of his success as a conductor and as a Broadway composer. Critics disparaged two of his three symphonies, accepting only the Age of Anxiety as a valid work, and the Mass he wrote for the Kennedys was dismissed quite rightly as an embarrassment of excess. Eclectic and occasionally glib, Bernstein lacked the concentration at his peak to sustain a major concert work in which there are no distractions of stage and showmanship.

There are two exceptions in the canon – the platonic Serenade for violin and orchestra, championed by Isaac Stern, and the Chichester Psalms, commissioned by the progressive Dean of an English cathedral. Bernstein rose to this challenge with mischievous ingenuity. He composed verses from three Psalms in biblical Hebrew, a language older than Christianity and unsung in consecrated Anglican premises. The texts overflowed with lyrical exaltation and the love of one God – words that are a joy to sing and to hear, with a delicious solo for boy treble as the central section, framed by a Davidian harp and percussive cross-rhythms. Bernstein finished the work in May 1965, premiered it in England in July, took it into studio as soon as he got home and had the LP in stores for Christmas. 'How good and pleasant it is, for brothers to dwell together in unity,' was the underlying ecumenical message.

43. *Elgar: Cello Concerto (with Elgar: Sea Pictures)*
Jacqueline du Pré, London Symphony Orchestra/John Barbirolli
EMI: London (Kingsway Hall), 19 August 1965

England's greatest concerto was recorded variously by Casals, Fournier, Tortelier and Rostropovich without ever finding a foothold abroad. One stiflingly hot afternoon in August 1965 a gawky twenty-year-old with a dazzling smile and waist-length blonde hair waltzed into Kingsway Hall, Holborn, to join Sir John Barbirolli and the London Symphony Orchestra in an EMI recording. The band were, for reasons internal, in murmurous mood, unsympathetic to young pretenders. The conductor had his work cut out to protect his debutante protégée.

After two tense and unpleasant sessions, with half the work in the can, Jackie asked to be excused and popped out to a Holborn pharmacy for headache pills. When she returned, she found the studio packed with onlookers. Word had whizzed round musical London that there was a phenomenon in the making and every musician within reach of a Tube station came crowding into the Kingsway dungeon to witness the finale. Few studio sessions have ever played to so live and large an audience.

Where Casals was masterful and possessive, du Pré entered the concerto gently and reflectively, becoming more expansive by degree until passion took over, arching high and low in search of catharsis. Elgar had infused the concerto, written at the end of the First War, with regret for a world destroyed. Du Pré found younger dimensions – pangs of love, fears of death – and swept all before her in a score that gives the soloist little more than five bars' rest from start to finish. If ever there was a definitive performance, this was it. Rostropovich, on hearing this record, erased the concerto from his repertory. The next generation of cellists made it their role model.

Du Pré went on to double stardom – in her own right as a soloist and as the wife of Daniel Barenboim, whom she married in Israel directly after the 1967 war. They went on to record the cello concerto together in Philadelphia in 1970, but presentiments of a terrible disease – she retired with multiple sclerosis in 1973 and died of it in 1987 – marred the second performance. The 1965 disc (paired with Janet Baker's soaring account of Sea Pictures) was Jacqueline du Pré's finest hour. On hearing the playback, she burst into tears and said, 'This is not at all what I meant.'

44. *Wagner: The Ring of the Nibelungen*
Vienna Philharmonic Orchestra/Georg Solti
Decca: Vienna (Sofiensaal), September 1958–November 1965

Sung over four evenings for fifteen hours, Wagner's Ring cycle was untenable on record before the LP, unprojectable before stereo and unaffordable on the kind of budgets labels allocated in the

1950s and consumers set aside for record spending. The Decca project began as a vision of a young producer, John Culshaw, who visited Bayreuth and was appalled at the amount of stage noise picked up by his microphones. If the Ring was to be done on record, he argued, it had to be done in studio. It took him six years to get the green light for a tentative Rheingold, the shortest of the pack.

Culshaw set up stall in a disused Viennese bathhouse with Europe's best orchestra a short bus-ride away. Such was the rarity of the Ring in English-speaking countries that Culshaw was the only member of the recording team who had seen a complete cycle on stage. His conductor was a prematurely bald Hungarian Jew who was based in Frankfurt and incurred the scorn of Vienna Philharmonic master-players. The risks were inordinately high but Georg Solti had an imposing grasp of the Ring, which Culshaw had reconceived as a purely aural concept, free of visual distraction. Sound engineer Gordon Parry was under instruction to simulate the effects of horses and anvils, where required, without supernumerary neighs and bangs. Everything was organized with the naked ear in mind.

The singers spanned three generations. Kirsten Flagstad, lured out of fjord retirement, sang Fricka in Rheingold; Brünnhilde was the soaring Swede Birgit Nilsson. Rhinemaidens included the young Lucia Popp and Gwyneth Jones; Christa Ludwig was Waltraute, Joan Sutherland sang the Woodbird. Wolfgang Windgassen was Siegfried, George London and Hans Hotter sang Wotan and Dietrich Fischer-Dieskau was Gunther in Götterdämmerung. Solti asserted a superhuman span over sessions that lasted seven years, never as subtle as Knappertsbusch or Furtwängler but more accurate throughout. The Decca Ring made his name internationally and made a case for a perfectionism of opera on record that could never be replicated on stage.

In an enterprise of such scope detail can be distortive, but such is the consistency of the dual control exercised by Culshaw and Solti that the smallest of parts reflects the greatness of the whole. The orchestral introduction to Götterdämmerung, followed by the singing of three Norns – Helen Watts, Grace Hoffman, Anita Välkki – is one of the most gripping sequences on record, not just as prelude but as autonomous drama, an act in its own right. Followed by a self-contained Nilsson at sunrise, saving her furies for last, the music exerts a trance-like effect, irresistible and ineluctable.

The Germanic world, fearing loss of heritage, responded with recorded Rings by Karajan in Berlin and Böhm in Bayreuth. An all-French centenary Ring, directed by Patrice Chereau and conducted by Pierre Boulez, was filmed in thirteen television episodes at Bayreuth in 1976. More Rings followed from Sawallisch, Haitink, Janowsky and Levine. None matched Solti for coherence, clarity or numinous wonderment at the world's creation and destruction.

No producer, either, emulated Culshaw's democratic mission. 'The sickness of opera,' wrote Culshaw, 'is that it is a very expensive and exclusive closed shop. Richard Wagner abhorred this attitude a hundred years ago and we are only now beginning to make the slightest progress towards a change. If, by as much as a fraction, the Ring on records has contributed to that change then I believe that all of us connected with it have reason to be pleased.'[7] His artistic ideal was vindicated by the biggest sales ever achieved for a classical performance (see p. 136), a result which meant that more people got to hear Wagner's Ring on record than ever saw it on stage.

45. *Rodrigo: Concierto de Aranjuez*
John Williams, Philadelphia Orchestra/Eugene Ormandy
CBS: Philadelphia (Town Hall), 14 December 1965

The century's most popular concerto, after Rachmaninov's second, was written by a blind man in a fascist tyranny and set in the courtly, escapist splendour of an eighteenth-century Bourbon

7. John Culshaw, *Ring Resounding: The Recording in Stereo of 'Der Ring Des Nibelungen'*, London: Secker & Warburg, 1967, p. 269.

garden. The outer movements are nothing much but the central Adagio swoons with unattainable yearnings. Four strums of the guitar, and the cor anglais takes off on its biggest solo since Dvořák's New World; much of the magic that follows lies in the dialogue between these two instruments. Rodrigo's heartstring theme inspired Miles Davis in Sketches of Spain (1960) and was fitted to the words 'mon amour' by French crooner Richard Anthony. Its attraction, said the composer, was rooted in 'a synthesis of classical and popular, in both form and emotion'. It was not so much unity, though, as hints of fragility and fragmentation that gave the theme its universal appeal.

Rodrigo, rendered sightless by diphtheria at the age of three, was living in poverty and no little fear (his wife was foreign and Jewish) in 1940 when he wrote Aranjuez for the national instrument, the guitar, and became an icon overnight. A capable pianist, he denied ever having tried to play the guitar and was not greatly offended when Spain's grand master, Andrés Segovia, rejected Aranjuez on the grounds that several passages were in the wrong key and some of the music made his guitar plink like a mandolin. (Rodrigo compensated him years later with a more ingratiating Fantasia para un Gentilhombre.)

For want of a Spanish star, the concerto was up for grabs. The Englishman Julian Bream made the early running on record with interpretations that stayed just the right side of schmaltz. But the man who set the stores on fire was a young Australian, John Williams, who had obtained Segovia's blessing on his way to London and his debut recording from the sharp-eared niece of Fred Gaisberg, Isabella Wallich. Williams, signed by CBS, epitomized Sixties cool in long dark hair and loose shirts. The label, for reasons unfathomable, put him together with the staid Philadelphia Orchestra, conducted by Eugene Ormandy, who was never seen out of suit and tie and knew all about classical pops from working with Rachmaninov. Whether by accident or design, the pairing produced a lasting hit, an attraction of opposites.

46. Stravinsky: The Edition – Sacred Works
Various artists and orchestras under the direction of the composer
CBS (Sony-BMG): New York and Toronto 1962–66

Igor Stravinsky was the first composer to have his complete works recorded while he was still alive. Not just alive, but in the process of exchanging the styles that made him famous – Russian ballet and neo-classicism – for the uncommercial outer fringes of acrid atonality. 'As he himself has pointed out, Igor Stravinsky has survived his own popularity,' wrote his friend Goddard Lieberson, president of Columbia Records, in 1962. 'He has neither succumbed to it . . . nor did he allow himself to be frozen in a popular period of his own music . . . he continues to be a vigorous young creator.'[8]

Stravinsky paid reciprocal tribute. Lieberson, he said, 'has almost single-handedly championed the modern composer rather than the established mediocrities amongst performers'. The recording project of his entire output, which began in 1947 and continued until his death in 1971, gave Stravinsky sole artistic control. He either conducted himself or, as he grew infirm, supervised the interpretation of his works under the direction of his skilled assistant, Robert Craft. His chief concern was textual fidelity. 'I love my music – excuse me,' he would say to any musician who deviated. 'Stravinsky had a relentless ear for nuance of performance and never gave his approval until he was completely satisfied,' reported Lieberson's wife, Vera Zorina. The performances are not always the most exhilarating or rhythmically consistent, especially in the furious dances of the composer's youth, but the authority is incontrovertible and, in the later works, indispensable for its connective thread between expressive lyricism and analytical modernism. The volume of sacred works contains some of his least-known pieces, which are also the most heartfelt.

8. All quotes taken from Goddard Lieberson and Vera Zorina's sleeve notes to the set.

Threni, though astringently atonal, could take its place unnoticed in the liturgy of any great Orthodox cathedral, so emphatic
is the shape that Stravinsky the conductor imparts to its arching
structure. The Canticum Sacrum, written for St Mark's in Venice,
a city the composer had chosen for his burial, applies a quirky,
tangential reverence to Catholic ritual, straining for relevance in a
modern age that would soon outlaw Latin as a language of prayer.
An Introitus in memory of his friend T. S. Eliot inhabits a meta-
phoric wasteland, though in colours much deeper than the poet's
pastels. Variations on a Bach Christmas chorale might easily have
been pitched at the seasonal gift market, though maiden aunts
would be startled by some of the sonorities. The freshness of
Stravinsky's invention in these largely unsung works is little short
of astonishing and the courage of CBS in fostering their recorded
completion was an act of faith that drew scant attention in the
mid-century but was soon to be extinguished by corporate
dictatorships.

47. *Mozart: Piano Concertos 22 and 25*
Alfred Brendel, Vienna Pro Musica Orchestra/Paul Angerer
Vox: Vienna, 1966

Alfred Brendel was a struggling pianist in 1950s Vienna who got
his break from an American fringe label. Vox, owned by 'George
de h. Mendelssohn-Bartholdy', was a two-bit outfit that employed
the Vienna Philharmonic under false names to get around legal
restraints and trawled the halls for hungry talent, of which there
was plenty. Brendel was put to work on Mussorgsky's Pictures at
an Exhibition and Balakirev's Islamey, a laughable pairing for an
artist of light, precise, Germanic touch, a pupil of the severe
Edwin Fischer. He followed that release with Liszt transcriptions
of popular opera tunes, a kind of Liberace hit parade. When both
of these records sold better than expected, Brendel was allowed to
tackle Schubert and Beethoven in substantial cycles.

The records that made his fame, though, were Mozart piano

concertos, played so light and fast that they rivalled newly-voguish 'authentic' performances. The conductor was Paul Angerer, a local composer. Brendel added a laconic angularity that treated the music with respect but also, at times, with a broad, infectious grin and, in the Allegro of the E-flat concerto, a barely suppressed giggle. The cockiness of Mozart, his contempt for lesser composers, comes through best in Brendel's playing. Without false reverence or flashy virtuosity, he brings forth a living, breathing Mozart who churns out new works as a tidal assault on prevailing mediocrity. The Vienna Philharmonic (by another name) responds intuitively to this empathetic approach and the interactive dialogue is consistently interesting – even more so in these relatively marginal concertos than in the more hackneyed works.

Brendel, along with another Vox pianist, Ingrid Haebler, was snapped up by a major label, Philips, for which he recorded the Mozart concertos all over again, some of them twice, with superior conductors, sound and the full panoply of record industry hype. He inherited Artur Schnabel's mantle as the philosopher-pianist, a pillar of the musical establishment and a published poet. His early Mozarts in garish Vox covers look puerile beside subsequent splendours, but Brendel allowed them to remain in circulation, a clue to his integral self.

48. Mahler: Das Lied von der Erde

Christa Ludwig, Fritz Wunderlich, Philharmonia Orchestra/
Otto Klemperer

EMI: London (Kingsway Hall: Ludwig), 7–8 November 1964,
(Abbey Road: Wunderlich) 6–9 July 1966

Mahler never lived to hear The Song of the Earth. 'Is it performable?' he asked Bruno Walter. 'Won't people want to do away with themselves on hearing it?' It was a work of anguish, triggered by the death of an infant daughter, the loss of his job in Vienna and the collapse of his health. Walter gave the 1912 premiere, a year after Mahler's death, and made the first two recordings, in

Vienna in 1936 (when no Austrian singer would take part for fear of Nazi sanction) and again in 1952 with the Austrian tenor Julius Patzak and the British mezzo-soprano Kathleen Ferrier, a recording that marked the beginning of the post-war Mahler revival. More than any other conductor, Walter exuded authority and serenity in this work, an assurance that all was not lost.

Klemperer, the composer's other acolyte, took an antipodal approach. Confrontational where Walter was compliant, averse to any ingratiatory urge, he let a dozen years slip by until he found the right pair of singers and an appropriately rigorist interpretation. His performance shocked the London critics, one of whom, John Amis, declared it to be 'so determinedly anti-Walter as to avoid practically any sentiment'. That, however, was Klemperer's point: a great work had to be open to contradiction and there was always more to Mahler than any mortal musician could monopolize.

He conducted the six songs stringently and with audible restraint, the orchestral sound crisper than Walter's Vienna cream, the heat lowered for simmering accuracy. The strangeness of the Chinese poems intensifies an aura of alienation. Hints at jollity and consolation are illusory: 'dark is life, is death'. Nature, in all its beauty, is something that every man must leave behind, and each floating line of oboe and clarinet is an ache of pain at future parting. Klemperer holds his line implacably until, two-thirds through the Abschied (Farewell), he allows emotions to flow freely. The catharsis arising from prolonged suppression is physically overwhelming, as Klemperer knew it had to be.

It was no easy matter to get the two soloists into studio since they had impossibly busy careers, so they were recorded separately. Christa Ludwig was the cleverest of mezzos and Fritz Wunderlich on the brink of world fame. Two months after making this recording he was involved in a freak domestic accident with a shotgun and died before the record was released. Tinged with pathos, this account of Das Lied acquired a stoic nobility which became, in time, the interpretative norm.

49. Mahler: Fourth Symphony
Cleveland Orchestra/Georg Szell
CBS: Cleveland (Severance Hall), 1966

Expert consensus, inasmuch as it can be trusted, holds that Cleveland made America's finest recordings in a decade when Bernstein hogged the limelight in New York and Ormandy sold the most records from Philadelphia. The source of excellence at Cleveland was Georg Szell, a man of narrow horizons and abrasive manner.

A Hungarian who learned his trade before the war at the progressive German Opera in Prague, Szell applied old-world rigour to Cleveland in much the same way that fellow Hungarian Fritz Reiner was doing in Chicago. Coming from Mahler's heartland both Reiner and Szell performed the symphonies long before Leonard Bernstein's much-trumpeted cycle and for very different reasons. Neither was much concerned with psychology and spiritual catharsis. For them, Mahler was a means of displaying extremes of dynamic range and the deadly accuracy of their orchestras.

Reiner recorded the fourth symphony in 1958 with the Simon-pure Swiss soprano Lisa Della Casa and a lofty detachment from its philosophical agendas. Szell, eight years later, asserted a pinpoint note-perfection from the problematic opening phrase – taken helter-skelter by the composer's associate Willem Mengelberg and lazy-languid by his pupil, Bruno Walter. Szell gripped the phrase in a metronomic vice that released the rest of the symphony to flow with limitless freedom. The gypsy fiddle in the second movement is just another beauty, not an anomaly, the Adagio is meltingly done, and soloist Judith Raskin arises angelically and sings without irony of the heavenly hosts at lunch, one of the most perplexing of Mahler's texts. This is Mahler without indulgence, played as written in a clinical interpretation. Many Mahlerians find it unsympathetic, preferring the wildness of Bernstein and Tennstedt or the dash of younger men – Abbado, Chailly, Gatti. Several adept Mahlerians came unstuck in this symphony – Solti,

Haitink (twice each), Boulez – and Klemperer's recording is un-
done by his unsympathetic soloist, Schwarzkopf. Szell's is the stone
by which other recordings are measured. It is immaculate in every
detail, almost inhumanly perfect.

50. Bach: Four Orchestral Suites
Concentus Musicus/Nikolaus Harnoncourt
Telefunken (Warner): Vienna, 1967

Never as familiar as the Brandenburg concertos, the Bach orchestral
suites (or overtures) are innately more significant, looking ahead
to symphonic form. Played only, if at all, by symphonic ensembles,
they were taken up in the mid-1960s by a dissentient Viennese
cellist who wanted to change the world's view of Viennese sound.

Nikolaus Harnoncourt, a descendant of Habsburg emperors,
aimed to recreate the pointed rhythms and correct tonality of the
baroque period on original instruments that he found in antique
stores. 'He never wanted to start a revolution,' said Harnoncourt's
friends, 'but one broke out anyway.' Harnoncourt's Bach was
brisk, elegant, deft, unpretentiously danceable. It had scholarly
credentials and audience appeal, a rare confluence of interests, and
the people it attracted were, on the whole, a generation younger
than the concert-hall crowd. He recorded the Brandenburg in
1963, the suites four years later, on the eve of a US tour that
earned his ensemble enough money to allow its members to quit
their jobs in symphony orchestras and apply themselves to recreat-
ing a vanished past.

Less obsessed with dashing speed than other early-music conductors, Harnoncourt pitched for a blend in which the plangency
of his flutes pitched nicely against the shiny timbre of his strings.
At his most prosaic, in the overture to the first Bach suite, he
matches Herbert von Karajan in perfectionist perversity. But when
the players start bouncing off each other, as they do in the Gavotte,
the music lightens up and becomes altogether friendlier, draw-
ing the listener into the conversation. That participatory ethos,

more than any scholarly bent, was the unique selling point of the early music movement – before, like all revolutions, it grew leadership structures.

A reticent man of intellectual mien, Harnoncourt was not cut out to be a record industry pin-up in Salzburg shop windows. When Karajan banned him from the festival in a fit of misplaced jealousy, he took up a post on the periphery of the star parade, teaching historical practice at the city's Mozarteum. Many of his students went on to found period ensembles of their own, acknowledging him as a father of the movement. Harnoncourt, after Karajan's death, conducted the Berlin and Vienna Philharmonic orchestras and was embraced by the record establishment.

51. *Vivaldi: Four Seasons*
Academy of St Martin in the Fields/Neville Marriner
Decca: London (St John's, Smith Square), September 1969

More than 400 recordings have been made of the Venice schoolmaster's pot-boiler, a piece that represents the epicentre of public taste, safe and sweet. The range extends from pea-soup full-orchestral by Herbert von Karajan and the Berlin Phil to sixteen spartan instruments of the Drottningholm Baroque Ensemble in the Swedish icecap. The first big seller was a 1955 performance by I Musici of Rome, with Felix Ayo as soloist, a record so successful that it was remade four years later in stereo.

But the Four Seasons was still an esoteric fad, not yet a tourist staple, until it fell into Academy hands. In the late 1960s Neville Marriner's Academy pitched a style that was midway between traditional smooth and the scratchy investigations of radical period instrumentalists. Having worked through a raft of 'ice-cream composers', the ensemble alighted on Vivaldi and ran smack into a brick wall. Nothing they played during an expensive morning session seemed to please anyone in the band and tempers were fraying when the players dispersed for lunch. St John's is a Palladian church located in the heart of London's political district, five minutes' walk from Parliament, an area liberally stocked with quiet places of liquid refreshment.

On their return from lunch, several musicians seemed visibly the worse for wear. On the red light, Alan Loveday, the New Zealand-born leader, took up his fiddle and played without pause for forty blistering minutes. His one-take wonder hit the racks with a rush and started selling in shoals. It made the Academy Britain's most sought-after musical export and Vivaldi a dinner-party accessory for aspiring hostesses the world over. Every star fiddler packed Four Seasons onto record. Isaac Stern played it like Mozart. Nigel Kennedy chopped it into pop-length CD tracks, Anne-Sophie Mutter posed for a sexy cover, Viktoria Mullova worked her hair wild with a raw-gut band. James Galway had the solo transcribed for flute, muesli masquerading as music. Among the 400 versions, Loveday's stands out for its to-hell-with-it attitude, something any musician must feel after running the syrup five times.

52. *Ecco la Primavera: Florentine Music of the Fourteenth Century*
David Munrow, Early Music Consort of London
Decca: London (West Hampstead Studios), April–May 1969

David Munrow was a musician like no other. As a pit player at the Shakespeare Theatre in Stratford-upon-Avon, he conducted researches into Elizabethan and pre-medieval music, enthusing colleagues to join him in higgledy-piggledy consorts that played music unheard for half a millennium. Before Munrow, such artefacts were dismissed as primitive. Thanks to Munrow, they became common heritage, rewriting musical chronology from Bach backwards and attracting a completely different attendance, more involved than the staid recital-hall crowd.

It was a post-school trip to Peru and Bolivia that awoke Munrow to indigenous instruments. Acerbic, sharp-witted and adroit at playing anything that came to hand, he formed his Consort with close chum Christopher Hogwood and magnetized media attention. The pieces he played danced and swayed; his art was physically irresistible. He cultivated a breed of counter-tenors to sing with his Consort – James Bowman, Nigel Rogers and Martyn Hill. He recorded for a dozen labels and, on free days, would pitch in at modern-orchestra sessions with Neville Marriner's Academy. Tragically, and at the second attempt, Munrow committed suicide under pressures of work and private confusions in 1976, at the age of thirty-three.

His output was so vast that less than half of his sessions have reached CD. Many of his pieces were first recordings, the scores created from manuscripts that Munrow found in medieval libraries. Florence in the fourteenth century was a Munrow speciality. Once the Wall Street of Europe, the finance centre for wars and sciences, it was also the seedbed of Renaissance, with wealthy Medicis pumping fortunes into art and music.

The composers Francesco Landini and Andrea Zacchara da Terama were stars of the day. Munrow treated them as living contemporaries, taking their music at note value and making no claim for its genius. The scores were written to entertain the rich, and he played them without pretension, here tonight, gone tomorrow. The naturalness of his dialogue with dead composers struck a chord in the Beatles era when relationships between generations were being reordered and barriers were falling between musical genres. As a consequence of Munrow's fame, pop musicians took to messing around with sackbuts, rebecs and crumhorns to achieve a peculiar effect on psychedelic tracks.

53. Magnificathy: The Many Voices of Cathy Berberian (works by Monteverdi, Debussy, Cage, Berberian, etc.)
Cathy Berberian with Bruno Canino (piano)
Wergo: Milan, November 1970

The most versatile singing voice of the twentieth century left hardly a recorded trace. Cathy Berberian (1925–83) could sing anything from baroque to the Beatles. An American of Armenian origin, not unlike Callas who was American and Greek, Berberian hung out with cutting-edge composers and furnished them with a vocal range that stretched from growl to squeak. She married Luciano Berio, taught him English and introduced him to James Joyce. Berio used her voice as Matisse did his wife, making art and finding a style at one and the same time. Berberian also drew works from Cage, Milhaud, Maderna and Stravinsky, who wrote Elegy for JFK for her unique ability to project a communicative immediacy to whatever she sang.

This passionate pathbreaker, a stranger to recording studios, can be heard mostly on recondite reissues of radio recitals. In this Milan programme at the peak of her powers, Berberian set out to display the fullness of her versatility. She delivers straight-recitative Monteverdi, a Gershwin Summertime to outweep Ella's and a Surabaya Jonny that is a woman's world apart from Lotte Lenya's (CD 30, p. 194): Cathy is no bruised wimp, but a sexual avenger. Her own composition Stripsody, a vocalization of the noises that characters make in newspaper cartoons, is the climax of the recital, but its cult value lies in a baroque setting of Lennon and McCartney's Ticket to Ride, which, apart from being file-sharingly comic, recontextualizes the Beatles as post-medieval troubadours in an unspoiled landscape. The record should carry a health warning: these performances are inimitable – do not try to make them at home.

54. Alkan: Piano Music
Ronald Smith
EMI: London (Abbey Road), March 1971

Charles-Valentin Morhange, known as Alkan, locked himself in his apartment for twenty-five years and grew a long beard after being refused a directorate at the Paris Conservatoire. He wrote a funeral march for his parrot and a symphony for solo piano, creeping out at night to play unheralded recitals at the Salle Pleyel that were attended by the finest pianists of the day. He was found dead beneath a collapsed bookcase, an accident caused (it was said) by his reaching for a tome of the Talmud which was kept on the top shelf. Busoni called him one of the five great composers for piano after Beethoven. That is about as much as anyone knew of Alkan until Ronald Smith brought him back to life.

Smith, a Kentish musician with fading eyesight and flying fingers, was shown some Alkan by the composer Humphrey Searle, who worked for the BBC. Intrigued by the perversity of the music – which other composer could have written an ironic requiem for his parrot? – Smith dug out more scores in French libraries and played them on the radio and in lecture recitals. The music was doubly intractable. Alkan as a young man had set out to show Chopin and Liszt that he could play them off the keyboard. In 1844 he was the first to depict a railway train in music. Later he was so far ahead of his time in tonal contrast and chordal accumulation that Wagner and Mahler, Stravinsky and Scriabin, are all anticipated in his dense and often disturbing scores.

Alkan, for all his eccentricities, was evidently a visionary of sorts. In the Grande Sonate, opus 33, he not only depicts four stages of a man's life at twenty, thirty, forty and fifty, but argues in a quasi-Faust section with Goethe in a prodigious eight-part fugue. Smith was not the only one to uncover his genius. An American, Raymond Lewenthal, recorded Alkan for CBS around the same time. But Smith also wrote the definitive biography and drew so many connections between Alkan and composers past and present that it would be impossible ever again to delete him from memory.

55. Haydn: Paris Symphonies
Philharmonia Hungarica/Antal Dorati
Decca: Marl, Germany (St Boniface), 1971

Among those who fled Hungary after the 1956 Soviet invasion were hundreds of musicians. Eighty of them formed an orchestra in Vienna but struggled to get work. The composer Nicolas Nabokov, a cousin of the novelist Vladimir, arranged funding from the Rockefeller and Ford Foundations and persuaded the prewar Hungarian exile Antal Dorati to conduct the new ensemble. Dorati, back in Europe after a long spell with US orchestras, was trying to convince Decca to let him record 104 symphonies by the hitherto uncommercial Joseph Haydn. His proposal coincided with the plight of the refugees and one of the great recording projects duly resulted.

The small Westphalian town of Marl gave the orchestra a residency and the church of St Boniface provided a pellucid acoustic. Many of the symphonies were first-time recordings and the performances, while played on modern instruments, followed the latest scholarly editions by Haydn's biographer, H. C. Robbins Landon. The tempi were light and airy, a world apart from the lugubrious norm of German orchestras, and the unprepossessing substance of the symphonies was refreshingly different from the weight of expectation that attended a work by Mozart or Beethoven. To call one symphony The Bear, another The Hen and the next The Queen indicates a certain levity on the composer's part. Frothier and less well known than their London successors, Haydn's Paris symphonies caught the ear on record and returned to public performance for a while. One of them, no. 86 in D major, played havoc with key signatures in a way that suggests the composer was trying to test the ears of his musicians and audience. Dorati and the Hungarians were plainly having a ball.

At the final recording session, in December 1972, Dorati announced that half a million Haydn records had been sold. That figure quickly quadrupled, becoming Decca's second biggest hit after the Ring. The once-homeless orchestra basked in fame as one of Europe's most prestigious ensembles – until the Cold War ended, at which point the German government stopped its subsidy and the band was dissolved.

56. Dvořák: New World Symphony (with Dvořák: Eighth Symphony)
Berlin Philharmonic Orchestra/Rafael Kubelik
DG: Berlin (Jesus-Christus-Kirche), June 1972

In 1948, shortly after the communists flung Jan Masaryk from a Foreign Ministry window, Rafael Kubelik flew out of Prague with his family knowing they might never return. Kubelik's name was known to most Czechs. His father, Jan, had been a world-famous violinist who returned to die among his people under Nazi occupation. Rafael was a marvellously sensitive conductor, much loved by musicians in Prague and Brno and later on around the world.

As a political asylum seeker, he had rocky spells at Chicago and Covent Garden before finding a world-class orchestra at Bavarian Radio and a recording career on Deutsche Grammophon. A tall, willowy man, he had a deceptive ability to conjure warm sonorities from orchestras, sometimes at the expense of attacking edge. His Mahler cycle errs on the side of gentility and his Brahms, while gorgeously coloured, glosses over the gloomier depths as if unwilling to countenance audience distress.

In Czech music, however, he shed all restraint and gave vent to ceaseless yearning. In the darkest hours of the Cold War he proclaimed publicly that he would live to see the Czechs regain their freedom and he performed their heritage with messianic fervour. Dvořák's Ninth, from the New World, written while homesick in America, acquired urgency in Kubelik's hands, a sense of past joined to future, bypassing the tense present. Taking on the Berlin

Philharmonic, Karajan's beauty-first boys, he elicited playing of high risk and explosive reactiveness from players who were playing at the edge of their seats. The principal flute in these sessions, young James Galway, repeats the opening theme with pent-up energy, as if he would burst if kept waiting by the conductor for another instant. The last two symphonies were released as the first in a Dvořák symphonic cycle on DG (István Kertész was doing another on Decca).

Kubelik retired with arthritis in the mid-1980s but when Soviet communism collapsed in 1989 he returned home, stooped with age and pain, to conduct Smetana's My Homeland at the Prague Spring. The last work he conducted, before his death in 1996, was the New World symphony.

57. Schubert: Die Schöne Müllerin
Dietrich Fischer-Dieskau with Gerald Moore
DG: Hamburg, 1972

Forget the singer for a moment. This recording begins and ends with the accompanist. *Am I too Loud?* was the title of Gerald Moore's memoirs. A Watford kid in his early twenties, he wandered into an HMV studio in 1921 and found himself tinkling as backdrop for Pau Casals and Elisabeth Schumann. Over the years he grew assertive. In 1943 *The Unashamed Accompanist*, his first book, raised public awareness of the uneven partnership that exists between recitalists and their pianists.

Moore worked with every soloist of consequence, but the surmounting relationship was the one he formed with Dietrich Fischer-Dieskau, who, more than any singer, made the Lied the centre of his life and the Lieder cycle a metropolitan fixture. The refined German baritone found his ideal foil in the rough-spoken Moore, who took the music as it came and would go to the cinema after a particularly gruelling rehearsal. Moore gave no quarter to his starry partner. When Fischer-Dieskau forgot his words in Auf der Bruck and gave an imploring look at the piano Moore, trotting along in a horsy rhythm, whispered: 'Sorry, I'm too busy riding.' Behind the bluff exterior he hid an acute sensitivity for the weighting of a musical phrase.

After Moore retired in 1968 – serenaded on his way by Elisabeth Schwarzkopf and Victoria de los Angeles singing Rossini's Cats' Duet at a Royal Festival Hall gala (recorded by EMI) – Fischer-Dieskau lured him back to the studio for one last crack at the Schubert cycles (their swansong, he called it). Moore played with dynamic spontaneity and Fischer-Dieskau, who had refrained from singing Schubert for several years, sang as if surprised by each line. At times, at Thanksgiving at the Brook, one can practically hear two hearts beat in harmony. 'The rhythm that [Gerald] particularly praised in me was one of his own principal virtues,' noted Fischer-Dieskau. 'He walked hand in hand with his partner, whose main-stay of meter and breath was never sacrificed. He never lost himself in details but always followed to the end the larger line initiated by the composer.'[9] On this occasion, knowing they would never work together again and relieved of career anxiety, the pair gave rein to impulse and created the performance of their lives.

58. *Canto Gregoriano*
Monks of the Benedictine Monastery of Santo Domingo de Silos
EMI: Santo Domingo de Silos, Burgos, March 1973

One baking Madrid afternoon in the late 1980s, as gridlocked drivers steamed at the wheel, a sound came over the radio that chilled them to their seats. Some bright deejay, alert to traffic chaos, spun an old LP of a bunch of monks at their daily devotions. His intervention caused a vertical drop in highway blood pressure and a beatific smile to spread at major intersections. EMI picked up the recording in 1993 and pitched it at club deejays to play at closing time, sending E-fuelled youngsters home on a spiritual

9. Dietrich Fischer-Dieskau, *Echoes of a Lifetime*, London: Macmillan, 1989, pp. 328–9.

cloud. Canto sold a million within a month of US release. Three out of five sales went to under-twenty-fives. The monks turned down a $7.5 million follow-up offer.

What had touched the world's hearts was the ethereal immaterialism of their secluded world and something primal in the music they sang. The tropes of Roman Church chant are attributed to Pope Gregory I, who died in the year 604, but it seems unlikely he could have written so much in a papacy of fourteen years. Some trace the melodies to an earlier source – Solomon's Temple in Jerusalem. If they are right, the racing pulses of the late twentieth century were slowed miraculously by some of the earliest known sounds of Man's communion with the Creator.

59. Bach: Sonatas and Partitas for Solo Violin
Nathan Milstein
DG: London (Conway Hall and Wembley Town Hall),
February–September 1973

Certain recordings are definitive in the sense that they deter all comers. More than one eminent violinist has declared that he will never attempt the Bach sonatas and partitas after hearing Milstein on DG, so glistening is the beauty, so daunting his authority.

Milstein was the first musician to leave Russia under communism, allowed out in 1925 with his friend Vladimir Horowitz as ambassadors for the new regime. Where the pianist was an overnight star, Milstein's appearance was modest and his virtuosity discreet. A man of limitless curiosity, he might easily be found half an hour before a recital in a bookstore or café, pursuing an unrelated quest. Rachmaninov, hearing him play the Bach E-major partita, was so overwhelmed by the range of expression that Milstein conjured from a single line of music that he converted three movements of the work into a piano suite for himself. Milstein's approach was unaffectedly engaging, as if he had something important to tell you but he wouldn't keep you a moment longer than necessary.

Each concert was, for Milstein, an act of reconsecration. 'I never gave more than thirty performances a year in my life,' he told me. 'I had a duty to refresh myself between recitals, to bring something new to my audience.' I heard him play with undimmed perfection and not a flash of exhibitionism well past his eightieth birthday.

Recording made him nervous and he gave up in mid-life, relenting here to play solo Bach in long stretches, which he would not permit to be edited or technically improved. He played as he spoke, conversationally, eyes twinkling, ever alert to the possibilities that a new inflexion could bring to the meaning of life. The opening of the Adagio of the G-minor sonata is, in Milstein's hands, a world entire, truly unrepeatable.

60. *Drumming; Six Pianos; Music for Mallet Instruments, Voices and Organ*
Steve Reich
DG: Hamburg (Rahlstedt, Musikstudio 1), January 1974

Minimalism was a 1960s West Coast fad based on esoteric Eastern practices that involved professional musicians sitting around uttering endless equivalents of 'Om'. The pioneers, Terry Riley and LaMonte Young, were counter-cultural characters, incapable of dialogue with classical record executives of the time. 'I rarely did music,' said Riley, 'without being stoned.'

The next phase of minimalism was led by Philip Glass, a New York cab driver who dreamed up operas, and Steve Reich, a many-sided composer who grew out of hypnotic immersion in shifting rhythms and proceeded to study indigenous cultures. Reich returned from Ghana with Drumming and from Californian gamelan groups with Music for Mallet Instruments, Voices and Organ. Drumming got a ninety-minute ovation at the Museum of Modern Art in New York and a German friend of the composer's alerted Deutsche Grammophon.

DG, against its deep conservative grain, flew Reich's ensemble to Hamburg in January 1974, a dark midwinter when Germany was gripped by Baader-Meinhof urban terrorism, spy scandals and artistic indeterminacy. Reich's musicians, among them the composers Cornelius Cardew and Joan LaBarbara, hit the drums and changed the world. The three-LP set, released that summer, broke the atonalist hegemony that had dominated contemporary music since 1945. More constructively, it also questioned the Western reference points of classical music by introducing tropes and rhythms from other cultures. To the innocent ear, Reich's music is monotonous, but prolonged listening reveals microscopic changes to texture and momentum, the beginning of an exploration that led Reich into the textual and spiritual complexities of Different Trains and Tehillim. DG did not make another minimalist record for twenty years, but this album broke the modernist ice, and brought down the prolonged ascendancy of academic asceticism.

61. Beethoven: Fifth Symphony
Vienna Philharmonic Orchestra/Carlos Kleiber
DG: Vienna (Musikvereinsaal), March–April 1974

Fate knocking on the door, Beethoven's Fifth was a symbol of freedom and resistance from the day it was written. It was the first complete symphony ever recorded – by Arthur Nikisch and the Berlin Philharmonic in November 1913 – and it is among the most performed. From a rack of more than 100 recordings, ranging from the portentous to the anorexic, it is absurd to speak of any single performance as definitive, but this recording is the one that most conductors regard as the benchmark.

Carlos Kleiber was a law unto himself, working only when (as he put it) his fridge was empty and often failing to turn up for work over some minor disagreement. Overshadowed by an authoritarian father, Erich Kleiber, who had run the Berlin State Opera in the 1920s and left some remarkable recordings of his own, Carlos restricted himself to his father's repertoire, aiming to outdo Erich at his unflappable best.

Erich Kleiber had made a famously controlled recording of the

Beethoven Fifth on Decca with the Amsterdam Concertgebouw in 1952, capturing the tricky opening triplet so adroitly that no other phrasing seemed possible. Carlos set out to trump that performance. His triplet is demonstrably quicker – six points faster on the metronome – and his fermatas much more flexible. The performance is filled with foreboding, rippling with an unnamed terror and manic wildness. The slow movement is gentle, though still tense, and it is only in the finale that Kleiber allows a possibility of hope. The Vienna Philharmonic, shocked out of safe routines, follow him blazingly like troops in battle to a conclusion that remains in doubt to the very last.

The sessions dragged out over two months while Kleiber was in Vienna studying *Tristan und Isolde*. He alternated in rehearsal between frustrated rage and personal concern, pushing players to their limits while cradling them with smiles and coffee-break conversation. By the end, they were prepared to give him their all. The result is a record universally revered, eclipsing the father, and unique to the prodigious son.

62. *Brahms: Viola Sonatas*
Pinchas Zukerman, Daniel Barenboim
DG: New York (Manhattan Center), November 1974

Exclusive label contracts ruled out any group record of the Kosher Nostra, a gang of mostly Jewish jet-setters that generated excitement in the late 1960s in concert and on television, in a series of documentary films by Christopher Nupen. A signature performance of Schubert's *Trout* Quintet by Barenboim (piano), his wife Jacqueline du Pré (cello), fellow-Israelis Itzhak Perlman (violin) and Zukerman (viola) and the Indian conductor Zubin Mehta (double bass) never made it onto record, though it exists in millions of visual memory banks.

This multilateral musical friendship can be heard only in twosomes – too little, and often recorded too late to capture the concert frisson. An exception is this unusual encounter with

Brahms, played on the wrong instrument and arguably on the wrong continent, since Brahms never set foot in America.

Barenboim was in New York at the same time as Zukerman who, equally adept on viola and violin, suggested they fill a blank day with the last works of Brahms, a pair of sonatas written for clarinet but inscribed by the composer as equally valid for viola. Deutsche Grammophon, compiling a centennial Brahms cycle, took up the project. In most other hands, this would have been just another box-filler.

But Barenboim's life had been blighted that year by his wife's tragic illness and his playing has a nervous, numinous edge to it that provokes in Zukerman so anxious a tone of reassurance that they close the first movement of the F-minor sonata in a tremulous fadeout. The Andante becomes an act of mutual encouragement, taken at a pace that precludes pressure, a refortifying conversation. After that, they start to enjoy themselves, two young men in New York with the world at their feet, oblivious to the perils of mortality. The E-flat major sonata, lovelier and more languorous at first, turns into a race for the finish, a thrilling conclusion to a great composer's life. The record was produced by Gunther Breest, a future power player in the record industry, and everything about it feels just right.

63. *Korngold: The Sea Hawk*
National Philharmonic Orchestra/Charles Gerhardt
RCA: London (Abbey Road), 1972–4

With a Hollywood deal that let him keep copyright in every note he wrote, Korngold invented a lexicon of musical emotions for motion pictures. Starting with Errol Flynn swashbucklers, he simulated Wagner for bombast, Mahler for conflict, Strauss and Puccini for love. He was not the only such maker of moods; Franz Waxman and Miklós Rózsa were likewise inventive and derivative by turn. Waxman made his name with a Tristan-like miasma for *The Bride of Frankenstein*; Rózsa peppered his scores for Alexander Korda and

Alfred Hitchcock with Hungarian discords. Korngold, though, was a class apart. He had come to Hollywood with a high reputation in Vienna and was regarded by studio bosses as a glittering asset.

A wunderkind who had a ballet commissioned by Mahler (it helped that his father was a powerful music critic), Korngold wrote the biggest hit opera of the 1920s, Die Tote Stadt, and was Max Reinhardt's preferred musical partner in the theatre. Enticed to Hollywood by the great director in 1935, Korngold found he had sacrificed status for dollars as orchestras slammed their doors on his works. A cello concerto that he extracted from the 1946 film *For Deception* was shunned as facile. The violin concerto, premiered by Heifetz the following year, was derided as 'more corn than gold'; its opening solo stemmed from *Another Dawn* and its finale from *The Prince and the Pauper* (both 1937). Korngold died heartbroken in 1957, unable to come to terms with his rejection by the custodians of musical quality.

His rehabilitation began a quarter of a century later with this compilation of movie highlights played by a pick-up orchestra of London studio professionals conducted by the veteran record producer Charles Gerhardt. The LP was produced by Korngold's son, George, and engineered by the brilliant Kenneth Wilkinson, pioneer of the Decca Sound. The three men shared a conviction that there was more to soundtracks than mere emotional exploitation. Clichéd as his effects might sound in isolation, Korngold had been taught a mastery of orchestration by Alexander von Zemlinsky, one of the great composer-conductors, and every score he wrote displays structural soundness and thematic originality. This recording rekindled interest in Korngold and, beyond him, in the generic potential of film music as an art in its own right. Whatever its value, Korngold invented film music as a sub-genre. Without Korngold there would have been no John Williams; without John Williams no *Star Wars*.

64. *Strictly for the Birds*
Yehudi Menuhin, Stéphane Grappelli
EMI: London (Abbey Road), 21–23 May 1975

Long before anyone came up with the term 'crossover', the world's most famous classical violinist met the foremost jazz fiddler in a BBC TV studio for a 1971 Michael Parkinson Christmas Special. Neither man was at ease. Menuhin feared that Grappelli would consider him 'a useless colleague who had never played jazz and could only remember one popular tune'. Grappelli, lacking formal tuition, worried 'what Menuhin would make of my technique'.

'Before starting to play,' recalled producer John Mordler, 'Yehudi would perform all sorts of Yoga type exercises.' Grappelli looked on astounded. 'I'll do the same as Le Père Menuhin,' he said, essaying a kind of belly dance. 'Perhaps it will help!' The ice broken, they picked up their fiddles and started testing each other.

Grappelli played freely and from memory, Menuhin had his improvisations strictly notated. 'Stéphane,' said Mordler, 'had that wonderful way of stretching as well as shortening notes and bar lines and, from time to time, hitting just below the note and then sliding upwards. Yehudi did not quite manage to master that same freedom. While Stéphane would play mostly by heart, Yehudi, being unfamiliar with many of the numbers, had his music written out, including the "improvisations", the style of which would otherwise have been quite alien for him.'

The repertoire covered music from their common boyhood in the Twenties and Thirties – Gershwin, Jerome Kern, Cole Porter. Their symbiosis was generational rather than stylistic and there was much sliding around that offended classical purists, but when a pair of top fiddlers take on the Nightingale in Berkeley Square it stops the traffic and the genre cops are forced to take down artificial barriers. One way or another, this record set the parameters for cross-cultural collusions. Grappelli was so taken by the experience that he wrote and played a new Minuet for Menuhin.

For Menuhin the disc was just another big seller in a lifelong string of successes. For Grappelli it marked the difference between hunger and ease. 'These recordings created a new lease of life for Stéphane,' said Mordler. 'He told me that this was the first time in his long career that any records of his had been sold by the thousands, and he suddenly found himself earning undreamed-of royalties. So he also made sure that they contained some of his own compositions. Normally, he would write these in the taxi on the way to the studio.' One such number was titled 'Johnny aime', pronounced 'M', a covert tribute to his studio producer, who spent the rest of his career as head of the opera house at Monte Carlo.[10]

65. *Russo: Street Music; Three Pieces for Blues Band and Symphony Orchestra (with Gershwin: An American in Paris)*
Corky Siegel (harmonica, piano), San Francisco
Symphony Orchestra/Seiji Ozawa
DG: Cupertino, California (Flint Center at
DeAnza College), May 1976

Not many American jazzmen made it onto a classical label. Bill Russo, though, had a foot in both camps. A member of the Stan Kenton Band and founder of the Chicago Jazz Ensemble, Russo wrote a piece called Titans for Leonard Bernstein and an English Concerto while living in London in the early 1960s, working for the BBC. Back in Chicago a young conductor heard him play at John's Bar in the summer of 1966 and suggested he come and play at the Ravinia Festival, where he was music director.

Seiji Ozawa was new on the American scene, refreshingly iconoclastic. A winner of the Koussevitsky Competition at Tanglewood, he had understudied Bernstein at the New York Philharmonic and Herbert von Karajan in Berlin. In his early thirties, he wore Haight-Ashbury flowered shirts and a Beatles haircut. The

10. John Mordler, email to the author, 31 August 2005.

following summer he premiered Russo's second symphony at Tanglewood and commissioned Three Pieces, which, rehearsed by the New York Philharmonic, had players leaping out of their seats between movements to applaud. 'Hardest thing I ever did,' said Russo. Ozawa was trading up from festivals to the San Francisco Symphony, where two European labels came vying for his favours and Russo was high on his recording programme. He opened with Street Music, a blues concerto that smelt of downtown tenements on a rainy night, instantly evocative and without the obvious gimmicks of a movie score. It is constructed formally as a concerto around a sensually irresistible harmonica solo.

The Three Pieces were deftly balanced between band and orchestra and beautifully played on both sides. Everyone seemed to be having a good time. But the record was not a hit, and the label wanted no more. The music would have vanished off the backlist, but over the years it acquired minor cult status as a high point in the stuttering dialogue between symphonic music and jazz, a conversation that had been running ever since Gershwin's day. Russo joined composer Gunther Schuller in keeping the links alive in a putative Third Stream but he wrote little more on the classical side. At his death in 2003, the Mayor of Chicago named 16 April as William Russo Day.

66. Janáček: Katya Kabanova
Elisabeth Söderström, Petr Dvorsky, Vienna Philharmonic
Orchestra/Charles Mackerras
Decca: Vienna (Sofiensaal), December 1976

The Australian Charles Mackerras saw his first Janáček opera, Katya Kabanova, as a British Council student in Prague in October 1947. He conducted its UK premiere at Sadler's Wells in 1951, an event which introduced English audiences to Janáček a quarter of a century after his death. Rafael Kubelik, music director at Covent Garden, had a follow-up hit with Jenůfa. Leoš Janáček was suddenly talked about as a major twentieth-century creator, but the record industry was not interested, reckoning that the composer's new fans would be satisfied with scratchy Supraphon imports.

Another quarter of a century passed and Janáček was being performed worldwide before a record company commissioned a Janáček cycle. Mackerras, now music director of English National Opera, was sent by Decca to Vienna, where players in the Philharmonic insisted they had never heard of him. An economy-class, nearly all-Czech cast was assembled, none of them known abroad, the exception being the Swedish soprano Elisabeth Söderström, who had taken on the title role at Glyndebourne. Despite these inequalities, the sessions were harmonious. The grim Slavonic drama of a woman who finds love outside marriage but cannot live with the consequences held everyone in its grip. Söderström, of Russian parentage, sang luminously and Petr Dvorsky was a lover to die for. Some at Decca had their doubts, but Janáček was now taking root on the US stage (though the Met did not see Katya until 1991) and Mackerras was cleared to conduct the rest of the operas in an award-winning, ground-breaking cycle.

67. Holst: Wind Suites
Cleveland Symphonic Winds/Frederick Fennell
Telarc: Cleveland (Severance Hall), 4–5 April 1978

Gustav Holst's Planets (see CD 69, p. 240) was a gift to the record industry. Premiered during the final weeks of the First World War, the great astrological suite was used as a display piece for every technological innovation from electrical recording onwards. Holst, a music teacher at St Paul's Girls' School in Hammersmith, west London, was bemused by its success, concerned as he was more with intricacy of texture than with spectacular effects.

A meek man of simple, rustic tastes, Holst loved writing wind suites for military bands, reworking folk tunes in country pastels and delicate turns of light and shade. The suites were taken up by brass bands in British mining villages and seldom heard in polite society until a shift occurred in recording destinies and they became the gateway to a shining future.

By the late 1970s Edison's invention was heading for obsolescence. Records scratched too easily and every superficial blemish was magnified by increasingly powerful amplifiers and speakers. Scientists aimed to avoid needle contact by converting sound to computer digits and reading it back through a laser eye. An American professor, Thomas Stockham, patented a Soundstream recording machine and tried it out at the Santa Fe opera festival. Two Clevelanders, Jack Renner and Robert Woods, asked to borrow it for their first professional recording and then had the effrontery to ask the professor to adapt it to their needs. Stockham cheerfully obliged and the device was tried out on the reeds, brass and percussion sections of the Cleveland orchestra.

The original manuscripts of Holst's suites had recently resurfaced after being lost for decades and were found to be peppered with anticipations of great themes from The Planets. The Cleveland musicians played with silky smoothness and the dynamic span from soft to loud was delicately calibrated, astonishing ears that had grown used to LP compression. This was the first digital release on LP, an amuse-gueule for what was about to be served up. Reviewers marvelled at the reduction of hiss and crackle and manufacturers cracked ahead with digital research. Five years would pass before compact disc displayed digital sound to full advantage, but this was the harbinger, like Mercury in The Planets, the bringer of good fortune.

68. *Britten: Peter Grimes*

Jon Vickers, Heather Harper, Jonathan Summers, Royal Opera
House Chorus and Orchestra/Colin Davis
Philips: London (Royal Opera House), April 1978

The composer, they say, is always right – especially when he is a
fine conductor. Well, not always. Benjamin Britten was a subtle
interpreter of symphonic music and opera. In 1959 he made for
Decca what was seen as the benchmark recording of Peter Grimes,
his breakthrough opera that had taken the stage eight weeks after
the war ended and swept the rest of the world soon after. Britten
wrote the role of Grimes for his partner Peter Pears. So long as the
composer lived, Pears was held to be peerless in the role and there
was no deviating from his depiction of the homicidal fisherman as
a morally ambiguous figure, as much a victim of social isolation as
he was a vicious killer. The opera was rooted in the two men's
anguish, as pacifists during the war and as gay men in a jurisdiction
that criminalized them. Grimes was, to a degree, their credo. To
tamper with it was tantamount to heresy.

In the year that followed Britten's death, the Royal Opera House
Covent Garden dared to break the mould. A new production by
the young Australian Elijah Moshinsky cast the Canadian tenor
Jon Vickers as a different Grimes: a complete monster, terrifying
in his amorality, unmitigated by any hinted attraction to young
boys. The Ulster soprano Heather Harper, a Britten loyalist, was
cast opposite him as Ellen Orford, a frigid virgin incapable of
offering Grimes any kind of consolation. Vickers, a devout Christian, abhorred the evil of Grimes in every fibre of his rock-solid
voice, so much more menacing than Pears' reedy tones. He pro-
fessed to hate the work but he sang throughout with transcendent
purity and passion, more evident here than in other operas. The
orchestral interludes, so essential to the creation of atmosphere, are
chillingly conducted by Colin Davis with a pit orchestra at the
peak of its form. There was resistance to the production from
the Britten faithful and the recording was paid for largely by the

company itself. More than any established tradition, it was this recording that fixed Grimes in the world's repertoire in the fragile decade after a composer's death, when reputations are actuarially reassessed and downgraded.

69. *Holst: The Planets (with Elgar: Enigma Variations)*
London Philharmonic Orchestra/Sir Adrian Boult
EMI (Kingsway Hall and Abbey Road), May–July 1978

Six weeks before the end of the First World War a young conductor, Adrian Boult, was sitting hunched over a score when Gustav Holst burst into his room, saying he had been given the Queen's Hall orchestra and chorus for Sunday morning by a generous friend. 'We are going to do The Planets, and you have got to conduct,' exclaimed the composer. The orchestral parts were copied out in class by his pupils at St Paul's Girls' School in Hammersmith, two of whom played the score four-handed for the unconvinced Boult as he struggled to master it in a matter of days.

The premiere, on 29 September 1918, drew some of London's top musicians to a deserted hall that was being readied for an evening performance. Holst's celestial grand tour required no astrological understanding. Charwomen scrubbing the corridors downed brushes in Jupiter and began dancing. In Neptune, musicians said they heard sounds from another galaxy, the fading chord of the women's chorus representing the ultimate in ethereality. The Planets became the most performed orchestral work by any British composer and an indispensable hi-fi spectacular. 'You covered yourself with glory,' said Holst after the first performance, and Boult carried on doing so for six decades more.

He recorded it five times, lastly and most effectively in the months before his ninetieth birthday. There was always an impassiveness to the willowy British conductor with the wire-brush moustache that seemed to belie passion, but Boult had learned from his mentor Arthur Nikisch how to conjure a massive climax from a tiny stick movement and the variations of light and shade are literally out of this world. Each planet in this performance extrudes a distinctive colouring and the echoes of war in Mars and Venus have never been more explicit, a reflection of the conditions in which they came into being. As for Saturn, the bringer of old age is not a pathetic dependant in a nursing home but a dignified man who has lived his time fully and is able to rage at its fading.

On CD, EMI coupled The Planets with Boult's 1970 recording of the Enigma Variations with the London Symphony Orchestra, itself the most commanding rendition since the composer's and Toscanini's (CD 8, p. 169). The pairing was issued in a series titled, without exaggeration, Great Recordings of the Century. Boult died, aged ninety-four, in 1983, the last link to the English musical renaissance.

70. Berg: Lulu
Teresa Stratas, Paris Opera Orchestra/Pierre Boulez
DG: Paris (Institution de Recherche et de Coordination
Acoustique/Musique), March–June 1979

Alban Berg died of a blood infection in December 1935, aged fifty, with his second opera unfinished and, his widow insisted, unrealizable. Two acts were staged in Zurich in 1937 but Helene Berg so long as she lived would not let anyone see the sketches for a finale in which Lulu, the original material girl, gets murdered by Jack the Ripper amid scenes of unexampled decadence.

Helene's reticence was triggered by her discovery of a terrible secret. Berg, while writing Lulu (and much else) had been conducting a passionate affair with a married woman in Prague. The score is seeded with hints of their physical love – the notes representing his initials and Hanna Fuchs-Robettin's intertwined sensuously at key junctures. Helene, incensed at the betrayal, both marital and creative, had the sketches locked in a publisher's vault and, in her will, issued an absolute ban on any further expansion of the third act. The publishers had other ideas. They showed the sketches long before her death to a capable Austrian composer,

Friedrich Cerha, who brought the opera to completion within weeks of her funeral.

The lame-duck estate made a feeble attempt to defend her will, settling for a promise by the publishers that the two-act version would 'remain available' alongside the full-frontal Lulu. Berg's last masterpiece finally made it onto the stage in Paris on 24 February 1979 and its recording won every available award for opera of the year.

Lulu, hypnotically rendered by the slinky Teresa Stratas, was revealed as a parable of twentieth-century femininity, tugged between irreconcilable desires for status, security and erotic satisfaction, always a mistress, never a wife, no man safe in her vicinity. The Greek-Canadian soprano gave the performance of her life. 'I had a fever and was drugged up with cortisone,' she recalled. 'I didn't want to sing – couldn't sing . . . I did what I was supposed to do: I stood there and sang.' She was Lulu to a tee.

The supporting parts were stunningly cast – Yvonne Minton, Hanna Schwarz, Robert Tear, Franz Mazura, Kenneth Riegel – and the conductor, Pierre Boulez, gave rein to a taut eroticism tinged by dread presentiments, the sexiest music of his life. This record established the three-act Lulu as the world standard, her nemesis one of the darkest scenes ever to be seen on an opera stage.

71. *Mahler: Tenth Symphony*
Bournemouth Symphony Orchestra/Simon Rattle
EMI: Southampton, (Guildhall) 10–12 June 1980

In 1974 a kid of nineteen won a cigarette-sponsored conducting competition. The prize was two years with a seaside band. 'During the Bournemouth period I very seriously toyed with the idea of giving up altogether,' said Simon Rattle, but at the end of his tenure he got to make a record for EMI.

Rattle chose Gustav Mahler's deathbed symphony, a fragmentary work completed by BBC producer Deryck Cooke and conductor Berthold Goldschmidt. Their attempt was denounced by Mahler's disciple Bruno Walter and ignored by Bernstein and Kubelik, who were performing the first recorded cycles.

Rattle, a decade later, studied the Tenth with Goldschmidt and developed the sketches further with composers Colin and David Matthews. Leading an orchestra that had all but sapped his confidence, he shaped a monumentally assured and surprisingly well-played account of a composer's struggle with love, faithlessness and death. The opening Adagio is tautly controlled to avoid self-pity; the two Scherzos are febrile and the Purgatorio inadequately ominous. But the finale, with its heavy death beats, is terrifyingly convincing, an apotheosis of sorts to Mahler's message.

The recording proved central to Rattle's career. Within a year he was appointed chief conductor in Birmingham, an orchestra that he moulded to his youthful and eclectic personality. Mahler's Tenth was the work he nominated when the Berlin Philharmonic asked him for a date in 1987. The players vetoed the work on the grounds of its contentiousness and Rattle backed down. He finally got them to rehearse the work in 1996. Throughout rehearsal, they muttered, 'It's ghastly . . . it's not by Mahler.' The concert changed their minds. Three years later the players elected Rattle music director in Berlin.

72. *Mozart: Clarinet Concerto*
Academy of Ancient Music/Christopher Hogwood
Decca: London, 1980

Christopher Hogwood was the acceptable face of early music, a conductor who never allowed dogmas of authenticity to overwhelm inherent musicality. When he persuaded Decca to let him record practically the whole of Mozart's orchestral opus – symphonies, concertos, interludes, the lot – it was assumed that nothing in the performances would frighten habitual record buffs who knew their Mozart back to front.

The clarinet concerto scared the pants off them. Hogwood and his soloist, Antony Pay, took the view that the work had never been intended for clarinet, a relatively new and high-pitched instrument that was just coming into use in 1789. The first movement was specifically sketched, in G major, for basset horn, and ten weeks before his death Mozart told his wife, Constanze, that he was orchestrating the rondo finale for Anton Stadler's basset clarinet, which had an extended lower range. To play it on a modern clarinet was, in Hogwood's view, anomalous to the point of ridicule.

Pay played it sweet and low. In less assured hands, the basset clarinet sounds growly, but so mellifluous was Pay's tone and so accomplished Hogwood's accompaniment that their performance established not just an ulterior appreciation of a much-loved work but a new tolerance in record shops for period practice as a whole.

73. *Lutoslawski: Paganini Variations*
Martha Argerich, Nelson Freire
Philips: La Chaux-au-fonds, Switzerland, August 1982

Paganini's twenty-fourth caprice for solo violin, itself a variation on an original theme, was diversified by such inventive minds as Brahms, Liszt, Szymanowski and, most lyrically, Rachmaninov. Later twentieth-century variations came from Blacher (1947), Lloyd Webber (1977) and Poul Ruders (1999), none wholly enchanting. The one to leave its mark was written by two young composers in Nazi-occupied Warsaw, where Poles were banned from attending concerts and under constant menace.

Witold Lutoslawski and Andrzej Panufnik transcribed some 200 standard orchestral works for piano and played them four-handed in cafés. One afternoon, Panufnik told me, they were hauled off the keyboard and slammed up against a wall by SS men, a pistol to their heads.

Lutoslawski looked after their library of scores. During the 1944 uprising his house burned down. The five-minute Paganini

Variations was the only manuscript to survive. 'He must have carried them with him,' said Panufnik.

The work's essence lies in the interplay of two restless spirits. The original theme gets subverted in its opening chords with daring dissonances – forbidden sounds at the time, a blazing protest against the homogenizers of art who were denying a whole nation the pleasures of music. That part of the dialogue is political; the rest is sporting and competitive: two rising, rival composers striking sparks off one another. The suite is so short that one wants to hear it twice (and pianists usually oblige). It is hard to believe that such wit and fun could prevail under constant mortal threat.

Lutoslawski went on to fashion an elegant orchestral version of the score, but it is the piano original that packs the punch. Martha Argerich, winner of the 1965 Warsaw Chopin Competition and an empathetic interpreter of Polish music, gives the most sparkling account on record with her close friend, Nelson Freire.

74. Bach: Mass in B Minor
Monteverdi Choir, English Baroque Soloists/John Eliot Gardiner
DG: London (All Saints' Church, Tooting), February 1985

Early music was a revolution in more than name. People who played period instruments and studied original texts were, from the outset, democratic to the point of anarchy, arguing throughout rehearsals and continuing the battle in pubs and learned journals. A conductor, historically the enforcer of unity, became an umpire between instrumental experts, barely primus inter pares. Soloists were reduced to level pegging with ensemble players.

The movement's egalitarianism was anathema to many in a record industry that lived and died upon the star system. But as the revolution gathered pace, especially among young listeners and new customers, labels were forced to take note and record the unthinkable: a major classical work without a single star. John Eliot Gardiner's 1985 account of the B-minor Mass was the industry's ice-breaker.

Gardiner was an entrepreneurial man, setting up ensembles and drumming up work for his musical factory. But he was also a facilitator, providing opportunities for fine musicians who might never otherwise have found voice on record. All his solos here are sung by rank-and-file members of the Monteverdi Choir, lustrously so; Nancy Argenta and Michael Chance lead a willing, flawless pack. The orchestra of twenty-eight is led by Gardiner's first wife, Elizabeth Wilcock. The tempi are almost twice as fast as Karajan's, transforming the atmosphere from sententious to infectious, practically from the opening downbeat. The clincher is the Qui Tollis chorus, light and airy yet spiritually uplifting. This was truly a revolutionary record, giving the impression that anyone could play and sing Bach – as everyone should.

75. *Horowitz*
Vladimir Horowitz
DG: New York (East 94th Street), 24–30 April 1985

Vladimir Horowitz had more comebacks than Lucifer. Every decade or so, the demons would take over and he would be medicated out of action or hospitalized. Manic depressive and awkwardly gay, he was the epitome of the wacko pianist in a polka-dot bow-tie who lived on a diet of boiled fish and played concerts only at 4.30 in the afternoon. He was also the most natural of artists, blessed with a touch that defied gravity and an ability to extend notes beyond the power of pedals: once heard, never forgotten. Nathan Milstein, his friend from boyhood, felt that Horowitz was never aware how extraordinary he was. On stage, he seemed mystified by the thunder of applause.

His last comeback, in his eighty-second year, was filmed in his own living room on East 94th Street by the Maysles brothers, a pair of discreet documentarists. Word spread that Horowitz was in remarkable form. His agent, Peter Gelb, called CBS and RCA and drew a blank. The corps were being run by new suits who knew not Horowitz. Gelb then tried Deutsche Grammophon, recruiting the pianist's lifelong RCA producer Jack Pfeiffer for the sake of comfort and continuity. The sessions stretched out over six afternoons and evenings but Horowitz sounded fresh throughout.

No pianist has ever taken the Busoni transcription of a Bach chorale so slowly, note by note, revealing its giant carapace, nor has anyone, the composer included, filled Rachmaninov's G-sharp minor Prelude with such glassy foreboding. Mozart and Chopin are treated as if they were still alive, tormented romantics in a technological laboratory. Scriabin is played with the benefit of personal acquaintance and massive affection. When the producers pointed out a wrong note on playback, the pianist said: 'I don't want perfection. I'm not Heifetz. I'm Horowitz.'[11] It was the closest this odd, introspective pianist ever came to artistic self-characterization.

76. *Verdi: Otello*

Placido Domingo, Katia Ricciarelli, Justino Diaz, Chorus and Orchestra of La Scala/Lorin Maazel
EMI: Milan (Conservatorio di Milano), 29 July–2 August 1985

The contrast between the two reigning tenors of the late twentieth century was pronounced. Domingo was a polyglot professional with 100 roles to his credit, the first singer of modern times to tackle Wagner's heroes as well as French and Russian dramas. Luciano Pavarotti was an unsophisticated powerhouse who sang his own language in thirty operas and sold more records than Caruso.

Otello was Domingo's defining role, the one Italian summit that he strutted above his arch-rival Pavarotti, who dodged the role until too late. Domingo took possession of the part as a young man in the early 1970s, a sultry Spaniard acting the Moor without face paint, singing with tenderness and venom. His marbl'd heavens duet with Iago was a surefire showstopper.

11. Harold Schonberg, *Horowitz*, London: Simon & Schuster, 1992, p. 268.

Domingo made four recordings of Otello – two with James Levine, in 1976 and 1996, the first too callow and the latter too knowing. At the midpoint between, he was about to film the opera with Franco Zeffirelli on location in Apulia when a terrible earthquake struck Mexico City, where much of his family lived. Friends and relatives were left injured and homeless. Domingo cancelled a year's engagements to raise funds. I caught up with him on set, in a ruined castle at Barletta, southern Italy. Dust-caked and distracted, his helpless rage was channelled, when the cameras turned, into the fury of a conquering hero whose love for his wife is turned by a worm of jealousy. The rest of the casting was compromised. Katia Ricciarelli was a domestic celebrity, married to Italy's leading chat-show host. Justino Diaz was an old pal of Domingo's. Neither had the acting skills to bring Desdemona and Iago to life as, for example, Rysanek and Gobbi had done on EMI's set, conducted by Serafin.

But Domingo was irresistibly Otello. At dawn on the ramparts overlooking the glassy Adriatic, or in a dungeon with the skulking Iago, his presence was awe-inspiring, a man transformed, transcending his private concerns. His second-scene cry 'Abasso le spade!' (Lower your swords) ripples with heroic desperation. Off set, he was continuously on the phone to Mexico.

The sound recording hit a trail of snags. Carlos Kleiber ducked out after disagreements over casting. Lorin Maazel, his replacement, tried to persuade Zeffirelli to allow him to insert some Moorish incidental music that he had wishfully composed. The director told Ricciarelli that she was too fat. EMI switched its soundman at the last minute to a set of Classic Rock sessions in London. Despite the ructions, the recording was immaculate. 'The battlements scene with Domingo and Ricciarelli was absolutely beautiful and I had never heard an opera chorus like La Scala's,' said sound engineer Tony Faulkner. Domingo contributed a sleeve note, venting the opinion that Otello 'is for grown-up singers'. The shaft was aimed directly at Pavarotti's playful midriff.

77. *Pärt: Cantus in Memoriam Benjamin Britten*
Royal Scottish National Orchestra/Neeme Järvi
Chandos: Dundee (Caird Hall), 23–24 August 1987

The tectonic plates of cultural history are heard shifting here. Arvo Pärt, a technician at Estonian Radio, was a philosophical individual who sought ways of using music as a means of resistance to the Soviet occupation of his country. He started composing twelve-note rows in the manner of Western atonalists and, when all that achieved was to get him banned, he turned to older sources. Profoundly religious, he drew upon the simplicities of medieval church music in his third symphony of 1973, dedicated to Neeme Järvi, his country's foremost conductor. Its monodic themes, set in Sibelian topography (Helsinki is a short hop across the Baltic from Tallinn), were ice-meltingly lovely, unpunishable by any communist criterion.

Pärt developed the style in a Cantata Symphony the following year and achieved an apotheosis of sorts when, in 1976, upon the death of Britten – a composer notorious for pro-Soviet sympathies – he wrote a short public eulogy for a colleague with whom he was unacquainted and out of sympathy. The Cantus in Memoriam Benjamin Britten splits a string ensemble into separate halves, each side descending very slowly down the scale of A minor, to the tolling of a single bell. Its ethereality was both an antidote to the dialectical materialism of state communism and a solemn assertion of the dignity of the individual in a system that claimed to own all souls.

Across the world, unknown to Pärt, New Yorkers Steve Reich and Philip Glass were offering a parallel response to Western materialism in a form of repetitive minimalism. In Poland, Henryk Mikolai Gorecki was writing his 'holy minimalist' third symphony (CD 88, p. 261). In Britain, Michael Nyman turned from serialism to minimalism. Composers on both sides of the Cold War were thinking similar thoughts. Neeme Järvi defected to Sweden with a repertory richer and more eclectic than any Western conductor.

He recorded Pärt on a small English label with a modest Scottish orchestra and no fanfare whatsoever. Cantus came out in a disc of music by Estonian composers. A year later, Soviet power collapsed and Estonia was set free.

78. Gershwin: Porgy and Bess
Willard White, Cynthia Haymon, London Philharmonic
Orchestra/Simon Rattle
EMI: London (Abbey Road), February 1988

George Gershwin's tale of tough love among the underclasses was anathema to opera houses. Turned down by the snooty Met, it had a modest premiere in Boston in September 1935 and transferred to the Alvin Theater, on Broadway, for 124 nights. When the show lost its $70,000 investment, Gershwin lost heart. After his death in July 1937 Porgy hovered in limbo between commercial theatre and repertory opera, the establishment clinging to the first-night verdict by Olin Downes in the *New York Times* that 'Mr Gershwin . . . has not completely formed his style as an opera composer.'

The Met considered Porgy for the 1976 US bicentennial year, but went cold on the idea for much the same reasons as before. Amends were finally made in February 1985 (Simon Estes and Grace Bumbry in the name roles), but it was the following summer, in a much unlikelier setting, that the work achieved universal recognition.

Simon Rattle, the rising British conductor, had been pestering Glyndebourne, the fat-cat summer festival, to engage with society red in tooth and claw. Trevor Nunn, head of the Royal Shakespeare Company and director of Andrew Lloyd Webber musicals, loved the Porgy story; Willard White and Cynthia Haymon took the title roles. Six weeks of rehearsal in the Sussex countryside was a festival of multiracial interaction in England's green and pleasant. On opening night stuffed shirts dissolved into helpless tears and the Glyndebourne Chorus sounded like gospel. Rattle pinned the rhythms just right, between opera and honky-tonk, and there wasn't a weak link in the cast. Harolyn Blackwell's Summertime was pitched so sweet and high it was practically out of her skin and Bruce Hubbard was deep in every sense as Jake. The perpetual motion of trains and ships about to leave is nervously innate to Rattle's beat. This was an opera that was on its way. The recording, two years later in Abbey Road, struggled to recapture the original excitement but it nevertheless conveyed a moment in performing history when colour and class ceased to matter and artists and audience were brought together by their common humanity.

79. Halévy: La Juive
José Carreras, Ferruccio Furlanetto, Dalmacio Gonzalez,
Julia Varady, June Anderson; Philharmonia Orchestra,
Ambrosian Chorus/Antonio de Almeida
Philips: London, 1–8 August 1986; Munich,
19–26 February 1989

One of the most popular operas of the nineteenth century, La Juive fell out of rep because few modern houses could find or afford to pay three lyric tenors, each capable of carrying off a big scene. The opera is immense, well over four hours long, and its early influence was vast – not only on Berlioz, Gounod, Bizet and Saint-Saëns, but on the impressionable young Richard Wagner, much as he despised its Jewish theme. It is an essential study score of the high noon of grand opera. Eleazar was the last role that Caruso sang on stage, at the Met, on Christmas Eve 1924.

With the rise of Nazism the work fell out of favour – its last Paris performance was in 1934 – and when normality was restored it had been completely forgotten, but for a few scattered concert performances. Its absence irked the New York Friends of French Opera, a group that put on one-nighters at Carnegie Hall. Money was raised, and Erik Smith of Philips assembled a credible cast under Antonio de Almeida, probably the world's foremost authority on French opera, owner of an unrivalled private library of first-edition scores (now at Trinity College, London).

De Almeida made some cuts to keep the costs manageable on three discs and split the session over three years and two venues to accommodate the busy diaries of its star performers. Despite these constraints, the performance is stylistically authentic and narratively compelling. Carreras, in prime voice, leads the tenorial pack; Julia Varady (Mrs Fischer-Dieskau), slightly too full and shrill, plays an epic heroine, forced to choose between her faith and her life. The set pieces are wonderfully rendered, never better than in Eleazar's rapt prayer, O Dieu, Dieu de nos pères, and the succeeding paschal cavatina. The recording sold in meagre quantities, chiefly to aficionados and rarity collectors, but its release reminded the opera world of La Juive's existence and revivals were staged in Vienna and New York during the 1990s. The Paris Opéra finally took it back in 2007.

80. Bruckner: Seventh Symphony
Vienna Philharmonic Orchestra/Herbert von Karajan
DG: Vienna (Musikvereinsaal), 23 April 1989

Hitler shared a birthplace, Linz, with Anton Bruckner and considered his seventh symphony to be the summit of German music, equal to Beethoven's Ninth. Once he won the war, he was going to rebuild Linz as the cultural capital of Europe. He blamed the Jews, wrote Joseph Goebbels, for making Brahms more popular than Bruckner.

The seventh symphony, an elegy on the death of Richard Wagner, chimed with Hitler's mood as the war went against him. Lyrical and in the key of E major, it descends into a solemn Adagio in C-sharp minor, employing four Wagner tubas to underline the source of all sorrows. Bruckner's was the last music played on Berlin radio before the city fell; it symbolized death, and transfiguration.

Decades later, pain-stricken and strife-torn, the most powerful conductor on record fell out with the Berlin Philharmonic and switched his next Bruckner concert to the rival Viennese. Herbert von Karajan was eighty-one years old and visibly ailing. His performance shocked admirers for its lack of immaculate sheen, the absence of what players called his 'ice-cold perfectionism'. There were fractured entries, a stressed roughness to the strings, a farm-yard earthiness. The recording had none of his personal stamp yet Karajan, whether out of arrogance or humility, gave it his approval.

Alongside epic performances by Klemperer, Furtwängler and Giulini, this stands out as an extraordinary interpretation, driven impulsively to the edge of understanding. If the opening Allegro Moderato is over-bright, the very slow Adagio veers towards the sepulchral and the Scherzo and finale are profoundly unsettling. It is impossible to know what was going through the maestro's mind, but he seemed to be showing that imperfection was a necessary part of life, that grief and lament were not things of beauty, and that all must accept their fate. This was to be Karajan's last record. Three months later, he was dead.

81. Rossini: Opera Arias
Cecilia Bartoli, Vienna Volksoper Orchestra/Giuseppe Patane
Decca: Vienna (Konzerthaus), July 1989

It says much for the supremacy of Maria Callas that no soprano came within one-tenth of her sales. The nearest contender was a young mezzo who, like Callas, had an unmistakable sound and an immovable will. Bartoli was spotted at nineteen at a Milan cattle-market audition by the veteran Decca producer, Christopher Raeburn. Two Rossini arias, from Tancredi and L'Italiana in Algeri, left him 'spellbound'. Raeburn cast her in a Barber of Seville but he also booked Bartoli for a solo album of Rossini arias, a daringly premature exposure for an artist barely tested on stage.

The child of two chorus singers at Rome Opera, born in 1966, Bartoli danced flamenco before she began voice training, independence and vivacity shining through as defining traits. Publicists tried to deck her in the usual paraphernalia, but Bartoli would kick off her shoes and shuck into jeans. Although she took advice from such experienced conductors as Daniel Barenboim and Nikolaus

Harnoncourt, she resisted directors with a vengeance and drove Jonathan Miller right out of the Met.

By restricting herself to five months' work a year, she kept her voice fresh, her fees high and her privacy intact. Only Bartoli could have made best-selling albums out of obscure arias by Scarlatti, Vivaldi and Gluck. Only Bartoli could, in an age of record desperation, refuse gold-leaf blandishments and stick to the high classical repertoire that came to her so naturally. In Rossini she had no living rival, displaying a ruby-red depth of pitch and colour as the Italian Girl in Algiers, an all-conquering vitality and high vibrato as the heroine of Cenerentola. She brings a smile to the lips, even on record.

82. *Corigliano: First Symphony*
Chicago Symphony Orchestra/Daniel Barenboim
Warner: Chicago (Orchestral Hall), 15 March 1990

Medical science in the 1980s was helpless in the face of Aids. Thousands were swept to early, emaciated deaths and losses across the arts were severe, from Rudolf Nureyev to Rock Hudson. But in the years before the arrival of attenuating drugs, it was the non-famous victims who left the largest epitaph. A gigantic quilt was made up in Washington, DC, each square a lovingly celebrated life, and the exhibit itself a reproach to the modern world's conscience in the face of its first real plague.

Seeing the quilt gave John Corigliano the idea for a patchwork symphony in memory of tragically afflicted friends – the pianist who premiered his first concerto, a cellist he played with, a music industry executive who went mad with Aids dementia – each life eulogized in his symphony by a solo instrumental line.

The son of a concertmaster of the New York Philharmonic, Corigliano was one of those stubborn composers who resisted atonality and persisted with writing emotionally direct music. His symphony is patchy in both structure and content and, while its sentiments are held sternly in check (one movement was later furnished with a kitschy, otiose recitation), its topicality was unmissable. Barenboim gave a blazing premiere with America's loudest orchestra – soloists: Stephen Hough (piano), John Sharp (cello) – and the symphony took off like migrating swallows. It was performed 600 times by 125 orchestras in 17 countries, the first contemporary American symphony to reach China and one of the final contributions the record industry made towards unifying the human race in mourning and resistance.

83. Three Tenors in Concert
José Carreras, Placido Domingo, Luciano Pavarotti/Zubin Mehta
Decca: Rome (Terme di Caracalla), 7 July 1990

It was never a meeting of equals. José Carreras had been desperately sick with leukaemia and the other two, bigger voiced, were keen to give thanks for his recovery with a concert for children's cancer charities. 'Both Placido and I are very fond of this beautiful man,' said Pavarotti, sensing victory in a gladiatorial contest (at one stage, a judging panel was mooted, with scoreboards flashed to the audience after each aria).

No concert of three tenors had been aired in living memory and media organizations were slow to subscribe. There was a World Cup going on across the road and the tenors, all soccer fans, would sing only on a rest night. Decca, Pavarotti's label, finally stumped up $1 million to be split between the boys and their chosen baton, Zubin Mehta. Not bad for a night's work.

The tenors held themselves stiffly apart, each singing alternate favourites. Domingo climaxed with E lucevan le stelle from Tosca and Pavarotti with Nessun dorma from Turandot. The three came together at the very end in a twelve-song medley arranged by Hollywood's Lalo Schifrin and when the applause kept rolling, they came right back in O Sole mio. But the night was sealed with a three-man Nessun dorma, the television theme tune of the Italy World Cup. The audience delirium was unbounded and when the CD hit the shops it outstripped any classical release in history.

How good were the tenors? Berthold Goldschmidt, an octogen-arian composer who had worked in Berlin with the best opera singers of the 1920s and played celesta at the world premiere of *Wozzeck*, rang me during the live broadcast to say he had never in a long life seen such a prodigious display of virtuosic vocal technique.

84. Shostakovich: Twenty-four Preludes and Fugues Op. 87
Tatiana Nikolayeva
Hyperion: London (Hill Chapel, Hampstead),
24–27 September 1990

In the eye of Stalin's wrath, unable to start another symphony under constant vilification, Dmitri Shostakovich reverted to the deceptive simplicities of Johann Sebastian Bach. Sent to Leipzig to judge a piano competition for the composer's bicentennial festival of July 1950, he voted (as required) for the Soviet entrant. Aged twenty-six and stockily built, Tatiana Nikolayeva looked like a typical keyboard banger from the tractor farm, but she stupefied the judges by offering to play Bach's complete forty-eight preludes and fugues. They settled for the F-sharp minor and awarded her first prize.

Back in Moscow, Shostakovich called to say he had been uplifted by her performance and was composing his own preludes and fugues. 'At his request I telephoned him every day and he asked me to come to him to listen to him play the pieces he had just written,' she reported. In May 1951 he played the cycle for the approval of Tikhon Khrennikov's all-powerful Composers Union, with Nikolayeva turning the pages. It was a stiflingly hot day and Shostakovich was nervous. His recital was greeted by a barrage of pseudo-political criticism from a host of jealous nonentities and craven sycophants. On a show of hands, the Union refused to allow Shostakovich to give the cycle a public hearing.

The following summer Nikolayeva arranged to play the set to a different committee at a time when Shostakovich was out of town.

Some of the composers who attacked it on first hearing now applauded wildly. Nikolayeva was cleared to give the premiere at Leningrad in December 1952; Shostakovich wrote a private dedication in her score (omitted from the published edition). He never performed the full cycle himself in public, but a week before his death he called Nikolayeva and asked her to play some of the preludes at his next birthday concert.

She was the first to record the cycle outside Russia, communing with the music in an empty London church in a performance that drew together the disparate struggles of Bach and Shostakovich to master and dictate musical form. The set opens with eleven seconds of cavernous silence before a tentative theme edges out of the darkness, lulling suspicion in a C-major tonality and maintaining a dynamic level that never rises above mezzo-forte. As the theme gives way to its successors in rising fifths, the ear is tweaked by unexpected discordances, notes of desperation that are buried in the crevices of a towering concept, a masterpiece by any measure.

Nikolayeva had the composer's permission to make changes and would add or omit a repeat (in the fourth fugue, for instance) for structural elegance. Physically massive and missing several front teeth, she sat at the keyboard like a witness at a war crimes trial, indomitable and unforgettable. The recording won international awards and tour invitations. On 13 November 1993, in the interval of a public recital of the preludes and fugues in San Francisco, Nikolayeva collapsed in her dressing room and died, her testimony complete.

85. *Brahms: First Symphony*
Berlin Philharmonic Orchestra/Claudio Abbado
DG: Berlin (Philharmonie), September 1990

The Wall had been down for less than a year and already Berlin was divided again, between rich and poor, triumph and uncertainty. The ochre, octagonal Philharmonie hall, built as a symbol of Cold War defiance in a desolate bend at the end of the free world, was now in prime development land, throbbing to the drills of multinational corporations.

Herbert von Karajan was dead and his orchestra had elected Claudio Abbado, a reticent, socialist, modernist, stylish Italian. He had one concert to win over Karajan's adoring public, and this was it. Abbado chose the first symphony of Johannes Brahms, a work embedded in the German consciousness as an act of cultural continuity – so much so that many referred to it as Beethoven's Tenth. The hall was filled with old-timers, silvery hair and duelling scars, and clutching tight to past preconceptions.

Abbado wreathed them in beams with his opening statement of absolute security and unblemished sound. Only the occasional turn of a woodwind phrase gave any hint of subversive intent. The middle movements were sumptuously arrayed and the adagio opening of the finale had never sounded so lustrous, even under Karajan's laser eye. But when it came to the big tune, which the old man used to approach with many changes of gear and signals of redemption, Abbado held back the orchestra, tamping down the dynamics and allowing the melody to rise imperceptibly out of the preceding texture. When it broke, the world took on a different light, warmer and less aggressive. It was a Eureka moment, a new dawn. Next morning, with myself and others as witnesses, Abbado signed a long-term record contract with Karajan's former label and set about the process of transforming the orchestra. When he stepped down a decade later, hardly one of Karajan's players was left in the band and the performing ethos had evolved from archaically imperious to fashionably imposing. It remained, however, an elite institution – refusing to admit by audition players from the former East Germany or the eastern half of its own city. Fabulous as it was, the Brahms First was a false dawn.

86. Crumb: Black Angels (with Marta: Doom, A Sigh; Shostakovich: Eighth Quartet; etc.)
Kronos
Warner (Elektra Nonesuch): San Francisco, 1990

In the thick of the Vietnam War, a young violinist was lying in bed on the US West Coast when he heard on late-night radio a string quartet, Black Angels, that gave expression to all of his frustrations about the purposeless conflict. David Harrington decided there and then that he would try to change the face of contemporary chamber music and turn it into a force for change.

Modernism fell into two camps at the time, either deadly serial or intellectually vacant, obsessed with theory or simple to the point of infantility. Harrington felt that his quartet, Kronos, should play all styles non-judgementally. They performed abstruse Penderecki in San Quentin jail and an amplified version of Jimi Hendrix's Purple Haze within the hallowed walls of Carnegie Hall. Kitted out in spiky hair and designer gear, switching easily between acoustic and electronic instruments, Kronos gave hundreds of world premieres and introduced dozens of composers – Sculthorpe, Gorecki, Golijov, Volans, Franghis Ali-Zade, Piazzolla – to international attention.

The starting point, George Crumb's Black Angels, appeared on their second album, along with a wartime Shostakovich quartet, a protest against ethnic cleansing in Ceausescu's Romania and adaptations of pieces by Istvan Marta, Charles Ives and Thomas Tallis. There was no instant comfort to be had in eighteen minutes of Crumb. Grounded in a theme from Schubert's Death and the Maiden quartet and replete with classical quotations, the quartet opens with a buzzing of electric insects, not unlike Bartók's night music gone mad, and gravitates through a maze of simulations – 'sounds of bones and flutes', 'lost bells' – to a medieval pavane and echoes of the Dies Irae. Numbers are dotted like clues through the score, sevens and thirteens dictating the electronic sequences and each sequence relating symmetrically to those around it. After a while, the sheer logic of the work overcomes its disparities and the ear is allowed to hope for better times ahead. There is no better memorial in art to the warped, irresolute Nixon years and the recording was the foundation of all that Kronos sought to achieve.

I heard them play Black Angels on a Berkeley campus to a backpack audience who walked around the lawns as they would at a rock gig, selectively absorbing the passages that were personally meaningful. The flickering response did not affect the group's concentration. On the contrary, they were tuned intently to audience mood and switched to a jam session if one piece or other failed to grip. This was chamber music for the post-modern age of short attention spans and visual imagery. Crumb wrote the formula; Kronos did the rest.

87. Handel: Messiah
Philharmonia Baroque Orchestra/Nicholas McGegan
Harmonia Mundi: University of California at Berkeley (Hertz Hall), 4–7 January 1991

In the early music revolution, Messiah became a free for all with each ayatollah of alleged authenticity producing his own doctrine on record. You could have a carbon-dated performance conducted by Christopher Hogwood, a chorus of sixteen from Harry Christophers, the Handel-inscribed Foundling Hospital score from Paul McCreesh, lickety-split tempi from John Eliot Gardiner – anything, in fact, except much-loved mass performances that were ruled out by the mullahs as hopelessly heretical and politically incorrect for our age of musical austerity.

Into the disputational mayhem leaped Nicholas McGegan, an Englishman in California, with a do-it-yourself Messiah that laid out all known variants of Handel's lifetime performances on a set of CDs that let listeners at home choose their preferred combination. There is an hour's more music on McGegan's Messiah than on any other, and it can be used to recreate any of nine distinct versions. The aria 'But who may abide the day of His coming' is sung according to strict tradition by a counter-tenor, but the set contains bright alternatives by bass and soprano, each with substantive differences, as well as a plain recitative for those who prefer to pass on Handel's sublime tune. To have two versions of 'He was despised', for alto or soprano, is a bonus choice for any rapt Handelian and the set as a whole is one of the most entertaining musical parlour games ever invented.

McGegan's liberalism was, understandably, attacked by funda-mentalist maestros and scorned by their lapdog critics but the logic was impeccable and the musicianship inspiring. There is sensational singing from the still-unknown soprano Lorraine Hunt (later Lorraine Hunt Lieberson), mezzo Patricia Spence, counter-tenor Drew Minter and a Berkeley chorus ably led by the camp musi-cologist Philip Brett, who sought to prove elsewhere on flimsy evidence that Handel was unremittingly gay. Scholarship, gossip and glamour – just what the composer ordered.

88. Gorecki: Third Symphony
Dawn Upshaw, London Sinfonietta/David Zinman
Nonesuch: London (CTS Studios, Wembley), May 1991

Henryk Mikolai Gorecki, a composer unknown, penetrated the pop charts in 1993 with a third symphony that sold three-quarters of a million CDs, its soprano finale composed around a girl's inscription on a Gestapo cell wall. Wearing his shyness like a shield, the lame-legged Pole from Katowice faced a round table of journalists in Brussels, speaking halting German, unable to explain his success. My memory is of a small, dark man adrift on a floodtide he had inadvertently unleashed. 'My symphony has nothing to do with the war,' he insisted, 'it is a symmetrical lament of a child for its mother, a mother for its child.'

Gorecki had written his third symphony seventeen years before as a Catholic response to atonal modernism, on the one hand, and to the monochrome communism that held his country in an iron vice, on the other. Meditative more than minimalist, the symphony was performed at contemporary music festivals to general derision and recorded twice on regional labels without much recognition. It took Dawn Upshaw's voice with the London Sinfonietta and an exceptionally perceptive conductor to achieve spiritual trans-cendence.

The recording process was fraught. The sessions were booked for St Augustine's Church, Kilburn, on a busy junction in north-west London, but engineer Tony Faulkner warned that street noise would wreck the atmosphere and moved it to a Wembley studio at considerable extra cost. The crew were told the recording would be cancelled unless they accepted a half-fee; Upshaw was advised by her agent to take cash instead of royalties. Producer Colin Matthews, accomplished composer and Mahler scholar, took the crew down the road for a cheap curry when the last take was in the can and everybody forgot all about the disc.

By Christmas the following year it was selling at the rate of one a minute on Oxford Street. Gorecki became the target of a bidding war by music publishers and promptly clammed up, producing no further scores for a decade. The symphony failed resoundingly in live performances, its success confined to record. But its composer could go home content, knowing that he had outsold most of the world's pop stars.

89. Mahler: Sixth Symphony
London Philharmonic Orchestra/Klaus Tennstedt
EMI: London (Royal Festival Hall), November 1991

No one who saw Klaus Tennstedt conduct will forget the prefatory uncertainty. The orchestra would sit on stage, half-expecting can-cellation as minutes ticked past the appointed hour. Then, rushing out of the wings, almost stumbling over his feet, this ramshackle figure would mount the podium and, with the most sheepish of grins, pitch into a performance that was like no other, before or since. The essence of his art was spontaneity, anathema to the perfectionist ethos of the recording studio.

Tennstedt (1926–98) was a natural, a non-intellectual who grasped the principles of conducting from his father, concertmaster in the small town of Halle, and took it up when a hand injury ended his violin career. Mistrusted by the communists, he found provincial obscurity in West Germany before a chain of coincidences propelled him to an explosive US debut in Boston, after which the world and its record labels were at his feet. Tennstedt responded with a massive nervous breakdown. He found succour in the music of Gustav Mahler, which became the leitmotiv of his anxious life.

Tennstedt's Mahler was wholly intuitive, ignorant of critical theory and infused with personal experience. The Sixth, he once told me, anticipated in its opening bars the tramp of Nazi jackboots and in its bleak finale the impotence of the individual against state tyranny. These insights were integrated subliminally into performances, without explicit gesture or rehearsal explanation. A Tennstedt concert was enriched as much by momentary impulse as by cogitated foresight.

His approach to Mahler was narrative, event relentlessly succeeding event until the pressure grew unendurable and catharsis broke. In the Sixth he balanced the opening movement terror with passages of profound compassion, upping the pace to a frenzied Scherzo, yielding to an Andante of unexampled tenderness. In the bleak finale, none bleaker in the whole symphonic repertoire, he allowed chinks of consolation. A BBC Proms audience stood motionless through the ninety minutes of Tennstedt's Sixth, petrified by its intensity. A 1983 EMI studio recording at Kingsway Hall lacked the high-wire risk that Tennstedt courted and was over-polished at the editing desk. This live concert performance, taken after his return from throat-cancer treatment, is less wild than usual but deepened with an irresistible finality. Cancer and self-doubt soon brought Tennstedt's art to a tragic, stuttering close.

90. Goldschmidt: The Magnificent Cuckold
Roberta Alexander, Robert Wörle, Deutsche Symphonie-Orchester/Lothar Zagrosek
Decca: Berlin (Jesus-Christus-Kirche), November 1992

Awash with Three Tenors profits, Decca set out in search of composers whose music was banned by the Nazis and deserving of resurrection. The producer Michael Haas was directed to an old man, Bertold Goldschmidt, who was living in the same two-room flat in Belsize Park, northwest London, that he had first rented as a refugee in 1935. Goldschmidt, Haas came to realize, was not just a surviving witness of Weimar art but one of its foremost voices. His opera, Der gewaltige Hahnrei, had triumphed in Mannheim in February 1932 and was on its way to the Berlin State Opera when Hitler brought down the curtain on works by Jews.

Haas selected the opera as a cornerstone of Entartete Musik, a series named by the Nazi title for proscribed and 'degenerate' works. Goldschmidt, nearing ninety, supervised the recording sessions in Berlin. He walked about picking wild tomatoes on the waste ground above Hitler's bunker and sat with me in Kurfürsten-damm cafés arguing that nothing much had changed. The Nazis were a brief, tragic aberration, a footnote in history.

His opera was a comedy of marital jealousy, melodically woven around the irresistible but virtuous wife Stella, sung by the American soprano Roberta Alexander. The febrile opening theme places Goldschmidt in familiar territory, between Weill and Hindemith, with harkings ahead to Britten and Shostakovich. The fun of the affair is grounded in a lascivious array of musical seductions, as much from the orchestral woodwind as from the singing characters – though the third-act opening 'Du und ich und ich und du' is a virtuosic comic set-piece.

Lothar Zagrosek conducted with subtle fervour and the opera received a huge ovation at a final public performance at the Philhar-monie. It was also staged at the Komische Opera, sixty years behind its intended debut. The Cuckold sold well on record and served as the series flagship but corporate cuts in the mid-Nineties put a summary end to Entartete Musik, the record industry's last great educational venture.

91. *Verdi: La Traviata*

Angela Gheorghiu, Frank Lopardo, Leo Nucci, Royal Opera House Orchestra and Chorus/Georg Solti

Decca: London (Royal Opera House), December 1994

Georg Solti was making a sentimental return to Covent Garden, which he had ruled in the 1960s, with an opera that he had somehow never conducted and was having to study from scratch. The director was Richard Eyre, head of Britain's National Theatre, a man who hated the artifice of opera and had never directed one before. Eyre was appalled to discover, on entering the opera house, that a singer earned ten times as much on stage as the greatest Shakespearean actress. There was a puritan bitterness to Eyre's approach that augured ill for the opera.

Serendipity intervened. A soprano from nowhere, a Romanian railworker's daughter, had caught the eye of Covent Garden's casting director weeks after leaving the Bucharest conservatory. Big-eyed, beautiful and with a ferocity reminiscent of Callas, Angela Gheorghiu ticked all the boxes for vocal and dramatic power and was being hotly pursued for all manner of roles by Placido Domingo, among others. Solti and Eyre agreed that she was the ideal Violetta.

Backstage, her life took a different turn. A French-Sicilian tenor, Roberto Alagna, flew in from his wife's funeral to sing Gounod's Romeo. Sparks flew backstage. Before long, he married Gheorghiu. 'The public is lucky to have us,' proclaimed Alagna. Jonathan Miller, the British stage director, called the celebrity pair 'the Bonnie and Clyde of opera'. They got fired, like Callas, from the Met. All that, however, lay ahead.

Solti, sensing an extraordinary debut, badgered the BBC to screen the opening night. Andrew Porter, the veteran critic, wrote:

'I encountered one of those performances when only the present seems to matter: when memories fade and any connoisseurship and comparisons are laid aside.'[12] Decca rushed in with a recording crew.

Rough as some of the live recording may be, Solti's command of the opera is wondrously compassionate and the secondary roles are extremely well sung, but it is Gheorghiu who catches the ear with a magnetism unheard for a diva generation. Her sotto voce entry 'E strano' combines pathos and fear with sexual confidence of a blazing voltage. As with Callas in Tosca, you feel that nothing is beyond this woman, including murder. Lustrous and faultless in voice and articulation, casting memories of Sutherland and Pavarotti (likewise on Decca) deep into shade, Gheorghiu possesses the role of Violetta with shattering conviction and you do not need the audience eruption to confirm the sighting of an ascendant comet.

92. *Bruckner: Fifth Symphony*
Royal Scottish National Orchestra/Georg Tintner
Naxos: Glasgow (Henry Wood Hall), 1996

A new classical label appeared in 1988 selling CDs at one-third of the usual price, a mere impulse purchase. The orchestras were remote, the conductors and soloists obscure. The discs came from Hong Kong and seemed to be pitched at the growing and somewhat indiscriminate Asian-tiger taste for high culture.

Critics greeted Naxos with collective disdain. What changed their tune was a cycle of Bruckner symphonies that called up mighty reminiscences of old masters: Klemperer, Furtwängler, Karajan. From the fifth symphony's opening footfall, the immaculate phrasing, idiomatic pacing and resolute passion announced an interpretation of unarguable authority.

The conductor, Georg Tintner, was a name unknown even to

12. Decca booklet accompanying the CD.

obsessive spotters of maestro movements. Evicted in 1938 from Vienna, where he had conducted at the Volksoper, Tintner wandered fruitlessly around New Zealand and Australia, impressing musicians with his rigour and offending managements with a rigid adherence to principle. In his mid-seventies, he had found some contentment with an orchestra in Nova Scotia, Canada, but his driving ambition seemed doomed to failure when a meeting with Klaus Heymann, the Naxos owner, clicked into gear.

Heymann had begun recording the symphonic repertoire systematically, one composer after the next. He had pencilled in two German conductors and the New Zealand Symphony for Bruckner but neither maestro could get on with the musicians, who were in stroppy mood. Tintner flew out to attempt the Bruckner sixth and ninth symphonies in New Zealand but the players misbehaved and the sessions had to be abandoned. Heymann approached several British orchestras, none of whom was prepared to risk their reputations on an unfamiliar conductor.

It was the Scots who broke the ice, warming to Tintner's other-worldly fervour, itself reflective of Bruckner's peasant naivety. Tintner's interpretation, however, was morally prophetic, conceived on a scale as large as a Gothic cathedral. After the opening Adagio, the first movement Allegro portends human suffering and redemption; the middle movements are a fertile canvas of rustic civilization and the finale, in this masterly performance, weaves together not only the disparate themes of an eighty-minute work but, in fleeting echoes, the history of music from Bach to Beethoven. It actually sounds as if Tintner had been waiting all of his life to give this performance. The Scottish orchestra, in fine form, completed the cycle over the next two years, apart from three works that went to the National Symphony Orchestra of Ireland. Acclaim mounted with each release. A set of Bruckner masses was planned and the English National Opera was contemplating a Tintner Parsifal when the conductor, aged eighty-two, flung himself off a high-rise balcony while in the throes of terminal cancer. His Bruckner symphonies sold half a million copies, far more than any set before or since.

93. *The Hyperion Schubert Edition*
Various artists with Graham Johnson (piano)
London, 1987–98

Ted Perry, a minicab driver with musical dreams, set up his label in a dreary corner of southeast London with a little loan from a friend. Once solvent, he asked the world's best Lieder singers to sing all 631 Schubert songs. So brash was the request, and so sincere, that although stars were exclusive to big labels, they got out of their contracts and trundled off to belt-and-braces Hyperion to join the integral edition. It helped that Graham Johnson, one of the world's most trusted accompanists, was selecting the programmes, carefully balancing familiar songs on each release with the esoteric.

Janet Baker, Elly Ameling and Brigitte Fassbänder came out of retirement for one last song; Dietrich Fischer-Dieskau, past singing in his seventies, narrated episodes in Die schöne Müllerin. Arleen Auger, critically ill, sang a sensational set with piano and clarinet. Lucia Popp, also tragically cut short, cut her last track. Margaret Price and Peter Schreier, Thomas Hampson and Edith Mathis, joined an ever-swelling party that blossomed into a set of forty discs, with an accompanying book of song texts.

Beside them sparkled a bevy of budding singers, spotted by Johnson on the way up. Ian Bostridge, Christine Schäfer, Matthias Görne and Simon Keenlyside were the Lieder talent of the future, learning as they sang. Bostridge is ideally innocent in Mein! and Ann Murray is magical in Rückweg. Some of the more famous names are on the verge of being past it but this is not a set to be judged by its parts, or even by their sum. Hyperion's Schubert Edition is one of the great achievements of the classical record industry, the more impressive for having been achieved by a one-man band in the back of beyond. It is an historic monument, unique and unsurpassable.

94. Beethoven: The Nine Symphonies
Tonhalle Orchestra/David Zinman
Arte Nova: Zurich (Tonhalle), December 1998

Arturo Toscanini, in the early 1950s, established the Beethoven symphonies as the summit of a conductor's recorded achievement and the cornerstone of every classical collection. The ceiling was swiftly lowered by mass imitation. Herbert von Karajan, who recorded the cycle energetically with EMI's Philharmonia Orchestra around the same time, went on to repeat it four more times. His 1962 Berlin DG set, recorded as the Wall went up, defined a certain materialist defiance both of communism and of all-purpose American consumerism. Karajan aspired in his Beethoven assaults to ever-greater purities of sonic perfection and proofs of his commercial dominance.

Otto Klemperer, in London, countered the Karajan effect with spiritual verities from a prior age, his recalcitrant tempi a reflection of the composer's growling misanthropy. Ego inflation then set in as just about every conductor with a record deal demanded a Beethoven box of his own. Haitink, Solti, Josef Krips and André Cluytens were quick off the mark, followed by Bernstein (twice), Vaclav Neumann, Kubelik, Böhm, Wolfgang Sawallisch, Colin Davis, Neville Marriner, Walter Weller, Charles Mackerras, Gunter Wand and Kurt Masur. Abbado had two cracks at the cycle, as did his arch-rival Muti. Christopher Hogwood led an onslaught from period instrument bands, followed by Gardiner, Norrington, Roy Goodman and a million-selling set from Harnoncourt. The shelves groaned with Beethoven excess, and still the inflationary maestros demanded more.

Simon Rattle preached early-music teachings to the Vienna Philharmonic, new tricks to old dogs, in an unsatisfying hybrid compilation. Daniel Barenboim sought to apply Furtwängler mannerisms to the Berlin Staatskapelle with equally varied effects. Interpretation turned to pastiche. Finally, patience ran out and record labels slammed down the shutters. Rattle and Barenboim were supposed to be the last, sustained by their celebrity and a public curiosity to discover what they might add to the canon.

Then, from a bargain-basement label, came a breath of fresh air. David Zinman, a long-underrated American conductor who had served at Baltimore and Zurich, was captivated by a scholarly restoration of Beethoven's original manuscripts prepared by a British musicologist, Jonathan del Mar, with meticulous attention to the composer's writ. Zinman laid claim to first recording rights amid considerable scepticism. Any doubts are dispelled by the opening of the Eroica, its tempi brisk and textures coolly transparent when compared either to Rattle and Barenboim or to any of the notionally more authentic period instrument versions. In Zinman's hands this was, in between the moving and numinous episodes, music to dance to.

It would be specious to list examples of excellence, for they are endless. The opening of the Fifth has the most natural sweep since Kleiber's; the Pastoral is irresistibly enticing; the Seventh is momentously structured; and the Adagio of the Ninth has a cameral quality of extraordinary intimacy. These are performances that feel spring-cleaned, played with brio and wide-eyed surprise in a crystal-clear digital acoustic. There was no vanity to this enterprise, no overweening maestro ego. Zinman directed from the page, with few personal superimpositions. Del Mar lists the points in each symphony where a listener can actually hear the difference – a thrilling novelty.

Many of the players in the Zurich orchestra boast Czech and Hungarian surnames, sharing a central European heritage with the Vienna Philharmonic. This is expertly accomplished Beethoven, user-friendly, up-to-the-minute in its scholarship and fresh as an Alpine meadow after rain. It is a classical record rarity, a genuinely new release.

95. Stravinsky: Rite of Spring (with Scriabin: Poem of Ecstasy)
Kirov Orchestra/Valery Gergiev
Philips: Baden-Baden (Festspielhaus), 24–27 July 1999

Igor Stravinsky recorded his notoriety earner twice, at bewilderingly different tempi. Pierre Monteux, who conducted the riotous 1913 premiere in Paris, also made two inconsistent recordings. The composer derided modern interpreters, singling out Karajan and Boulez for personal abuse; no account, it seemed, would satisfy him.

The score itself is contradictory, on the one hand Stravinsky's mathematically precise markings and on the other the bucolic savagery of the sacral dance, itself a metaphor for the innate unruliness of Mother Russia. This is not a piece that can be performed safety-first. Unless it feels dangerous, the performance must flop. On record, Bernstein and the extremely young Rattle (with the Youth Orchestra of Great Britain) come closest to the requisite wildness.

One summer's night in Rotterdam, I saw a pair of Georgian pianists pound through the two-piano version of the Rite, shattering nerves and windows around the town. Once they had finished, Valery Gergiev strolled backstage to a rehearsal piano and played the piece again privately, two-handed and with chilling menace. The fury of the dances was held in check until near the end, the muttered threat of violence more terrifying than a veritable bloodbath. This suppression of desire seemed to get to the heart of the Stravinskian dichotomy.

I spent until four in the morning walking the streets of Rotterdam with Gergiev, discussing the relative merits of Stravinsky and Prokofiev (whom he, at the time, preferred). Of Caucasian origin, raised within the self-enclosed Soviet aristocracy (his uncle was Stalin's favourite tank designer), Gergiev had no access to the mindset of the French-nannied Westernized Stravinsky and no sympathy for such luxuries. His grasp of the Rite was intuitive: he knew whereof it sprang, in the taunting rituals of tribal rivalry that created his country. Those rituals lie at the heart of the Rite, wild and wary, belonging to a civilization that predates civilization. This is Gergiev's habitat and he rules it like a lion. Nothing is respected in this performance except the deference owed to a conqueror. The phrasing – so complicated that many maestros rewrite the score without bar-lines – is rendered with casual mastery. The Kirov orchestra play like musicians possessed. There has never been a Rite like this.

96. Berlioz: Symphonie Fantastique
London Symphony Orchestra/Sir Colin Davis
LSO Live: London (Barbican Hall), 29–30 September 2000

When the writing appeared on the wall and it became clear that large record labels had no further interest in classical music, orchestras were in despair. How would people ever hear of them again, or tell them apart, without the oxygen of record hype? What would become of venerable reputations? Was this the final spin?

The London Symphony Orchestra produced, quite literally, the first solution to this conundrum. Instead of hassling record labels for work, they recorded live concerts with their principal conductor, paying the musicians nothing more than their normal concert fee but promising a small royalty on future sales, if profitable.

Colin Davis, who conducted the first Berlioz cycle on record for Philips in the 1970s, was revisiting his early triumphs with the benefit of mature reflection. His cycle contained many memorable performances, among them a superbly sung Les Troyens, itself a rarity on record. But no work focused so much of the conductor's experience and the orchestra's energy as the psychedelically colorific Fantastique, a sound world that had intoxicated every great conductor from Mahler and Toscanini to the present day (Bernstein, in his CBS recording, added an impromptu lecture titled 'Berlioz Takes a Trip'). Davis's 1974 recording had topped the critical listings for three decades. To eclipse that outstanding performance, he added textural refinement and expanded the aural dimensions of the fantasy, tinkering with the directionality of key effects. The distant dialogue of shepherds (solo oboe and cor anglais) at the opening of the Scene in the Country gets widescreen vision in this account. The rolling and tolling of drums is never aurally expected.

The calculation of spatial difference and the fizz of live performance sets this recording apart from studio productions. The producer and engineer were major-label veterans James Mallinson and Tony Faulkner. The release made the top ten in Japan and, while it made little money for the players, it established the own-label brand as a viable option for orchestras in a world after classical recording.

97. *Shostakovich: Fifteenth Symphony*
Cleveland Orchestra/Kurt Sanderling
Erato: Cleveland (Severance Hall), 17–18 March 2001

Ambiguity was built into the way Shostakovich wrote his symphonies. To official ears, they sounded a hymn of praise to the Soviet system while, to Russian audiences, they communicated an empathetic detachment, a sorrow shared, a kind of samizdat. Coded numbers and initials conveyed an ulterior agenda, amplified to outright rebellion in the composer's reported conversations.

Despite widespread clues to his double life, Western conductors wilfully misinterpreted Shostakovich for their own ends. Power-crazed Karajan claimed the anti-Stalin Tenth as the symphony he would most like to have written himself. Haitink performed the cycle with small-nation neutrality. Solti was all bluff and bluster, Previn filmic, Ormandy banal, Bernstein spectacular.

After the fall of communism, interpretation turned excessive as each note was searched for hidden meaning and scholars squabbled in rival camps. Ambiguity, once a half-secret, lost its charge in the glare of acrimonious public debate. Shostakovich became a football for frustrated musicologists and unredeemed ex-communists.

The one veteran who knew the truth refused to talk about it – except to orchestras in rehearsal. Kurt Sanderling, a Hitler refugee, had served as second conductor at the Leningrad Philharmonic. His boss, Mravinsky, got to premiere most Shostakovich symphonies but was never intimate with the composer. Sanderling, who conducted the second runs, was a close confidant.

Facing American orchestras, who knew nothing of the fear and deprivation of Soviet life, he would patiently explain how a tuba wickedly portrays a party apparatchik on his first junket abroad, or a piccolo ironically punctures the arrogance of power.

In his late eighties, Sanderling took on the deepest Shostakovich enigma – the final symphony that begins with a parodied phrase from Rossini's William Tell and ends, after many near-blank pages, in Mahlerian fragmentation. Was this despair? Defiance? Defeat? Sanderling presented a landscape of bleak beauty, a dying man's tour through his life's journey, rich in self-quotation and a gathering sense that all had not been in vain. There is no messianic message, no vain hope offered to successors – just a treasure trove of musical beauties and mysteries, the stuff of life. Cleveland took the work to heart and played without false inflection as the symphony found, at last, a meaning beyond meaning.

98. Ligeti: Atmosphères, Aventures (Music from the Film 2001)
Berlin Philharmonic Orchestra/Jonathan Nott
Teldec: Berlin (Philharmonie), 13–16 December 2001

The Hungarian modernist György Ligeti was astonished to learn that his music had found a global audience in Stanley Kubrick's space fantasy, *2001: A Space Odyssey* (1968). He went to see the film and was justly incensed. Not only had Atmosphères and other pieces been taken without his permission, but a section of Aventures had been electronically distorted. He sued, was hammered down by Hollywood lawyers and was advised by his publishers to settle for $3,500 – 'a despicable amount'. Later he said:

'I liked the film. The way it used my music I accept artistically.'

This was no ordinary soundtrack, for Kubrick had completely altered the way music was applied in movies – no longer as an enhancement of emotion, but as a dimension in its own right. Ligeti was played without a word of dialogue for sixteen out of the film's closing twenty-one minutes, a screen exposure other composers would die for.

After the legal settlement, the director continued to raid the Ligeti oeuvre, copiously and with permission, taking a section of Lontano in *The Shining* (1979) and Musica ricercata in *Eyes Wide Shut* (1999). Ligeti attended the German premiere of the last film, the director's widow sociably on his arm.

Because of the litigation, no soundtrack CD could be issued for *2001* and, by the time it could, the original performances were no longer up to contemporary standard. A Swiss Maecenas, Vincent Meyer, put up money for all of Ligeti's orchestral music to be recorded on Sony Classical by the Philharmonia and Esa-Pekka Salonen, only for Peter Gelb to shut the project down. Ligeti meanwhile fell out with the orchestra and Salonen. Teldec offered him Europe's foremost orchestra, but isolated him from the proceedings to prevent composer interference. The Berlin Philharmonic played clinically and with staggering exactitude under the British conductor Jonathan Nott, every so often creating an original soundscape that might appeal to a film auteur. The music, 'static' in the composer's estimation, harks at times to the fluttering night music that Bartók conjured from the never-sleeping countryside.

99. *Purcell: Dido and Aeneas*
Le concert d'astrée/Emmanuelle Haim
EMI Virgin: Metz (Arsenal), 14–16 March 2003

The record industry refused to recognize women conductors. A token few cut a disc or two but no female music director was ever given a record contract and nothing seemed about to change when the industry went into freefall. But out of the blue came two women of divergent background and broke the antiquated mould. Marin Alsop, a Leonard Bernstein pupil, bestrode a spate of American repertoire for bargain-label Naxos so successfully that she was given a Brahms cycle. Emmanuelle Haim, a French keyboard player, took charge of Handel's Rodelinda at Glyndebourne in the summer of 2001 and won a conducting contract with EMI Virgin.

As William Christie's harpsichordist, Haim had previously caught the eye of Simon Rattle and Claudio Abbado. She formed her own Concert d'astrée and was soon in demand as a guest conductor with mainstream symphony orchestras. No prisoner of period doctrine, she set about casting Purcell's tragic masterpiece with grand opera voices – Susan Graham and Ian Bostridge – and engaged Rattle's Berlin chorus master Simon Halsey to lead her vocal ensemble, while using period instruments in the pit and directing herself from the harpsichord.

Despite the risk of big-name showboating, the performance, rapt and lyrically pure, was a collaboration of equals. Graham sounds completely at ease in the baroque and Bostridge sheds preciousness for a muscular virility. There was no shortage of diva competition on record from Janet Baker, Maria Ewing, Jessye (believe it or not) Norman, Emma Kirkby and Kirsten Flagstad, but Graham in this performance was prima inter pares and that was its crowning virtue. The emotion as Dido is 'laid in earth' is the more overpowering for being purely aural, her death unseen. It would be the last occasion when a recorded opera triumphed over all stagings.

100. Debussy: Preludes
Pascal Rogé
Onyx: La Chaux-de-fonds, Switzerland (Salle de musique),
January 2004

Amid the collapse of classical recording, two former executives lunched over their shrunken future. Paul Moseley, marketing man at Decca, met Chris Craker, a producer of some 400 records whose boutique label, Black Box, had gone belly-up in a corporate takeover. What about the artists? they asked one another. What about all those rising stars who had received massive promotions from major labels and were now, in mid-life, consigned to the scrapheap? Surely a famous name must count for something in the new economy.

For their new enterprise, named Onyx, Craker and Moseley recorded Viktoria Mullova (ex-Philips), Barbara Bonney (ex-DG) and the Borodin Quartet (ex-EMI) in music they had never tackled before. Mullova pitched into Vivaldi with hair flying into the faces of a feral early-instrument band. Bonney sang Bernstein, the Borodins played a sixtieth anniversary recital. But the real catch was Pascal Rogé, who, dumped by Decca, recorded the Debussy Preludes that had filled his mind since the age of eight.

Rogé was the archetypal master of French pianism, heir to the Cortot panache, the subtlety of Casadesus. Style was paramount in his Preludes. A hair out of place, a soupçon of wrong flavouring, and the whole effect would be ruined. Each Prelude was a separate course, warm or cool, sombre or *bien amusant*.

Relieved of major-sales expectations, Rogé played as he wished, intent upon the text and subtext of a set that is seldom played entire. The Preludes, he said, were written for the player: 'I can't conceive what the listener can enjoy, compared to the voluptuous delight of creating all those sounds, perfumes, *colours* . . . Sometimes I even feel guilty about experiencing so much pleasure in public. It's almost indecent.'[13]

From the 'slow and grave' pace of Delphic dances to the 'animated' playing of the wind on the plains, the pianist is concerned solely with picture and mood. The 'profound calm' of a submerged cathedral is brought wondrously to the mind's eye; the satiric homage to Samuel Pickwick is rendered po-faced, and twice as comic for that.

This was, by several measures, a milestone recording on musical merit as well as being an indicator to whatever might lie ahead for

13. Sleeve note to CD.

the transmission of music in a post-recording age – a model for modest ventures by major artists, a thin but resistant chain of continuity. Before the record was out, Chris Craker claimed a top job at Sony-BMG and Onyx gained major-league distribution. It marked a glimmer, more likely a chimera, of new beginnings.

PART III

Madness: 20 Recordings that Should Never Have Been Made

What is a bad recording? Not one made by bad musicians or poorly played. Such things, rife as they are, are unworthy of criticism. The rotten records that we remember and cherish are those which were produced with the best of intentions and performed by the finest artists yet which, in one particular or other, stray so far from the intended purpose that they present a caricature of recording, a Versailles mirror in which everything is warped.

Every record collector has a cabinet of such horrors. I have picked twenty from the bottom drawer, records which expose in different ways the fallibilities and vanities of the record business yet endure, in their vain perversity, as distinctive artworks. My selection, while generally subjective (though augmented by consultation with many artists and producers), is indicative of the things that can go wrong when we aspire to the highest.

1. Bach: Concerto for Two Violins and Orchestra
Jascha Heifetz, RCA Victor Chamber Orchestra
RCA: Hollywood, 14 and 19 October 1946

The Bach double concerto is a dialogue between two violinists of unequal temperament. David Oistrakh recorded it unforgettably with his son Igor, the Vienna concertmaster Arnold Rosé with his ill-fated daughter, Alma (murdered by the Nazis in Auschwitz). Yehudi Menuhin recorded it with his teacher Georges Enescu, less successfully with the Frenchman Christian Ferras, a fellow Enescu pupil, and late in life with a twelve-year-old Chinese boy from his own school, Jin Li. Isaac Stern picked the young Pinchas Zukerman, who went on to redo the work with his Israeli friend, Itzhak Perlman. The choice of partner is as much a social gesture as an artistic one.

Heifetz, being Heifetz, recorded it with himself. His performance is ear-gougingly odious, lickety-split fast from the start to demonstrate the soloist's disdain for baroque simplicity and accompanied by a studio ensemble whipped together (most of the time) by the metronomic film composer Franz Waxman, who was no genius at inflexion. The Adagio is treacly-sweet and the finale seems driven by a desire to get off set and out into the Californian sunshine. Like a day at the dentist's, you can hardly imagine it will ever be over.

Heifetz kept the orchestra only for so long as it took him to record the primo part; he then stayed on to play the second violin part against his original pressing, wearing steel headphones on his skull and a look (judging by the session photograph) of a racing driver at the starting grid. At certain points in the second lap he was either not listening or unable to keep pace with himself. At others he suffers a sudden change of mind and ignores the first violin altogether. In the home stretch his tone goes mechanically cold. As an exercise in narcissism, one Heifetz in the lily pond to another, this performance can hardly be worsted.

The master-violinist may well have regretted the exercise for, fifteen years later in Walthamstow Town Hall, he re-recorded the Bach Double with a London pick-up orchestra conducted by Malcolm Sargent (whom he despised) and a soloist, Erick Friedman, who was the only violinist Heifetz acknowledged as his pupil. Second time round, the concerto sounds almost beautiful.

2. Beethoven: Triple Concerto
Sviatoslav Richter, David Oistrakh, Mstislav Rostropovich,
Berlin Philharmonic Orchestra/Herbert von Karajan
EMI: Berlin (Jesus-Christus-Kirche), September 1969

It was a dream team, the most formidable troika ever put together for Beethoven's unpretentious and seldom performed concerto for violin, cello and piano in the humdrum key of C major. EMI, having recaptured the world's most sought-after, relaunched him with the cream of Soviet soloists, three stars who worked together often but never abroad. The project cost a mint – Karajan alone demanded a £10,000 advance – but this was one of those sessions where money was no object. This was the record industry at its most ambitious, bringing together a line-up that would never be seen together on stage.

Hugs of greeting all round, and then it all went wrong. Oistrakh and Richter found Karajan's tempi portentous and felt the music was being travestied by the ultra-plush underpinnings of the super-sleek Berlin Philharmonic. The pair gave voice to their objections, only for Rostropovich to side with the man in power – 'falling over himself,' grumbled Richter, 'to do everything Karajan wanted'. The conductor complained that he could not hear the pianist. Richter retorted that the cello was over-prominent. Time was running out. 'Karajan had buggered us about with his schedule,' said a member of the EMI team. 'We had to get it all in the can in the one session.' Lacking conviction in each other, none of the soloists gave a hint of personal expression to his work. Oistrakh is unnaturally hoarse, Richter absent-minded and Rostropovich routine. The four carried on playing with and against each other until producer Peter Andry declared he had had enough. Oistrakh and Richter, ashamed of their performance, asked Karajan for one last take. 'No time,' said Karajan, 'we have to pose for the cover photographs.'

'It's a dreadful recording and I disown it utterly,' exclaimed Richter, and so it is – a textbook example of musical non-communication, all the notes in place and none of them meaningful. Any pleasure in the making of music seems to have evaporated. Not that many critics seemed to notice. Dazzled by the hype and for want of a superior recording, the reviews were raves and the sales hit half a million. It took years for a conscientious record label to come up with a credible alternative, pairing the well-attuned Beaux Arts Trio with the Leipzig Gewandhaus orchestra under Kurt Masur (Philips).

3. Elgar: Enigma Variations
BBC Symphony Orchestra/Leonard Bernstein
DG: London (Watford Town Hall), April 1982

Even by his own flamboyant standards, Leonard Bernstein's late attack on the Enigma Variations was some way beyond outrageous. It was not a work he had performed much or cared for. He undertook it as a chance to appear live on BBC television after a long absence and he seemed to regret it the moment he agreed.

Bernstein was at his lowest emotional ebb, gripped by self-loathing and creative despair. The works he had hoped would flow after he gave up the New York Philharmonic failed to convince the public, or himself. As a guest conductor, he was an exotic peacock, not senior enough to command elder statesman status.

He turned up half an hour late for rehearsal with an orchestra he had never met before, and picked fights immediately with musicians and attendants, behaving like an alcoholic boor with a bad headache. He slouched into the Enigma at just over half the prescribed tempo – 36 crotchets (quarter-notes) a minute instead of 63 (had he dyslectically misread the score?). The first variation, dedicated to the composer's wife, he conducted sluggishly without affection. The second was neurotically frenetic, the third simply bored. By the time he reached the Nimrod adagio he was going so slow it felt like backwards, a monstrous travesty of a minor masterpiece, though not without incidental beauties and a certain erotic languor. A work that should have lasted half an hour dragged on for just under thirty-eight minutes.

The musicians were incensed. Bernstein had made porridge out of a piece of national heritage for no apparent reason except perversity. He told the orchestra he would never work with them again. Several players broke into applause. On the cover photo, he snarls into camera. There was simply no excuse for what he had just done.

4. Klemperer: Merry Waltz; Weill: Threepenny Opera Music; Hindemith: Nobilissima Visione Suite
Philharmonia Orchestra/Otto Klemperer
EMI: London (Kingsway Hall), October 1961

Composers who conduct are nuisance enough, but conductors who compose in their spare time are a positive menace. Mahler and Strauss are the notable exceptions but their success gave licence to the rest of the profession. Even those with creative talent and detachment were bulging with so huge a repertoire that they were unable to tell what was theirs and what had already been composed by someone else.

Which did not stop them scribbling. Wilhelm Furtwängler wrote three symphonies of grandiose pretensions and very little originality, their structure Brucknerian, their themes shadowing Hindemith and Strauss. Felix Weingartner, Mahler's successor in Vienna, composed seven operas and symphonies. Victor de Sabata, director at La Scala, was an avid composer. Bruno Walter published several pieces.

Otto Klemperer's efforts fall into early (1920s Berlin) and late (1960s London), the first period overshadowed by Kurt Weill, the latter thick with undigested Mahler. In his dotage, EMI indulged him with a catalogue entry as a composer. The Merry Waltz was taken from an unperformed early opera. It sounds like an amateur musician trying to copy Ravel's La Valse from faulty memory, with digressionary nods to Franz Schreker and Richard Strauss and a metronome borrowed from Franz Lehár. Deftly played, it sounds almost worthwhile, though never quite catching the ear. Just as you are about to say 'not a bad composer, then', Klemperer lights into Kurt Weill and Hindemith and the difference is night and day. The real composers not only have something to say but Klemperer the conductor can sense the underlying tensions and gives their music a grandeur that is plainly lacking in his own.

It seems mysterious that Klemperer, the most critical of conductors, could not hear his own shortcomings. He hired the Philharmonia and Royal Festival Hall at his own expense to try out his symphonies and, out of mercy, the orchestra refused to take a fee. Appreciating the kindness, he told the orchestra's manager: 'I would be glad to be remembered as a conductor and a composer. But, without wishing to be arrogant, I would only want to be remembered as a *good* composer. If people find my compositions weak, it is better not to be remembered.' This record defies that wish. It should have been strangled at birth.

5. Mahler: Second Symphony (Resurrection)
Jessye Norman, Eva Marton, Vienna Philharmonic/Lorin Maazel
CBS: Vienna (Musikvereinsaal), January 1983

Gustav Mahler, despite his late popularity, is the victim of more awful recordings than any other symphonist. One can easily assemble a cycle of total calamities. There is a First symphony with Ozawa (or Mehta, or Rattle) containing the Blumine movement that Mahler intentionally left out, and a Second from Sinopoli with an unrisen Resurrection. The Third has been wrecked by the wrong type of mezzo (Leinsdorf, Järvi), while Bernstein's Fourth with a boy treble and Walter's with the vocally untrained Desi Halban are tremulously remote from the composer's instruction.

Kondrashin's Moscow horns howl off-tune in the opening fan-fare of the Fifth, a symphony that Scherchen cut by several minutes to accommodate a perversely elongated Adagietto. Horenstein's Sixth is poorly played by the Stockholm Philharmonic. The Boulez Seventh is disinfected of humanity. Almost every Eighth except Tennstedt's and Solti's crashes short of sonic realism and Karajan treats the Ninth like a concerto for orchestra, devoid of mortal angst. Placido Domingo pops up bizarrely in Salonen's account of Das Lied von der Erde, opposite an equally inapposite Swedish baritone. As for the Tenth, against the authoritative Deryck Cooke version, there are four speculative endings conducted by Slatkin, Barshai, Sieghart, Olson and others. Each and any of these record-ings could qualify as an all-time worst Mahler effort but the one that sticks most vividly in memory was a session of the Resurrection that I attended in Vienna, where Lorin Maazel was serving in Mahler's shoes as director of the Opera. He quickly fell out with half the city, promising 'a gala every night' and delivering much that was unfocused and under-prepared, held together only by the clarity of his beat.

The Vienna Philharmonic played through gritted teeth and intrigued against Maazel behind a façade of imperial courtesies. The two outsized female soloists in the Resurrection conceived an instant mutual disregard and did not exchange one glance throughout the session. Maazel sacked the English producer, David Mottley, who, years later, told friends he still had nightmares of the conductor's glaring eyes. On a wintry Saturday night, the Musikvereinsaal was chilled with disaffection. The effect of a rotten atmosphere on a redemptive work of art is indescribably subversive. No matter how sweetly the violins sing and the winds hum, the missing humanity cannot be simulated. The dreariness of this performance defies belief and when the big girls get up to belt their worst, you somehow feel that everyone in the orchestra and chorus wished they had taken up accountancy or plumbing for their livelihood. If ever there was a recording that no one wanted to be part of, this is it.

6. *Kreisler: Concertos in the Baroque Style*
Fritz Kreisler, Victor String Orchestra/Donald Vorhees
RCA: New York (Lotos Club), 2 May 1945

Fritz Kreisler loved his little jokes. Loath to warm up alone in his dressing room for a concerto, he would slip into the back desk of the violins to play along in the first piece on the programme, delighted when his presence caused the conductor to miss a beat.

A composer of slushy encores – Liebesleid, Schön Rosmarin – Kreisler footled around on long train journeys with baroque relics, reorchestrating a Paganini concerto and writing several pieces in the style of Vivaldi, Pugnani, Martini, Couperin and Dittersdorf. Unethically, he passed them off as the genuine article but so little was known at the time of these ancient composers that music historians and critics accepted his 'discoveries' as the real deal, to Kreisler's immense amusement.

Unable to keep a secret, he shared the jokes with chums such as Enescu, Heifetz and Albert Spalding, finally acknowledging his authorship in 1935. Critics exploded with outrage and the English clique, led by pompous Ernest Newman, never forgave him. Kreisler, to keep them twittering, recorded some of the fakes in the last sessions of his life.

Modern ears will find it hard to fathom how the music world was fooled for so long by his fakeries. The music sounds nothing like Vivaldi, the melodies too ornate, the phrase patterns imprecise, the expression exaggerated. Oversweet, under-nourished and un-expectedly inelegant for so consummate a phrase-maker, the music lacks so much as a nugget of an idea, substituting gesture for substance and scarcely bothering to affect a pre-romantic pronunci-ation. For a violinist of such exquisite tone and civilized taste, this is an unworthy pitch for posterity, a travesty of an epitaph. But it is also a salutary reminder that even the most exquisite artists can be prone to terrible lapses of taste.

7. *Schubert: Winterreise*
Peter Pears, Benjamin Britten
Decca: London (Kingsway Hall), October 1963

Peter Pears was the love of Benjamin Britten's life and the dominant member of a forty-year partnership that lasted until death. Without Pears as friend and lover, interpreter and mediator, Britten would never have managed his immense talent so efficiently, or coped with the demands of a world he viewed as innately hostile. Pears stands deservedly above criticism in the roles that he inspired. As Peter Grimes he represented the human face of a child killer. As Aschenbach in Death in Venice he conveyed the agony of a creator as virility and originality fade. There were other ways of approaching these roles, but all were pitted against the example of Pears. In the Serenade for tenor, horn and strings, he was likewise in a class of his own.

Singing other music, though, was another matter. Pears pitched himself as the premier English singer of German Lieder, the man who taught the English to love Schubert and Brahms. With Britten at the piano, he was a hot recital ticket and the public basked in their celebrity. Critics sat through these occasions in haemorrhoidal agony, for the pair could not be reviewed apart and any adverse remarks about Pears would bring savage personal retaliation from Britten, who nurtured grudges as other men tended rose gardens. As a result, Pears got away with blue murder.

Safely dead, the pretence of competence need not be maintained. Pears, in Lieder, hardly got through one song unblemished. To reach a high note, he strained or blared. At the low end, he growled and snuffled. His delivery was nasal, as if one nostril were permanently blocked. His German was imprecise and his entries inelegant. In song after song he teetered at the edge of wrong notes like a tightrope walker on Temazepam. Britten leaped in to save him with a beautifully turned rubato, most daringly in Einsamkeit, where Pears was going it alone down a dead man's gulch. To test how bad he is, compare the crawly way he approaches a phrase in Der Lindenbaum to the crisp attack of such concurrent masters as Hans Hotter and Dietrich Fischer-Dieskau.

Much of his Winterreise is frankly unpleasant, barely above amateurish. Sensitive friends like Covent Garden's Earl of Harewood conceded that Pears' voice 'took some getting used to' and got ostracized for their comments. Others kept their mouths shut. The comedian Dudley Moore created, in the revue Beyond the Fringe, a hilariously strangulated English Lieder singer whose resemblance to Pears was, to those in the know, deadly. This record, a Decca Legend, is, in a morose and masochistic sort of way, almost twice as funny as Dudley's sketch.

8. Albinoni: Adagio; Pachelbel: Canon; Corelli: Christmas Concerto; Vivaldi: Concertos
Berlin Philharmonic Orchestra/Herbert von Karajan
DG: Berlin (Philharmonie), September–November 1983

Every conductor of consequence imparts a personal sound to his orchestra, a wordless transference. In most cases, it amounts to an aural subtlety, the way an office atmosphere changes when the chairman is around. With Herbert von Karajan, however, the personal focus was explicit. Karajan imposed on orchestras an idea of sound that was literally unnatural: without human imperfection. Every line was clean, every parabola mathematically precise, every dimension conforming to a hidden masterplan. The Karajan sound transcended differences of period and style, the individuality of composers and their national and ethnic idiosyncrasies. A Karajan orchestra made the same noise in Schütz as in Strauss.

His repertoire was founded on the nineteenth century, an epoch that idealized romanticism to the point of morbidity. Karajan applied a Burne-Jones brush to every score he touched, colouring the sound to a point of saturation where the ear cried out for a pastel variant. The formula fitted all forms of music, sometimes to the point of astonishment. Only Karajan could have made the atonal Six Pieces for Orchestra by Anton von Webern resonate with the melodic logic of Carl Maria von Weber. Only Karajan could have interpreted Mahler and Shostakovich without a scintilla of irony. The genius of the man was that whatever he touched sounded like Karajan. That, in turn, delighted record labels, which were able to deliver a product that consumers could trust, a brand beyond variation.

The stumbling block to this seamless record of success was Karajan's ventures into the baroque, a culture that he treated the same as all others. Ignoring the inherent roughness and haphazard instrumentation, Karajan drove his perfect band through the hoops of practised manoeuvres, insensitive to anomaly and anachronism. The results, to anyone with an ear for the ridiculous, are a monument to interpretative arrogance.

Vivaldi's Concerto alla rustica sounds as bucolic as a Mercedes engine and Corelli's music as Roman as apple strudel, a sugary squelch. The crowning glories of this early-digital disc were the orchestral sauce that Karajan poured ever so slowly over Tomaso Albinoni's sighing Adagio, making it sound like medicated minimalism, and the holy hokum that he made of Johann Pachelbel's Canon, a stately gigue (or jig) that he whirled off like a fin-de-siècle Viennese waltz.

A record like this defies criticism. It defines the best and worst of Karajan: his sleek lines and irresistible tempi to the credit side, his stubborn vanity to the dubious. He was blazingly proud of this best-selling compilation.

9. *Jazz Sebastian Bach (US title: Bach's Greatest Hits)*
Swingle Singers
Philips: Paris, 1962

Ward Swingle, a textbook American in Paris, was fooling around with friends over the Well-Tempered Clavichord when an under-lying rhythm hinted at something smokier. His clique of eight well-trained voices, accompanied by solo double bass and drums, began to vocalize their way through Bach's best-known tunes in a style that bisected barber-shop quartet and New Orleans speakeasy.

The debut LP shot into the pop charts and stayed there for eighteen months. Glenn Gould cabled his approval and Luciano Berio booked the group for Sinfonia, his sprawling modernist commentary on Mahler's Resurrection symphony. The singers, who had previously been doing oohs and aahs for Charles Aznavour and Edith Piaf, became chic and rich. Michel Legrand, composer brother of soprano Christiane, got them onto movie soundtracks. Quincy Jones steered them into pure jazz. In 1966 they starred at the Cannes Film Festival. Almost as much as the Beatles, they typified the musical 1960s until Swingle, fed up, moved to London and formed another group.

Four decades on, you have to wonder what artistic purpose was served by this pastiche. No harm done, jing-jing, doowah doowah, but turning sacred Bach into shower-room singing requires some form of validation if it is not to go down as a rather naff idea that made lots of money. Critically approached, the treatment amounts to nothing more than a traditional novelty record, like How Much is that Doggy in the Window? or the Singing Nun. Oddly, for a jazz disc, the rhythms are equalized to the point of monotony and the harmonies are predictable. It is the blend that appeals, but it gives way to a crushing depression that such fine voices should be used for such trivial purpose. The record industry issued the stan-dard justifications, pretending that these treatments would awaken a new generation to the glories of Bach. As usual, this was pure cant for the Christmas trade.

10. A Different Mozart
Dawn Atkinson (producer)
The Imaginary Road: Windham County, Vermont; Oakland,
California; Portland, Oregon, 1996

At first hearing, this sounds like the scores Mozart sold to Starbucks. On second sip, you recognize them vaguely from an elevator or airport lobby. Producer Dawn Atkinson, a Grammy and Emmy nominee for easy-listening Windham Hill albums, decided that Mozart was made of million-selling mush. 'A Different Mozart presents a kaleidoscope of instruments and approaches,' she proclaimed. The only approach audible is the kind that synthesizers write for the Muzak Corporation.

Staying awake through this kind of stuff would be hard enough, were it not for jolts to the nervous system delivered by Eine Kleine Nachtmusik reworked for glass harmonicas and four mandolins. The genius behind this adaptation is named as Todd Boekelheide, an Oscar winner for Milos Forman's film *Amadeus*, which he sound engineered. Then there is Tracy Scott-Silverman, described as 'the greatest living exponent of the electric violin', short-circuiting a piano sonata adagio to no intelligent purpose. There is also a banjo version of another Mozart solo.

None of this would be of consequence were it not for the secret authorship of track 5, a sleepytime adaptation of a theme from Mozart's A-major piano concerto. The composer is named as 'Val Gardena', which is an Italian ski resort. His real name is Chris Roberts, an Oregon record store attendant who became president of Deutsche Grammophon, Decca and Philips, which he proceeded to decimate of content, replacing classics with crossover and serious artists with teen sensations. Under a second pseudonym, 'Christopher James', Roberts played piano hesitantly and unattractively on this track. Under his own name, he bought a half-share in the label.

The strategy that destroyed classical recording is enshrined in this otiose disc, a muddle of idle thoughts passing for modern improvisation. In terms of the eco-damage this policy inflicted on the centenary balance of music and commerce, this can safely be counted the worst classical recording of all time.

11. *Verdi: Requiem*
Renée Fleming, Olga Borodina, Andrea Bocelli, Ildebrando d'Arcangelo, Kirov Orchestra and Chorus/Valery Gergiev
Decca: London (All Hallows Church), 11–15 July 2000

Critics may sometimes be accused of cynicism, but they cannot compete with the music industry for sheer brazen effrontery. When the St Petersburg conductor Valery Gergiev sought to record a Requiem as a climax to the centennial year of Verdi's death, he was told it would need a star line-up to have any chance of breaking even. Gergiev secured the luminous Renée Fleming as soprano and Olga Borodina as mezzo with the respected Italian baritone Ildebrando d'Arcangelo. He was casting around for a tenor when the label landed him with Andrea Bocelli, a blind Italian pop star who had graduated from syrupy San Remo ballads to the upper reaches of opera arias. Pavarotti, a generous soul, had pronounced him a colleague.

Blinded by a footballing accident at age twelve, Bocelli sold 45 million pop records and brought the elderly Elizabeth Taylor out in goose bumps. His debut Decca recital sold 5 million. He was eager to try a Verdi Requiem. Gergiev had his doubts. They were swiftly put to rest. Bocelli's inclusion, he told me, 'was a condition for making the record'.

Bocelli's solos started sweetly, if simplistically, his Ingemisco entry achieving serenity through severe vibrato control and restraint of showmanship. But whenever he had to reach for a note he would slide and swoop like a kid in a playground, oblivious to dignity and art. It was soon obvious that he lacked the technique to cope with Verdi's subtle shifts of emotion and, joined by the big guns in the great set pieces, Bocelli is exposed as cruelly as a Sunday-morning park footballer would be in the World Cup final.

To hear Fleming and Borodina cramp their exceptional voices to his limitations is an embarrassment to the listener and an indictment of the makers of this record.

Gergiev loyally avowed that 'the reason for B's success in pop world is that he feels for traditional values of music – beauty of tone, expression of emotion', and Bocelli's sincerity was never in question. He truly wanted to be a celebrated operatic tenor. The release sold in excess of 80,000 CDs, a hit in classical terms. But the popster's presence robbed the Requiem of seriousness and solemnity, creating a commercial travesty of Verdi's noble monument.

12. *The Jazz Album*
London Sinfonietta/Simon Rattle
EMI: London (CTS Studios, Wembley), December 1986–January 1987

Like every other conductor, Simon Rattle has blotted his record with a few stinkers, notably some badly cast Elgar and Mahler and an ill-advised bash at Duke Ellington. What sets this Rorschach specimen apart is that the conductor is touchingly proud of it, having lovingly selected its mismatched menu and handpicked his best mates among the soloists. Such pub fun does not necessarily yield a studio sensation.

The programme was all over the place. Starting with the obvious – Darius Milhaud's La Création du Monde and Gershwin's Rhapsody in Blue (in the original Ferdé Grofé jazz version), it takes a stab at Stravinsky's Ebony Concerto before degenerating into such vacant ephemeralities as Making Whoopee and Sweet Sue, intoned by an eclectic quintet called Harvey and the Wall-bangers. Whoever had the idea that this lot made a coherent record deserves to be taken out the back and educated in the realities of cultural relationships.

The unfortunate orchestra was the London Sinfonietta, formed to play ink-wet modern music and completely unable to swing or bend a line. Rattle dressed for the cover in a white tie and black-and-white suspenders, looking like a barmitzvah boy who has lost his way to the loo.

Neither of the instrumental soloists could wash the stiffness out of his shirt. Pianist Peter Donohoe and clarinettist Michael Collins followed a deadly beat to the bitter end and must have been relieved when the last of Bernstein's Prelude, Fugue and Riffs (what riffs?) was over. The record sold poorly, prompting EMI to consider calling in young Rattle's contract. The Jazz Album could have finished his career before it got going – a lesson to rising young conductors to temper impulse with wisdom, begged, borrowed or stolen. On the reissue cover, Rattle dresses mournfully in a black suit.

13. *Mahler for Dummies*
Klaus Tennstedt, John Barbirolli, Carlo-Maria Giulini
EMI Classics: Studio compilation, 1996

'Just goes to show that you can't outwit fate', preaches the booklet blurb in this cabbage-headed package. 'Get to Know the Real Mahler and Have the Ultimate Listening Experience', screams the yellow cover. Der, how, exactly?

Aimed at culture-bypassed residents of Silicon Valley, the Dummies were supposed to introduce workaholics to the pleasures they were missing – life, love and the whole damn thing – assuming they ever took a break from the computer screen. Heard of Mahler? This is all the Mahler you need to hear – 'the fun and easy way to explore the world of classical music'. Fun? Mahler? Somebody's program has just crashed.

The music assembled here amounted to cuts from exemplary performances of five Mahler symphonies. The accompanying notes, in eye-massaging big letters, reduce the composer's life to the terms of a personnel report: 'Perhaps not surprisingly, given his harsh childhood, Mahler developed a hostile abrasive personality that made the ladder of success all the harder for him to climb;

the surprise is that he managed to further his career anyway . . .'

Hard to tell whether this is music appreciation for the education-ally challenged or management babble for the vertically aspirant. Even a worn-out dork on a sofa with The Simpsons could surely tell the difference between being an artist and brown-nosing the human resources department. And what Mahler's social skills have to do with the emotional roller-coaster that is the starting point of each of his symphonies is something that only the programmers of these designedly half-witted productions could possibly explain.

The notes are peppered with inaccuracies, but they hardly mat-ter. In this peachy, preachy Stepford Wives world of techno-addled empty heads, Mahler has as much chance of breakthrough as a fur coat salesman in the Sahara.

14. Beethoven: Violin Concerto
Gidon Kremer, Academy of St Martin in the Fields/
Neville Marriner
Philips: London, January 1982

Before recording began, soloists used to improvise cadenzas, adding a few minutes of flashy individuality to the end of a concerto movement. When music went mechanical, so did performers. Fearful of being judged by originality, or lack of it, they all took to playing the same cadenzas – and in Beethoven that meant borrowing Fritz Kreisler's warm and whimsical interpolation to the composer's text. The Kreisler cadenza became so indispensable for soloists that the Third Reich was unable to ban it along with the rest of his works and a recording by the Berlin Philharmonic concertmaster, Erich Röhn, could still be taped in the final months of Hitler's Reich. Kreisler was everyone's companion in Beet-hoven, bar none.

Until Gidon Kremer broke the mould. A Baltic rebel, born in Riga in 1947, Kremer took up a five-minute cadenza by his friend Alfred Schnittke, who had written what amounted to an essay in his new style, known as polystylism. Schnittke had seen his symphonies banned by the Soviets but he knew they could not touch Beethoven. He created at the heart of the concerto an historical commentary on musical development. Starting with a theme from Beethoven's seventh symphony, he went into a phrase of Bach borrowed in the Alban Berg concerto, then into quotations from Bartók and Shostakovich and back into Beethoven and Brahms, wittily demonstrating a unity of purpose down the classical centuries, a brotherhood of great composers.

Kremer's performance was received with outrage. 'You can't mix up styles like that,' scolded Itzhak Perlman. Yehudi Menuhin was disparaging; Isaac Stern refused to utter Schnittke's name.

The ultra-classical Neville Marriner agreed to conduct a recording, which he described as 'one of the most delightful I have ever taken part in'. All seemed set for a gleaming launch when Philips panicked and, instead of branding the LP a world premiere, wiped Schnittke's name off the cover and put it on the market as just another Beethoven concerto.

Few were deceived. *Musical America* damned the cadenza as 'specious and incoherent nit-picking' and the Kremlin resumed its persecution of the composer. Kremer dropped the cadenza from his repertoire and it fell into disuse. What should have been a challenging addition to the classical repertoire turned into one of the worst record releases in memory, a classic case of corporate cold feet.

15. *Weill: September Songs*
Various artists
Sony Classical: Studio compilation 1997

Kurt Weill was an unlucky composer. Born in 1900 and dead at fifty, the coinciding dates of birth and death left him short of anniversaries. When his first centenary came around, it was eclipsed by millennium fireworks and aroused very little interest from opera companies, which looked down their noses at Weill for his success on Broadway.

His songs, though, never fell out of pop fashion. Frank Sinatra recorded a luminous September Song, Louis Armstrong sharpened Mack the Knife as trad jazz, Tony Bennett sang Speak Low and Sting worked his way around Threepenny Opera.

For the year 2000, two TV stations and Sony Classical assembled a revue of Weill cover versions by contemporary chart artists. It opened evocatively with a sombre PJ Harvey account of the Ballad of the Soldier's Wife, affectingly hoarse-voiced, but the programme swiftly degenerated. Elvis Costello attempted Lost in the Stars but lacked the breathing apparatus and was left gasping like an amateur climber at high altitude. Lou Reed growled all the romance out of September Song, Betty Carter was consistently off-key in Lonely House and a rare track of Weill himself singing Speak Low was wrapped in egregious accompaniment. Even the sound of Brecht singing Mack the Knife with a hurdy-gurdy in the background could not save the tribute from ridicule. Weill once said, 'Music isn't bad just because it's popular.' On this disc, it is.

16. Bizet: Carmen
Jessye Norman, Orchestre National de France/Seiji Ozawa
Philips: Paris (Grand Auditorium de Radio France),
13–22 July 1988

Every record is an illusion, but this album strained credulity to snapping point. Jessye Norman had never sung Carmen on stage. She was the wrong shape, the wrong colour of voice and completely the wrong personality for the sexy cigarette girl in the bullring. The idea that she could accomplish unseen what the eye would not permit on the stage was preposterous to rational critics, if not to record producer Erik Smith. Without erotic voltage her Carmen attempts charm, never Ms Norman's strong point, and when that fails she bludgeons poor Neil Shicoff into limp submission. Her Habanera plods to near standstill and her set-pieces with Shicoff seem to grow more distant with the passing of tracks.

Ozawa, an opera novice, faced an indifferent French orchestra and rebellious chorus. Paris in the heat of July did not improve moods and even the accomplished Mirella Freni as Micaela was prone to shriek, perhaps out of frustration. But record labels at the height of the CD boom were prisoners of their stars and few names were bigger than Jessye Norman. If Radio France was paying the bills what was the harm?

Surprisingly, quite a lot. Jessye Norman's prestige took a hit, and the unspoken pact between record labels and regular buyers – if you don't overdo the fakery, we won't ask too many questions – was undermined by this Carmen, an illusion too far.

17. *Moment of Glory*
Scorpions, Berlin Philharmonic Orchestra
EMI: Berlin (NLG Studios), 14 March 2000

When recording work dried up, big orchestras went begging. Labels that once felt privileged to pay the Berlin Philharmonic $100,000 for a Haydn symphony were refusing to take calls from its conductor. Tours, too, were suffering and some players were talking of leasing out their second homes as holiday lets.

In some desperation, they began talking to a German rock band, The Scorpions, with whom they had performed a celebrity stunt for the tenth anniversary of the fall of the Berlin Wall. The Scorpions, well past their prime, were thrilled to get classical recognition. Populist politicians in the Berlin Senate encouraged the orchestra in its self-abasement, waving banners of cultural diversity.

The band turned up with enough amplification to bring down the Wall all over again. 'Are you ready to rock?' they yelled at the ranks of musical professors, launching into a song in praise of oral sex. The lyrics were sung in basic, heavily accented English and the music was a blend of James Bond and post-sell-by-date Rolling Stones. The Berlin Philharmonic, led by its principal concertmasters, hacked somnambulistically through the simple accompaniments without sheen or smile. A live concert followed at Expo 2000 in Hanover.

Simon Rattle, the orchestra's incoming chief conductor, called the operation 'a terrible idea . . . horrible', and told players it must not be repeated – though it was classical managers from his own label, EMI, that had set up the collusion. While the revenues rolled in, orchestras across the deprived eastern half of Germany were being disbanded and musicians thrown on the dole.

18. Satie: Vexations
Reinbert de Leeuw
Philips: Haarlem, May 1977

There is stiff competition for the all-time accolade of worst sound on a classical record. Florence Foster Jenkins had a head start, a society dame who screeched her first and only record at the age of seventy-three. More august divas – Ernestine Schumann-Heink more than most – warbled long past their vocal prime, prompting listeners to check whether it was the turntables or their ears that had lost their balance. Victims of Karajan abuse – Helga Dernesch, Katia Ricciarelli – had their voices stressed beyond beauty by the unreasonable conductor demands.

The former Sony president Norio Ohga was not at his best as soloist in a Sony Japan recording of the Fauré Requiem. Count Numa Labinsky, who owned the Nimbus record label, sang Schubert execrably in its catalogue under the pseudonym Shura Gehrman (he also sang baroque arias in falsetto).

Early recordings of serial music go seriously out of tune as musicians struggle to adjust to unnatural dissonances; Schoenberg's CBS recording of Pierrot Lunaire is almost unlistenable. Even under the expert advocacy of Pierre Boulez, the extreme modernisms of Xenakis and Ferneyhough preclude the possibility of aural pleasure. French music eludes many fine maestros – try Solti's goulash recipe for Gaieté Parisienne – while offences committed by Soviet conductors against Bach and Handel deserve to be put on trial in The Hague.

Minimalism posed another set of confusions. What are we to

make of the recording of John Cage's 4' 33", a rumbling of ambient noise? Morton Feldman's second string quartet drones on interminably – the composer said it should last for ever – and Philip Glass seemed more than sanely repetitive until his music is set beside the arch inventor of musical boredom.

Erik Satie (1866–1925) was a Parisian eccentric who wore a velvet suit and bowler hat and proclaimed that music need not be listened to – it should play as background. The prototype was a piece called Vexations, which consisted of eighteen notes played 'tres lent' 840 times without hesitation or variation, for a day and a night.

Early performances were staged by John Cage and his friends as art events, or happenings, sometimes in the nude. The first complete solo performance was given in London, by Richard Toop, in October 1967. A Dutch activist, Reinbert de Leeuw, set about the recording with the solemnity of a sacred mission. No short cuts for de Leeuw. He filled a CD with Vexations, to be played end to end 15 times – an act of total incomprehension. In concert, Vexations has a certain intellectual validity, making a point about hypnotic effect and what people will tolerate in a public place. On record, it has no point at all, except the capacity to irritate. Adequately played, this is the stupidest classical recording ever made, and surely the least musical.

19. *Christmas with Kiri*
Kiri te Kanawa, London Voices (chorus master Terry Edwards),
Philharmonia Orchestra/Carl Davis
Decca: London (CTS Studios, Wembley), March 1985

Christmas came early for the record industry with a pair of First World War hits – O Little Town of Bethlehem sung by the Columbia Double Mixed Quartette and Sing O Heavens by the Victor Mixed Chorus. To launch electrical recording, Columbia released thousands singing Adeste Fideles at the Met in March 1925; Victor snapped back with a solo rendition of the carol by the peerless tenor John McCormack. Irving Berlin's *White Christmas* became the biggest selling song on record, twenty-five million sales just for Bing Crosby's version.

The Christmas record acquired, over time, pejorative connotations as star singers with two hours between flights churned out perennials without punch or passion – and still sold enough copies to the granny market to justify another set the following year. It seems almost invidious to single out one Christmas album from a pile that is topped by the Three Tenors Christmas Album, Herbert von Karajan conducting carols with Leontyne Price and every conceivable duet between classical and pop celebrities.

Invidious, perhaps, but *Christmas with Kiri* ticks most of the boxes. Fresh from her triumph at the ill-fated Royal Wedding between Charles and Diana, the Kiwi canary in the yellow pillbox hat was wheeled into studio to run the gamut from *Silent Night* to *Have Yourself a Merry Little Christmas*. Never a whizz at articulating her ps and qs, the soprano ladled out a soupy selection of traditional songs reorchestrated for the occasion by film conductor Carl Davis and accompanied with matchless indifference by the Philharmonia Orchestra and London Voices.

Set beside the mictrotimed rubato of Ernestine Schumann-Heink in *Silent Night* (1926) or Elisabeth Schumann's crisp and tender delivery of the *Coventry Carol* (1938) – a pair of serenities brought together in Naxos' *Christmas from a Golden Age* – this marks a demonstrable nadir. Not one track on this tedious compilation is sung with feeling or meaning. There is an absence of interpretative intelligence, which is all the more remarkable for the renowned ingenuity of the conductor and chorus master. The rhythms are inconsistent, unconvincing, life-draining. If there is a worse Christmas record somewhere on earth, I am grateful never to have heard it.

20. *Pavarotti: The Ultimate Collection*
Luciano Pavarotti
Decca: Studio compilation, 1997

The biggest tenor in history managed his opera career immaculately. Limiting himself to thirty roles, he sang what he knew, and sang it well. The only lapse was a late Otello – too late, and undertaken chiefly because this was Placido Domingo's signature role.

In concert as in opera, Big Lucy could not be faulted. Although he took on a range of ice-cream songs, there was an integrity to his selection and a preparedness to his performance. Nothing Pavarotti undertook was ill-considered, whether in terms of aptitude or public impact. Until the early 1990s he had, uniquely for a classical performer, a perfect record.

Then, for reasons probably connected with personal upheavals, he lost it. Each year at Mantua, his young secretary and eventual second wife organized an orgy of Pavarotti and Friends which brought the uncomfortable fat cat together in duets with sleek lions of the pop world, ostensibly in some charitable cause. George Michael and Joe Cocker, Mariah Carey and Boyzone, were just a few of his unsuitable partners.

Most odious of all was Pavarotti's duet with the dead. In this Ultimate Collection the great man took on a tape of Frank Sinatra in My Way. Sinatra was way past his best on this late track, the voice coarsened by tobacco, the tenderness wrinkled. Pavarotti, likewise, was a patina of his mighty self, covering his cracks with tasteless vibrato and barely bothering to pronounce English vowels. The effect is more embarrassing than unpleasant, like seeing an old man's nakedness haplessly uncovered. You don't want to look again, but you know it won't go away. This is a record of sorts, an indelible stain that will linger for all time on the voice of the century.

Concise Bibliography

Gerben Bakker, *The Making of a Music Multinational: The International Strategy of PolyGram, 1945–88*, AFM Working Paper, University of Essex, 2003

Kevin Bazzana, *Wondrous Strange: The Life and Art of Glenn Gould*, New Haven: Yale University Press, 2004

Herbert Breslin and Anne Midgette, *The King and I*, New York: Doubleday, 2004

Donald Clarke, *The Rise and Fall of Popular Music*, London: Penguin, 1995

Schuyler Chapin, *Musical Chairs*, New York: Putnams, 1977

John Culshaw, *Ring Resounding: The Recording in Stereo of 'Der Ring Des Nibelungen'*, London: Secker & Warburg, 1967

———, *Putting the Record Straight: The Autobiography of John Culshaw*, London: Secker & Warburg, 1981

Frederic Dannen, *Hit Men*, London: Muller, 1990

Clive Davis, *Clive: Inside the Record Business*, New York: William Morrow, 1975

Dietrich Fischer-Dieskau, *Echoes of a Lifetime*, London: Macmillan, 1989

Otto Friedrich, *Glenn Gould: A Life and Variations*, London: Lime Tree, 1990

Wilhelm Furtwängler (tr. Shaun Whiteside), *Notebooks*, London: Quartet Books, 1989

F. W. Gaisberg, *Music on Record*, London: Robert Hale, 1947

Roland Gelatt, *The Fabulous Phonograph, 1877–1977*, London: Cassell, 1978

Suvi Raj Grubb, *Music Makers on Record*, London: Hamish Hamilton, 1986

Peter Heyworth and John Lucas, *Otto Klemperer: His Life and Times*, vol. II, Cambridge: Cambridge University Press, 1996

John L. Holmes, *Conductors on Record*, London: Victor Gollancz, 1982

Joseph Horowitz, *Understanding Toscanini*, New York: Alfred A. Knopf, 1987

John Hunt, *The Furtwängler Sound*, Exeter: Short Run Press, 1985

Kees A. Schouhamer Immink, 'The Compact Disc Story', *Journal of the Audio Engineering Society*, vol. 46, no. 5, May 1998

Wilhelm Kempff, *Wass ich hörte, wass ich sah*, Munich: R. Piper & Co., 1981

Norman Lebrecht, *The Maestro Myth*, London: Simon & Schuster, 1991

——, *When the Music Stops*, London: Simon & Schuster, 1996

Brown Meggs, *Aria*, London: Hamish Hamilton, 1978

Pali Meller Marcovicz (ed.), *Deutsche Grammophon Gesellschaft: eine Chronologie*, Hamburg: DGG GmbH, 1998

George Martin (with Jeremy Hornsby), *All You Need Is Ears*, London: Macmillan, 1979

Peter Martland, *Since Records Began – EMI, the First 100 Years*, London: B. T. Batsford, 1997

Robert Metz, *CBS: Reflections in a Bloodshot Eye*, Chicago: Playboy Press, 1975

Bruno Montsaigneon (tr. Stewart Spencer), *Sviatoslav Richter, Notebooks and Conversations*, London: Faber and Faber, 2001

Paul Myers, *Leonard Bernstein*, London: Phaidon, 1998

John Nathan, *Sony: The Private Life*, London: HarperCollins, 1999

Jerrold Northrop Moore, *Sound Revolutions: A Biography of Fred Gaisberg, Founding Father of Commercial Recording*, London: Sanctuary, 1999

Charles O'Connell, *The Other Side of the Record*, New York: Alfred Knopf, 1947

Richard Osborne, *Herbert von Karajan: A Life in Music*, London: Chatto & Windus, 1998

Luciano Pavarotti (with William Wright), *My Own Story*, London: Sidgwick & Jackson, 1981

Robert Philip, *Performing Music in the Age of Recording*, New Haven: Yale University Press 2005

William Primrose, *Walk on the North Side*, Provo, Utah: Brigham Young University Press, 1978

Harvey Sachs, *The Letters of Arturo Toscanini*, London: Faber and Faber, 2002

Artur Schnabel, *My Life and Music*, Gerrards Cross: Colin Smythe, 1970

Harold Schonberg, *Horowitz*, London: Simon & Schuster, 1992

Elisabeth Schwarzkopf, *On and Off the Record*, London: Faber and Faber, 1982

Sam H. Shirakawa, *The Devil's Music Master*, New York: Oxford University Press, 1992

Erik Smith, *Mostly Mozart*, Winchester: privately published, 2005

Georg Solti with Harvey Sachs, *Solti on Solti: A Memoir*, London: Chatto & Windus, 1997

Brian Southall, *Abbey Road*, London 1997

Wolfgang Stresemann, *Zeiten und Klänge*, Frankfurt a/M: Ullstein, 1994

H. H. Stuckenschmidt, *Zum Hören Geboren*, Munich: R. Piper & Co., 1979

Joseph Wulf, *Musik im Dritten Reich*, Gütersloh: Sigbert Mohn Verlag, 1963

Walter Yetnikoff, *Howling for the Moon*, New York: Random House, 2003

Index

ALSO BY NORMAN LEBRECHT

"A dazzling piece of fiction. . . . It is a rare author who can write as sensitively, and pithily, about the wounding aftereffects of the Shoah as he does about music." —Forward

THE SONG OF NAMES

Martin Simmonds's father tells him, "Never trust a musician when he speaks about love." The advice comes too late. Martin already loves Dovidl Rapoport, an eerily gifted Polish violin prodigy whose parents left him in the Simmonds's care before they perished in the Holocaust. For a time the two boys are closer than brothers. But on the day he is to make his official debut, Dovidl disappears. Only forty years later does Martin get his first clue about what happened to him. In this ravishing novel of music and suspense, Norman Lebrecht unravels the strands of love, envy, and exploitation that knot geniuses to their admirers. In doing so he also evokes the fragile bubble of Jewish life in prewar London, the fearful carnival of the Blitz, and the gray new world that emerged from its ashes. Bristling with ideas, lambent with feeling, *The Song of Names* is a masterful work of the imagination.

Fiction/978-1-4000-3489-5

ANCHOR BOOKS
Available at your local bookstore, or call toll-free to order:
1-800-793-2665 (credit cards only).